GED® TEST MATHEMATICAL REASONING

FLASH REVIEW

Related Titles

GED® Test RLA Flash Review
GED® Test Science Flash Review
GED® Test Social Studies Flash Review
GED® Test Power Practice

GED® TEST MATHEMATICAL REASONING

FLASH REVIEW

NEW YORK

Published in the United States by LearningExpress, LLC, New York.

Cataloging-in-Publication Data is on file with the Library of Congress.

Printed in the United States of America

9 8 7 6 5 4 3 2 1

First Edition

ISBN 978-1-61103-008-2

For information on LearningExpress, other LearningExpress products, or bulk sales, please write to us at:
80 Broad Street
4th Floor
New York, NY 10004

Or visit us at:
www.learningexpressllc.com

CONTENTS

INTRODUCTION

About the GED® Mathematical Reasoning Test

The GED® test measures how well you can apply problem solving, analytical reasoning, and critical thinking skills alongside your understanding of high-school level math. The entire test is given on a computer. On the GED® Mathematical Reasoning test, you will have 115 minutes (just under two hours) to answer 45 questions. These questions will fall under two areas: Quantitative Problem Solving and Algebraic Problem Solving.

Quantitative Problem Solving questions cover basic math concepts like multiples, factors, exponents, absolute value, ratios, averages, and probability.

Algebraic Problem Solving questions cover basic topics in algebra, including linear equations, quadratic equations, functions, linear inequalities, and more.

> An online calculator, called the **TI-30XS MultiView**, will be available to you for most of the questions within the Mathematical Reasoning section.

Formulas

A list of formulas will be available for you to use during the test. However, it will NOT include basic formulas, such as the area of a rectangle or triangle, circumference of a circle, or perimeter of geometric figures. You will be expected to know these already. This is where this book comes in handy—it gives you practice with all of the formulas you will need to have memorized on test day.

How to Use this Book

GED® Test Mathematical Reasoning Flash Review is designed to help you prepare for and succeed on the official exam, where a strong knowledge of mathematics fundamentals is essential. This book contains more than 600 of the most commonly covered mathematics concepts, images, formulas, problems, and question types on the exam. The cards are organized by math topic for easy access.

GED® Test Mathematical Reasoning Flash Review works well as a stand-alone study tool, but it is recommended that it be used to supplement additional preparation for the exam. The following are some suggestions for making the most of this effective resource as you structure your study plan:

- Do not try to learn or memorize all 600 math concepts covered in this book all at once. Cramming is not the most effective approach to test prep. The best approach is to build a realistic study schedule that lets you review one math topic each day (refer to the Table of Contents to see where each new topic begins).
- Mark the topics that you have trouble with so that they will be easy to return to later for further study.
- Make the most of this book's portability—take it with you for studying on car trips, between classes, while commuting, or whenever you have some free time.

- Keep scratch paper on hand as you make your way through the book—you might need it to work out some of the more complex problems.
- Visit the official GED® test website for additional information to help you prepare for test day.

Best of luck on the exam—and in achieving your goals!

GED® TEST MATHEMATICAL REASONING

FLASH REVIEW

What is a *rational number*?

. . . .

Which of the following are not rational numbers?

A. $\sqrt{16}$

B. $\sqrt{-4}$

C. $\frac{0}{5}$

D. 0.875

E. $\sqrt{2}$

. . . .

What does it mean if *k* is a multiple of *m*?

A **rational number** is any number that can be expressed as a quotient or fraction of two integers. A rational number can be written as $\frac{p}{q}$, where p and q are integers and the denominator q does not equal zero. All integers are rational numbers as q can equal 1.

A. $\sqrt{16}$ is rational.

B. $\sqrt{-4}$, the square root of a negative, is imaginary and irrational.

C. $\frac{0}{5}$ is rational.

D. 0.875 is rational.

E. $\sqrt{2}$ cannot be written as a fraction so it is irrational.

A number k is a multiple of m if k can be written as m times another number. So if $k = mn$ for any integer n, then k is a multiple of n.

Ex: 20 is a multiple of 5 because $4 \times 5 = 20$.

What are the first five multiples of 8?

. . . .

What is the *least common multiple (LCM)* of two numbers or expressions?
What is the LCM of 6 and 8?
Note: "The least common multiple of 6 and 8" is written as LCM (6, 8).

. . . .

What is the least common multiple of 12 and 20?

The first five multiples of 8 are:

8 × 1 = **8**

8 × 2 = **16**

8 × 3 = **24**

8 × 4 = **32**

8 × 5 = **40**

• •

The **least common multiple** is the lowest multiple that both numbers have in common. LCM (6, 8) = 24 since 24 is the smallest number that is a multiple of both 6 and 8.

• •

Write out lists of multiples for each number, and the lowest number that is a multiple of both is the least common multiple:

12: 12, 24, 36, 48, **<u>60</u>**, 72

20: 20, 40, **<u>60</u>**, 80

So LCM (12, 20) = **60**

What does it mean if *v* is a *factor* of *w*? What are the factors of 12?

. . . .

How do you find the *greatest common factor (GCF)* of two numbers?

For example, how would you find the GCF of 70 and 105?

Note: "The greatest common factor of 6 and 8" is written as GCF (6, 8).

. . . .

What is the greatest common factor of 98 and 35?

If there is an integer k such that $v \times k = w$, then v is a factor of w.

Ex: 3 and 4 are factors of 12 since $3 \times 4 = 12$.

The complete list of factors of 12 is: **1, 2, 3, 4, 6, and 12**.

In order to find the **greatest common factor** of two numbers, write them both out as the product of all of their factors and then identify the factors they have in common. If they just have one factor in common, then that is the GCF. If they have two or more factors in common, then multiply those numbers together, and that product will be the GCF:

$70 = 35 \times 2 = \underline{\mathbf{7}} \times \underline{\mathbf{5}} \times 2$

$105 = 35 \times 3 = \underline{\mathbf{7}} \times \underline{\mathbf{5}} \times 3$

7 and 5 are the factors that 70 and 105 have in common, so multiply them together to get 35 as the GCF.

Write 98 and 35 out as a product of all of their factors:

$98 = 49 \times 2 = \underline{\mathbf{7}} \times 7 \times 2$

$35 = \underline{\mathbf{7}} \times 5$

The only factor they have in common is 7, so GCF (98, 35) = **7**.

What is the greatest common factor of the expressions $40v^2f$ and $17v^2f^2$?

. . . .

Sue's favorite number is the greatest common factor of 16 and 24. Mike's favorite number is the least common multiple of 12 and 16. What is the positive difference of Sue's and Mike's favorite numbers?

. . . .

What are *consecutive numbers, consecutive even numbers,* and *consecutive odd numbers*?

Write $40v^2f$ and $17v^2f^2$ out as a product of all of their factors:

$40v^2f = 5 \times 2 \times 2 \times 2 \times \underline{\mathbf{v}} \times \underline{\mathbf{v}} \times \underline{\mathbf{f}}$

$17v^2f^2 = 17 \times \underline{\mathbf{v}} \times \underline{\mathbf{v}} \times \underline{\mathbf{f}} \times f$

v, *v*, and *f* are the factors that these expressions have in common, so multiply them together to get $\mathbf{v^2f}$ as the GCF.

• •

The greatest common factor of 16 and 24 is the largest integer that divides evenly into both 16 and 24. The GCF of 16 and 24 is 8.

The least common multiple of 12 and 16 is the smallest number that both 12 and 16 are multiples of, which is 48. Subtract them to find the difference of **40**.

• •

Consecutive numbers follow each other in order, without any gap or space between them: 17, 18, 19 . . .

Consecutive even numbers skip the odd integers between them: 22, 24, 26 . . .

Similarly, **consecutive odd integers** skip the even integers between them: 21, 23, 25 . . .

The product of two consecutive integers is 182. If the smaller integer is *x*, write an equation modeling this situation.

. . . .

What is important to keep in mind when ordering negative numbers on a number line?

. . . .

For the following number, identify the name of which place value each of the digits are in (for example, units, tenths, thousandths, etc.):
91,234.5678

If the first integer is x, then the second consecutive integer is $x + 1$. Their product is $x(x + 1) = \mathbf{x^2 + x = 182}$.

. . . .

The negative numbers sit to the left of zero on a number line. The larger a negative number is, the farther to the left of 0 it lies. For example, –5 is a smaller number than –2, and it is farther to the left on the number line than –2.

. . . .

91,234.5678

9 = **ten-thousands**

1 = **thousands**

2 = **hundreds**

3 = **tens**

4 = **units** (sometimes called the "ones" place)

5 = **tenths**

6 = **hundredths**

7 = **thousandths**

8 = **ten-thousandths**

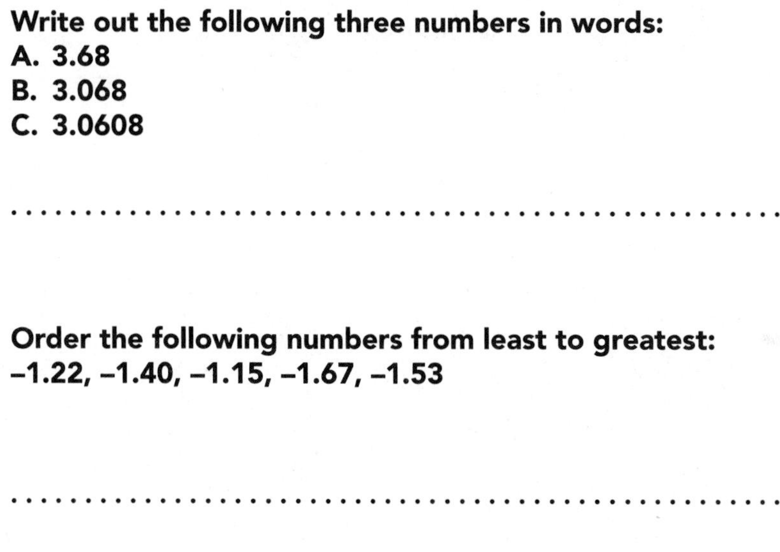

Write out the following three numbers in words:
A. 3.68
B. 3.068
C. 3.0608

. . . .

Order the following numbers from least to greatest:
–1.22, –1.40, –1.15, –1.67, –1.53

. . . .

What is important to keep in mind when ordering decimals on a number line like 0.1 and 0.09?

A. 3.68 = **three and sixty-eight hundredths**

B. 3.068 = **three and sixty-eight thousandths**

C. 3.0608 = **three and six-hundred-eight ten-thousandths**

Recall that with negative numbers, the larger the negative number is, the smaller its value:

–1.67, –1.53, –1.40, –1.22, –1.15

The place value that a decimal holds is more important than the value of the number. For example, 0.1 is bigger than 0.09 because 0.1 = 0.10, which is equivalent to ten hundredths (which is like a dime), whereas 0.09 is only equivalent to nine hundredths (which is like 9 cents).

Although 0.1 might look smaller than 0.09, 0.1 is actually the larger number. It has a number in the tenths position, while 0.09 only has a number in the hundredths position.

How should decimals be rewritten so that they can be compared? For example, what is the best way to compare 0.2, 0.009, and 0.08?

. . . .

Put the following list of decimals in order of least to greatest: 0.083, 0.109, 0.2, 0.0600

. . . .

Which point best represents $-1\frac{3}{8}$ on the number line below?

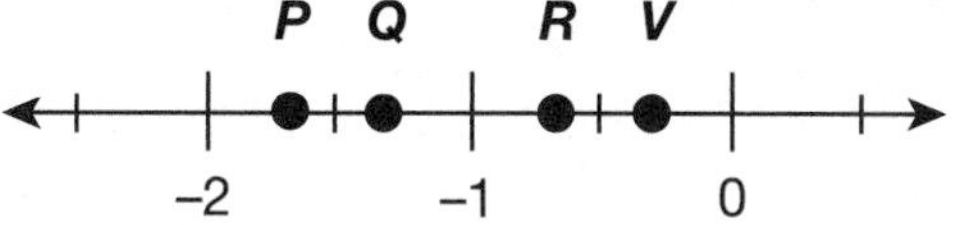

In order to compare decimals, add zeros after the last number to the right of the decimal until all of the decimals have the same number of digits to the right of the decimal point. Then, ignore the decimal point and compare the values of the numbers:

0.2 = 0.200

0.08 = 0.080

0.009 = 0.009

Since 200 is the largest number, 0.2 is the largest. 80 is larger than 9, so 0.08 is the middle number, and 0.009 is the smallest.

. . . .

0.0600, 0.0830, 0.1090, 0.2000

. . . .

$-1\frac{3}{8}$ is close to –1.5, which is halfway between –1 and –2. $\frac{3}{8}$ is smaller than $\frac{1}{2}$, so $-1\frac{3}{8}$ will be closer to –1 than –2, so **Q** is the correct answer.

Put the following list of fractions and decimals in order from least to greatest:
0.068, $\frac{2}{3}$, −1.7, $\frac{8}{5}$, 0.61, $-1\frac{2}{3}$

Write the decimals as fractions and add zeros so that they all have three places to the right of the decimal:

0.068 = 0.068

$\frac{2}{3}$ = 0.667

–1.7 = –1.700

$\frac{8}{5}$ = 1.600

0.61 = 0.610

$-1\frac{2}{3}$ = –1.667

In order: –1.7, $-1\frac{2}{3}$, 0.068, 0.61, $\frac{2}{3}$, $\frac{8}{5}$

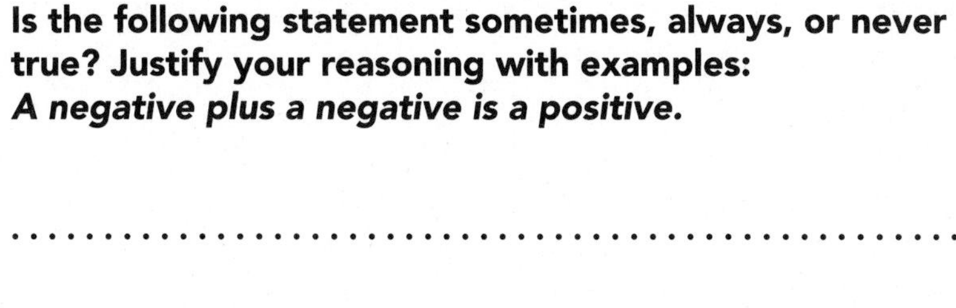

Is the following statement sometimes, always, or never true? Justify your reasoning with examples:
A negative plus a negative is a positive.

. . . .

Simplify: –10.5 + (–8) + (–20.07)

. . . .

Finish the following statement:
Subtracting a number is always the same as adding
________________.

This statement is *never* true. A negative plus a negative is always a bigger negative.

. . . .

A negative plus a negative is always a bigger negative, so the sum of these three negatives will be a larger negative. Line the decimals up, add, and give a negative sign to the answer:

$$\begin{array}{r} -10.50 \\ -8.00 \\ + -20.07 \\ \hline \mathbf{-38.57} \end{array}$$

. . . .

Subtracting a number is always the same as adding ***its opposite***.

Ex: 10 – 7 = 10 + (–7)

Ex: –8 – (–6) = –8 + 6

Convert the following subtraction problems into addition problems:
A. $-6x - (-17x)$
B. $-10y - 16y$

. . . .

Is the following statement sometimes, always, or never true? Justify your reasoning with examples:
A negative plus a positive is a positive.

. . . .

Simplify: $-16k - (-5k) + -8k - 10k$

Subtracting a number is always the same as adding its opposite:

$-6x - (-17x)$ becomes $\mathbf{-6x + 17x}$.

Once a problem is converted into an addition problem, the order of the numbers can be inverted:

A. $-6x + 17x = 17x - 6x$

B. $-10y - 16y = \mathbf{-10y + (-16y)}$

. . . .

This statement is *sometimes* true. When adding a negative and a positive number, subtract the absolute values of the two numbers and give the answer the sign of the larger number.

Ex: $(-2) + 5 = 3$, but $(-5) + 2 = -3$.

. . . .

First, convert the subtractions in the expression to addition:

$-16k - (-5k) + -8k - 10k =$

$-16k + 5k + (-8k) + (-10k)$

Now add the terms going from left to right:

$-11k + (-8k) + (-10k) =$

$-19k + (-10k) =$

$\mathbf{-29k}$

Subtracting negative and positive numbers can sometimes be confusing. What is the correct method to turn a subtraction problem into an addition problem?

Is the following statement sometimes, always, or never true? Justify your reasoning with examples:
A positive minus a negative is a positive.

Is the following statement sometimes, always, or never true? Justify your reasoning with examples:
A negative minus a negative is a positive.

Use the phrase "keep-switch-switch" to turn subtraction into addition:

"Keep" the sign of the first number.

"Switch" the subtraction sign to addition.

"Switch" the sign of the last number. For example:

4 – (–7) becomes 4 + 7 = 11.

–5 – 9 becomes –5 + (–9) = –14.

. . . .

This statement is *always* true. Subtracting a negative is the same thing as adding a positive, so "a positive minus a negative" is equivalent to "a positive plus a positive," which is a positive.

Ex: (20) – (–5) = (20) + (+5) = 25

. . . .

This statement is *sometimes* true. Since subtracting a negative is the same thing as adding a positive, "a negative minus a negative" is equivalent to "a negative plus a positive." When adding a negative and a positive number, the two numbers are subtracted, and the sign of the larger number is used.

Ex: (–2) – (–5) = (–2) + (+5) = 3, but (–20) – (–5) = (–20) + (5) = –15

Finish the following statement:
A negative number times a negative number will always equal a ________.

Finish the following statement:
A positive number times a negative number will always equal a ________.

Finish the following statement:
A negative number plus a negative number will always equal a ________.

A negative number times a negative number will always equal a ***positive***.

Ex: $-7 \times -3 = 21$

. . . .

A positive number times a negative number will always equal a ***negative***. (Think about spending \$10 three times in one day—you would spend \$30!)

Ex: $-\$10 \times 3 = -\$30$

. . . .

A negative number plus a negative number will always equal a ***bigger negative***. (Think about spending money twice.)

Ex: $-\$70 + -\$10 = -\$80$

Finish the following statement:
A negative number plus a positive number will always equal a ________.

Complete the following table, which illustrates the rules when multiplying and dividing positive and negative numbers:
Rule 1: (+) × (+) = (___) and (+) ÷ (+) = (___)
Rule 2: (–) × (–) = (___) and (–) ÷ (–) = (___)
Rule 3: (–) × (+) = (___) and (–) ÷ (+) = (___)

SIGNED NUMBERS

A negative number plus a positive number will always equal a ***number with a sign that agrees with the larger number***. A negative plus a positive is not always negative or positive! Ignore the signs, subtract the two numbers, and then use the sign of the larger number for the answer.

Ex: –20 + 35 = 15, but –35 + 20 = –15.

Rule 1: (+) × (+) = (**+**) and (+) ÷ (+) = (**+**)

Rule 2: (–) × (–) = (**+**) and (–) ÷ (–) = (**+**)

Rule 3: (–) × (+) = (**–**) and (–) ÷ (+) = (**–**)

What does it mean to find the *absolute value* of a number, and what does absolute value notation look like?

. . . .

When taking the absolute value of |6 – 8|, does the problem get changed to |6 + 8|?

. . . .

What are the values of the following expressions:
|6.3|
|–10|
–|–2|
|20 – 50|

ABSOLUTE VALUE

The **absolute value** of a number is the distance between that number and zero on a number line. Absolute value is written with a straight bar on either side of the number: $|-4|$. In this case, since –4 is 4 units away from zero on the number line, $|-4| = 4$.

No. When dealing with absolute value, evaluate all of the operations exactly as they are presented. The only time that a negative is converted to a positive is in the case of the final answer.

$|6 - 8| = |-2| = \mathbf{2}$

$|6.3| = \mathbf{6.3}$

$|-10| = \mathbf{10}$

$-|-2| = \mathbf{-2}$

$|20 - 50| = |-30| = \mathbf{30}$

Find $|x - y|$ when $x = 3$ and $y = -8$.

. . . .

Find $-|m - n|$ when $m = -10$ and $n = 25$.

. . . .

The expression $|x - y|$ when $x = 3$ and $y = -8$ simplifies to

$|3 - (-8)| =$

$|3 + 8| =$

11

The expression $-|m - n|$ when $m = -10$ and $n = 25$ simplifies to

$-|-10 - 25| =$

$-|-10 + -25| =$

$-|-35| =$

$-(35) =$

–35

What does it mean to reduce a fraction to *simplest form*, and how is this done?

. . . .

Reduce $\frac{75}{100}$ into simplest form.

. . . .

What is the difference between $\frac{5}{0}$ and $\frac{0}{5}$, and why is it important not to confuse them?

A fraction is in **simplest form** when its numerator and denominator cannot be divided by any like factor. In order to reduce a fraction into simplest form, divide the numerator and denominator by the Greatest Common Factor. For example, $\frac{24}{42}$ reduces to $\frac{4}{7}$ after 24 and 42 are both divided by their GCF, which is 6: $\frac{24 \div 6}{42 \div 6} = \frac{4}{7}$.

$\frac{75 \div 25}{100 \div 25} = \mathbf{\frac{3}{4}}$

$\frac{5}{0}$ means "5 parts of nothing," which is an impossible statement. Whenever the denominator equals zero, the value of a fraction is undefined. "Undefined" is represented with the symbol ∅.

$\frac{0}{5}$ means "0 parts of 5," which is equivalent to 0. Whenever 0 is in the numerator of a fraction, it is equal to zero.

Find the values of each of the following:

A. $\frac{13}{13}$ =

B. $\frac{0}{13}$ =

C. $\frac{13}{0}$ =

. . . .

For what two values of *x* is the following numerical expression undefined?

$\frac{12x}{x^2 - 25}$

. . . .

What is important to keep in mind when ordering fractions on a number line?

A. $\frac{13}{13} = \mathbf{1}$

B. $\frac{0}{13} = \mathbf{0}$

C. $\frac{13}{0} = \mathbf{\varnothing}$

Only the denominator is important when talking about undefined expressions. Find the values of *x* that make the denominator equal to zero. Set up the following equation to solve for *x*:

$x^2 - 25 = 0$

$x^2 = 25$

$x = 5$ and $x = -5$

Find a common denominator for all of the given fractions and rewrite them all with that denominator. Then compare the numerators.

Put the following list of fractions in order from least to greatest:
$\frac{17}{30}, \frac{11}{15}, \frac{5}{12}, \frac{2}{3}$

Convert these common fractions into decimals:

$\frac{1}{2} =$

$\frac{1}{3} =$

$\frac{2}{3} =$

$\frac{1}{4} =$

$\frac{3}{4} =$

$\frac{1}{5} =$

$\frac{2}{5} =$

Jonna runs $\frac{7}{10}$ of a mile every day. How many miles does she run in three weeks?

$\frac{17}{30} = \frac{34}{60}$

$\frac{11}{15} = \frac{44}{60}$

$\frac{5}{12} = \frac{25}{60}$

$\frac{2}{3} = \frac{40}{60}$

Therefore, $\frac{5}{12}, \frac{17}{30}, \frac{2}{3}, \frac{11}{15}$ is the correct order from least to greatest.

. . . .

$\frac{1}{2} = \mathbf{0.5}$

$\frac{1}{3} = \mathbf{0.3\overline{3}}$

$\frac{2}{3} = \mathbf{0.6\overline{6}}$

$\frac{1}{4} = \mathbf{0.25}$

$\frac{3}{4} = \mathbf{0.75}$

$\frac{1}{5} = \mathbf{0.2}$

$\frac{2}{5} = \mathbf{0.4}$

. . . .

Three weeks is 21 days, so $\frac{7}{10} \times \frac{21}{1} = \frac{147}{10} =$ **14.7 miles**.

What must fractions have in order for them to be added or subtracted?

What are the three steps of adding or subtracting fractions?

Find the sum of $\frac{1}{2}$, $\frac{1}{4}$, and $\frac{3}{5}$.

FRACTIONS

Fractions must have **common denominators** in order to be added or subtracted.

1. Use equivalent fractions to make common denominators.
2. Add/subtract the top numbers (numerators), and keep the denominator the same.
3. If possible, simplify the fraction by reducing it.

Find a common denominator of 20 and then add the numerators:

$\frac{1}{2} \times \frac{10}{10} = \frac{10}{20}$

$\frac{1}{4} \times \frac{5}{5} = \frac{5}{20}$

$\frac{3}{5} \times \frac{4}{4} = \frac{12}{20}$

$\frac{27}{20} = \mathbf{1\frac{7}{20}}$

$\frac{1}{3x} + \frac{x}{5} =$

Are the following statements true or false?

1. Fractions must have common denominators in order to be added and subtracted.
2. Fractions must have common denominators in order to be multiplied and divided.

What are the three steps for multiplying fractions?

Find a common denominator of 15x, and then add the numerators:

$\frac{1}{3x} \times \frac{5}{5} = \frac{5}{15x}$

$\frac{x}{5} \times \frac{3x}{3x} = \frac{3x^2}{15x}$

$\mathbf{\frac{3x^2 + 5}{15x}}$

1 **TRUE:** Fractions must have common denominators in order to be added and subtracted.

2. **FALSE:** Fractions do not need common denominators in order to be multiplied and divided.

1. Going straight across, multiply the numerators and write that product as the new numerator.
2. Going straight across, multiply the denominators and write that product as the denominator.
3. If possible, simplify the fraction by reducing it.

What is the product of $\frac{5}{12}$ and $\frac{6}{7}$?

$\frac{3x}{5} \times \frac{4}{9y} =$

What is a *reciprocal*?
Find the reciprocals of:
A. 1
B. $-\frac{3}{5}$
C. 6

$\frac{5}{12} \times \frac{6}{7} =$

$\frac{5 \times 5}{12 \times 7} =$

$\frac{30}{84} = \mathbf{\frac{5}{14}}$

$\frac{3x}{5} \times \frac{4}{9y} =$

$\frac{3x \times 4}{5 \times 9y} =$

$\frac{12x}{45y} = \mathbf{\frac{4x}{15y}}$

The product of any number and its **reciprocal** is 1. To find the reciprocal of a whole number, divide 1 by the number. To find the reciprocal of a fraction, flip it upside down.

A. **1** is the reciprocal of 1.

B. $\mathbf{-\frac{5}{3}}$ is the reciprocal of $-\frac{3}{5}$.

C. $\mathbf{\frac{1}{6}}$ is the reciprocal of 6.

How is the *reciprocal* of a mixed number found? What is the reciprocal of $3\frac{2}{5}$?

. . . .

What are the three steps for dividing fractions?

. . . .

How are mixed numbers divided? Divide $3\frac{3}{4}$ by $1\frac{3}{5}$.

In order to find the reciprocal of a mixed number, it must first be written as an improper fraction: $3\frac{2}{5} = \frac{17}{5}$. Then, the reciprocal of $\frac{17}{5}$ is $\mathbf{\frac{5}{17}}$.

1. Division of fractions is performed by multiplying the first fraction by the reciprocal of the second fraction.
2. Perform multiplication on fractions as required.
3. If possible, simplify the resulting fraction by reducing it.

Mixed numbers must be turned into improper fractions before they can be divided. Once the problem has been rewritten as the quotient of improper fractions, follow the rules for dividing fractions.

$3\frac{3}{4} = \frac{15}{4}$ and $1\frac{3}{5} = \frac{8}{5}$, so rewrite the problem as $\frac{15}{4} \div \frac{8}{5}$:

$\frac{15}{4} \div \frac{8}{5} = \frac{15}{4} \times \frac{5}{8} = \mathbf{\frac{75}{32}}$

What is the *quotient* of $\frac{5}{4}$ and $\frac{6}{7}$?

$\frac{7x}{5} \div \frac{3}{8} =$

$8\frac{1}{4} \div 5\frac{2}{3} =$

The quotient of $\frac{5}{4}$ and $\frac{6}{7}$ means $\frac{5}{4} \div \frac{6}{7}$:

$\frac{5}{4} \div \frac{6}{7} =$

$\frac{5}{4} \times \frac{7}{6}$

$\mathbf{\frac{35}{24}}$

$\frac{7x}{5} \div \frac{3}{8} =$

$\frac{7x}{5} \times \frac{8}{3} =$

$\mathbf{\frac{56x}{15}}$

Change the mixed numbers to improper fractions:

$8\frac{1}{4} = \frac{33}{4}$ and $5\frac{2}{3} = \frac{17}{3}$

$\frac{33}{4} \div \frac{17}{3} =$

$\frac{33}{4} \times \frac{3}{17} = \mathbf{\frac{99}{68}}$

Simplify: $\frac{1}{4}[\frac{5}{2} - \frac{1}{6}]$

The brackets indicate that $\frac{1}{4}$ is a factor that must be distributed to both terms in the brackets.

$\frac{1}{4}\left[\frac{5}{2} - \frac{1}{6}\right] =$

$\frac{1}{4}\left[\frac{5}{2}\right] - \frac{1}{4}\left[\frac{1}{6}\right] =$

$\frac{5}{8} - \frac{1}{24} =$

$\frac{15}{24} - \frac{1}{24} =$

$\frac{14}{24} = \mathbf{\frac{7}{12}}$

What is an *exponent* and how is it written?

. . . .

What does it mean to raise something to a *power*? What is "5 raised to the 4th power"?

. . . .

What happens when a negative number is raised to an even power? For example, what is the value of $(-2)^4$?

EXPONENTS

An **exponent**—written as a small number to the upper right of a "base" number or variable—indicates how many times a number should be multiplied by itself. For instance, 10^2 (read as 10 to the second power, or 10 squared) means 10×10, or 100; and 10^3 (read as 10 to the third power, or 10 cubed) means $10 \times 10 \times 10$, or 1,000.

. . . .

Raising something to a power means applying an exponent to a number or variable.

"5 raised to the 4th power" = 5^4

$5^4 = 5 \times 5 \times 5 \times 5 =$ **625**

. . . .

When a negative number is raised to an even power, the answer is positive. This is true because a negative times a negative is a positive, so an even number of negative signs will cancel out to be a positive:

$(-2)^4 = -2 \times -2 \times -2 \times -2 = 4 \times 4 =$ **16**

What happens when a negative number is raised to an odd power? For example, what is the value of $(-2)^3$?

. . . .

What does it mean to *square* a number? What is the value of "5 squared"?

. . . .

What does it mean to *cube* a number? What is the value of "10 cubed"?

When a negative number is raised to an odd power, the answer will be negative. All of the pairs of negative signs will cancel out to be positive, but there will be one negative sign remaining:

$(-2)^3 = -2 \times -2 \times -2 = 4 \times -2 = \mathbf{-8}$

Squaring a number means raising the number to a power of 2:

5 squared $= 5^2 = 5 \times 5 = \mathbf{25}$

Cubing a number means raising the number to a power of 3:

10 cubed $= 10^3 = 10 \times 10 \times 10 = \mathbf{1{,}000}$

How are $(-5)^2$ and -5^2 different?

. . . .

Evaluate:

A. $-(-9)^2$
B. -8^2
C. -5^3

. . . .

What does it mean to take the *square root* of a number *y*, and how is square root notation written?
What is the square root of 49?

When the negative sign is included inside the parentheses with the base, then the exponent applies to the negative sign as well. When the negative sign is not within the parentheses and is merely next to a base that has an exponent, then it is to be added to the answer after the exponent has been applied.

$(-5)^2 = (-5) \times (-5) = \mathbf{25}$

-5^2 means $-(5 \times 5) = \mathbf{-25}$

A. $-(-9)^2 = -(-9)(-9) = \mathbf{-81}$

B. $-8^2 = -(8 \times 8) = \mathbf{-64}$

C. $-5^3 = -(5 \times 5 \times 5) = \mathbf{-125}$

Taking the **square root** of a number *y* means finding the number that, when multiplied by itself, equals *y*. "The square root of *y*" is written as $\sqrt{y}$.

The square root of 49 is asking for the number that, when multiplied by itself, equals 49.

$7 \times 7 = 49$ and $-7 \times -7 = 49$

$\sqrt{49} = \mathbf{\pm 7}$

Why does the square root of a positive number always have two answers, a positive and a negative number? Use $\sqrt{25}$ to support your explanation.

Solve for x:
$x^2 - 64 = 0$

What is a *radicand*? For example, in $5x^2\sqrt{7}$ what is the radicand?

The square root of a number will have a positive and negative answer because when the negative answer is multiplied by itself, it will equal the desired positive number.

Consider $\sqrt{25}$:
$5 \times 5 = 25$
and $(-5) \times (-5) = 25$
So $\sqrt{25} = \mathbf{\pm 5}$

• •

Since this equation only has one variable, an x^2, isolate the x^2 and take the square root of both sides:

$x^2 - 64 = 0$
$x^2 = 64$
$\sqrt{x^2} = \sqrt{64}$
$\mathbf{x = 8}$ **and** $\mathbf{x = -8}$

• •

A **radicand** is the number under the radical sign. In $5x^2\sqrt{7}$, **7** is the radicand. It is important to be familiar with this word in order to follow the explanations for performing operations with radicals.

What is the correct way to add and subtract radicals? For example, how would the following be simplified?
$5\sqrt{7} - 3\sqrt{7} - 2\sqrt{11}$

. . . .

Is the following statement true or false? Justify your answer.
$\sqrt{50} + \sqrt{100} = \sqrt{150}$

. . . .

Simplify: $2\sqrt{5} - 3\sqrt{15} + 4\sqrt{5}$

Radicals can only be combined through addition or subtraction if the same number is under the radical sign. In that case, the coefficients of the radicals are added or subtracted, and the radicand remains the same:

$5\sqrt{7} - 3\sqrt{7} - 2\sqrt{11} = \mathbf{2\sqrt{7} - 2\sqrt{11}}$

• •

$\sqrt{50} + \sqrt{100} = \sqrt{150}$ is a **false** statement, because radicals can only be added if the same number is under the radical sign.

Thinking about this equation, $\sqrt{50}$ is a little bigger than 7, since $7 \times 7 = 49$, and $\sqrt{100} = 10$, so their sum is 17, but $\sqrt{150}$ is just a little bigger than 12 since $12 \times 12 = 144$.

• •

Radicals can only be combined through addition if the radicands are the same, so only the first and last terms can be combined:

$\underline{2\sqrt{5}} - 3\sqrt{15} + \underline{4\sqrt{5}}$

$\mathbf{6\sqrt{5} - 3\sqrt{15}}$

What is the correct way to multiply and divide radicals? For example, how would the following be simplified?
$5\sqrt{18} \times 3\sqrt{2}$

. . . .

Simplify the numerical expression $\sqrt{2}(\sqrt{18} - \sqrt{6})$.

. . . .

What does it mean if a number is a *perfect square*?

Unlike with addition and subtraction, the radicands do not need to be the same to multiply or divide radicals. Multiply the coefficients together and write this product outside the radical sign. Next, multiply the radicands and write their product under the radical sign. If possible, simplify the resulting radical.

$5\sqrt{18} \times 3\sqrt{2}$

$(5 \times 3)\sqrt{18 \times 2}$

$15\sqrt{36}$

$15 \times 6 = \mathbf{90}$

. . . .

Distribute the $\sqrt{2}$:

$\sqrt{2}(\sqrt{18} - \sqrt{6})$

$\sqrt{2} \times \sqrt{18} - \sqrt{2} \times \sqrt{6}$

$\sqrt{2 \times 18} - \sqrt{2 \times 6}$

$\sqrt{36} - \sqrt{12}$

$6 - \sqrt{4 \times 3}$

$6 - \mathbf{2\sqrt{3}}$

. . . .

A **perfect square** is a number that has an integer square root. A perfect square x can be written in the form $x = y^2$, with y being any integer.

For example, 25 is a perfect square because $5^2 = 25$.

What are the first ten perfect squares?

. . . .

Simplifying a radical is similar to reducing a fraction into simplest terms. How are radicals simplified?
How would $\sqrt{32}$ be simplified?

. . . .

In order to simplify radicals, it is important to know how a composite number can be broken up. Fill in the missing steps:

$\sqrt{20} =$

$\sqrt{\_\_ \times \_\_} =$

$\sqrt{\_\_} \times \sqrt{\_\_} =$

$\_\_\ \sqrt{5}$

A perfect square is a number that has an integer square root. Perfect squares can be written in the form y^2. The first 10 perfect squares are:

1, 4, 9, 16, 25, 36, 49, 64, 81, 100

When simplifying radicals, start by rewriting the radicand as a product of a perfect square factor and another factor. Then, take the square root of the perfect square and rewrite it as a product of that number times the square root of the remaining factor.

$\sqrt{32} =$

$\sqrt{16 \times 2} =$

$\sqrt{16} \times \sqrt{2} =$

$\mathbf{4\sqrt{2}}$

In order to simplify radicals, it is important to break down composite numbers into the product of a perfect square and another factor.

$\sqrt{20} =$

$\sqrt{\underline{4} \times \underline{5}} =$

$\sqrt{\underline{4}} \times \sqrt{\underline{5}} =$

$\underline{2}\sqrt{5} =$

$\mathbf{2\sqrt{5}}$

Simplify the expression $\sqrt{27x^2}$.

. . . .

What does it mean to take the *cube root* of a number *y*, and how is this notation written? What is the cube root of 8?

. . . .

What is $\sqrt[3]{64x^3}$?

$\sqrt{27x^2} =$

$\sqrt{\underline{9} \times 3 \times \underline{x^2}} =$

$\sqrt{9} \times \sqrt{x^2} \times \sqrt{3} =$

$\mathbf{3x\sqrt{3}}$

Taking the **cube root** of a number *y* means finding the number that, when multiplied by itself three times, yields *y*. It is symbolized with a radical symbol that has a 3 in the outside left corner of it: $\sqrt[3]{8}$. In order to find $\sqrt[3]{8}$, look for the number that equals 8 when multiplied by itself three times.

$\sqrt[3]{8} = \mathbf{2}$, since $2 \times 2 \times 2 = 8$.

$4x \times 4x \times 4x = 64x^3$

$\mathbf{4x} = \sqrt[3]{64x^3}$

Simplify:

A. $\sqrt[3]{27} =$

B. $\sqrt[3]{-125} =$

C. $\sqrt[3]{1{,}000} =$

What is the cube root of $\frac{1}{8}$ in fractional form?

Simplify $\sqrt[3]{16}$ in radical form.
Hint: Break 16 down into the product of a perfect cube and another factor.

A. $\sqrt[3]{27} = \mathbf{3}$

B. $\sqrt[3]{-125} = \mathbf{-5}$

C. $\sqrt[3]{1{,}000} = \mathbf{10}$

Since $\sqrt[3]{\frac{1}{8}} = \frac{1}{2} \times \frac{1}{2} \times \frac{1}{2}$, then $\mathbf{\frac{1}{2}}$ is the cube root of $\frac{1}{8}$.

Break the cube root of 16 down into the product of a perfect cube and another factor, then simplify:

$\sqrt[3]{16} =$

$\sqrt[3]{(8 \times 2)} =$

$\sqrt[3]{8} \times \sqrt[3]{2} =$

$\mathbf{2\sqrt[3]{2}}$

Is it possible to take the square root of a negative number? Justify your reasoning.

. . . .

Is it possible to take the cube root of a negative number? Justify your reasoning.

. . . .

Simplify: $\sqrt{45} + \sqrt{125}$

It is impossible to take the square root of a negative number because there is no way that the product of the two identical numbers can be negative:

(positive) × (positive) = (positive); (negative) × (negative) = (positive)

There is no way that a number can be multiplied by itself to produce a negative answer.

• •

It is possible to take the cube root of a negative number because the product of three negative numbers is a negative:

(negative) × (negative) × (negative) = (negative)

The cube root of a negative number will always be negative.

• •

$\sqrt{45} + \sqrt{125} =$

$\sqrt{9 \times 5} + \sqrt{25 \times 5} =$

$\sqrt{9} \times \sqrt{5} + \sqrt{25} \times \sqrt{5} =$

$3\sqrt{5} + 5\sqrt{5}$

$\mathbf{8\sqrt{5}}$

Simplify: $\sqrt{20}\sqrt{12}$

. . . .

How is $\frac{\sqrt{p}}{\sqrt{q}}$ **simplified?**

. . . .

Simplify the expression $\frac{\sqrt{76}}{\sqrt{38}}$.

$\sqrt{20}\,\sqrt{12} =$

$\sqrt{4 \times 5}\,\sqrt{4 \times 3} =$

$\sqrt{4}\,\sqrt{5} \times \sqrt{4}\,\sqrt{3} =$

$2\sqrt{5} \times 2\sqrt{3} =$

$(2 \times 2)(\sqrt{5} \times \sqrt{3}) =$

$4\sqrt{5 \times 3} =$

$\mathbf{4\sqrt{15}}$

$\frac{\sqrt{p}}{\sqrt{q}} = \sqrt{\frac{p}{q}}$ for positive numbers p and q.

$\frac{\sqrt{p}}{\sqrt{q}} = \sqrt{\frac{p}{q}}$ for positive numbers p and q. Using this property:

$\frac{\sqrt{76}}{\sqrt{38}} =$

$\sqrt{\frac{76}{38}} =$

$\mathbf{\sqrt{2}}$

What is the value of x^0?

Simplify: $5v^0$

What is the rule for simplifying the expression $x^a \times x^b$?

$x^0 = \mathbf{1}$. Any base with an exponent of 0 equals 1.

The zero exponent is only applied to the v and not to the 5, so $v^0 = 1$:

$5v^0 =$
$5(v^0) =$
$5 \times 1 =$
5

$x^a \times x^b = \mathbf{x^{(a+b)}}$

Example:

$x^3 \times x^6 =$
$x^{(3+6)} =$
x^9

Simplify $w^7 \times w^3$.

What is the rule for rewriting the expression x^{-a} with a positive exponent?
How is $2^{(-3)}$ written as an equivalent expression with a positive exponent?

Simplify by rewriting as an equivalent number with a positive exponent: 5^{-3}

Use the rule $x^a \times x^b = x^{(a + b)}$:

$w^7 \times w^3 =$

$w^{(7 + 3)} =$

$\mathbf{w^{10}}$

$x^{-a} = \frac{1}{x^a}$

$2^{-3} = \frac{1}{2^3} = \mathbf{\frac{1}{8}}$

NOTE: A negative exponent does not mean the answer is negative!

$5^{-3} = \frac{1}{5^3} = \mathbf{\frac{1}{125}}$

What is the rule for simplifying the expression $\frac{x^a}{x^b}$? Simplify $\frac{x^{10}}{x^6}$.

. . . .

Simplify: $\frac{8x^5}{4x}$

. . . .

What is the rule for simplifying the expression $(xy)^a$? Simplify $(4p)^2$.

$\frac{x^a}{x^b} = x^{(a-b)}$

$\frac{x^{10}}{x^6} = x^{(10-6)} = \mathbf{x^4}$

• •

Divide the coefficients and simplify the variables by using the rule

$\frac{x^a}{x^b} = x^{(a-b)}$:

$\frac{8x^5}{4x} = \frac{8}{4}(x^{5-1}) = \mathbf{2x^4}$

• •

$(xy)^a = (x^a)(y^a)$

$(4p)^2 =$

$(4^2)(p^2) =$

$\mathbf{16p^2}$

Simplify: $(4xy)^3$

. . . .

What is the rule for simplifying the expression $(x^a)^b$?
Simplify: $(x^3)^4$

. . . .

Simplify $(3x^2)^4$

Use the rule $(xy)^a = (x^a)(y^a)$:

$(4xy)^3 =$

$(4^3)(x^3)(y^3) =$

$\mathbf{64x^3y^3}$

$(x^a)^b = x^{(ab)}$

$(x^3)^4 =$

$x^{(3 \times 4)} =$

$\mathbf{x^{12}}$

Use the rule $(xy)^a = (x^a)(y^a)$ in combination with the rule $(x^a)^b = x^{(ab)}$:

$(3x^2)^4 =$

$(3^4)(x^2)^4 =$

$81x^{(2 \times 4)} =$

$\mathbf{81x^8}$

What is the value of x^1?
What are the values of 5.4^1 and $(-17)^1$?

. . . .

Which of the following is equivalent to $5^{0.5} \times 5^2$?
A. $5^{0.5} + 5^2$
B. 5
C. 5^1
D. $5^{2.5}$

. . . .

What is the correct way to raise a fraction to a power? For example, how is $(\frac{4}{9})^2$ calculated?

$x^1 = \mathbf{x}$

$5.4^1 = \mathbf{5.4}$

$(-17)^1 = \mathbf{-17}$

Choice **D** is correct. When multiplying terms with the same base, the exponents are added. Therefore:

$5^{0.5} \times 5^2 =$

$5^{(0.5 + 2)} =$

$\mathbf{5^{2.5}}$

Raising a fraction to a power is done the same way as raising a whole number to a power. Multiply that fraction by itself the number of times dictated by the exponent:

$(\frac{4}{9})^2 =$

$(\frac{4}{9}) \times (\frac{4}{9}) = \mathbf{\frac{16}{81}}$

What is the value of $(\frac{2}{5})^3$?

What is the value of $-(\frac{6x}{7})^2$ and how is that different from the value of $(\frac{-6x}{7})^2$?

What is the value of $\frac{x-5}{x^2+1}$ when $x = \frac{1}{2}$?

$(\frac{2}{5})^3 =$

$(\frac{2}{5}) \times (\frac{2}{5}) \times (\frac{2}{5}) = \mathbf{\frac{8}{125}}$

When the negative sign is on the outside of the parentheses, it is applied after the exponent has been fully applied:

$-(\frac{6x}{7})^2 = -(\frac{6x}{7})(\frac{6x}{7}) = -\mathbf{\frac{36x^2}{49}}$

When the negative sign is inside the parentheses, the exponent applies to it as well:

$(\frac{-6x}{7})^2 = (\frac{-6x}{7})(\frac{-6x}{7}) = \mathbf{\frac{36x^2}{49}}$

$\frac{x-5}{x^2+1} =$

$\frac{0.5-5}{0.5^2+1} =$

$\frac{-4.5}{1.25} = \mathbf{-3.6}$

Find the product of $x^2 - 6$ and x^4.

Which of the following is equivalent to $\frac{8^5}{8^2}$?
A. 8
B. 8^3
C. 8^7
D. 8^{10}

Simplify the expression $\frac{\sqrt[3]{9x} \times \sqrt[3]{18}}{3}$.

The first step is to distribute the x^4. Recall that when multiplying like bases, the exponents will be added.

$x^4(x^2 - 6) =$

$x^4(x^2) - x^4(6) =$

$\mathbf{x^6 - 6x^4}$

. . . .

By the laws of exponents, $\frac{x^a}{x^b} = x^{(a-b)}$

Therefore, $\frac{8^5}{8^2} = 8^3$, so **B** is correct.

. . . .

First, combine the cube roots:

$\frac{\sqrt[3]{(9x)(18)}}{3} = \frac{\sqrt[3]{162x}}{3}$

Then, break 162x down into the product of a perfect cube and another factor:

$\frac{\sqrt[3]{27}\,\sqrt[3]{6x}}{3}$

Finally, take the cube root of 27:

$\frac{3\sqrt[3]{6x}}{3} = \mathbf{\sqrt[3]{6x}}$

What is the general format of numbers written in *scientific notation* that have a value greater than 1?

. . . .

Write 623,080 in scientific notation.

. . . .

What is the general format of numbers written in scientific notation that have a value between 0 and 1?

SCIENTIFIC NOTATION

Scientific notation represents numbers in the format $m \times 10^n$, where $0 < m < 10$ and n is an integer; if the number is greater than or equal to 1, then n must be greater than or equal to 0. (**$n \geq 0$**).

Scientific notation represents numbers in the format $m \times 10^n$, where $0 < m < 10$ and n is an integer.

623,080 = **6.2308×10^5**

Scientific notation represents numbers in the format $m \times 10^n$, where $0 < m < 10$ and n is an integer; if the number is between 0 and 1, then n must be less than 0 (**$n < 0$**).

How is 0.0508 expressed in scientific notation?

. . . .

A specialized part for a manufacturing process has a thickness of 1.2×10^{-3} inches. To the ten-thousandth of an inch, what would be the thickness of a stack of ten of these parts?

. . . .

Calculate and write the answer in scientific notation: $(5.3 \times 10^{-2}) \times (8 \times 10^{5})$

Scientific notation represents numbers in the format $m \times 10^n$, where $0 < m < 10$ and n is an integer.

$0.0508 = \mathbf{5.08 \times 10^{-2}}$

$1.2 \times 10^{-3} = 0.0012$ and $10 \times 0.0012 =$ **0.012 inches**

$(5.3 \times 10^{-2}) \times (8 \times 10^5) =$

$(5.3 \times 8) \times (10^{-2} \times 10^5) =$

$42.4 \times 10^3 =$

$\mathbf{4.24 \times 10^4}$

Calculate and write the answer in scientific notation:

$$\frac{9 \times 10^{6}}{4.5 \times 10^{-2}}$$

SCIENTIFIC NOTATION

$\frac{9 \times 10^6}{4.5 \times 10^{-2}} =$

$\frac{9}{4.5} \times 10^{6-(-2)} =$

$\mathbf{2 \times 10^8}$

What does *percent* mean and represent?

What form must percentages be converted into in order to use them in calculations?

How do you change a fraction to a percent? Change $\frac{3}{8}$ to a percent.

PERCENTS

Percent means "out of every hundred." A percent represents a ratio that is out of 100. For example, 50% means 50 out of 100, or $\frac{50}{100}$.

Percent is a number that is "out of 100." Therefore, when computing with percents, they must either be written as a fraction over 100 or converted into a decimal. To change a percent into a decimal, move the decimal point two places to the left, and then remove the % symbol.

To change a fraction to a percent, divide the top number by the bottom number, multiply by 100, and add a percent symbol.

$\frac{3}{8} = 0.375$

$0.375 \times 100 =$ **37.5%**

When given a statistic that *v* items have a certain trait out of a group of *w* items, what is the best way to calculate the percent of items with that trait?
(Ex: If three out of four students walk to school, what percent of students walk to school?)

. . . .

Five out of every six women in Huntington have a high school diploma. What percentage of women has a high school diploma?

. . . .

Change the following to percentages:
A. 1.4
B. 0.3
C. 0.0875

The term "out of" indicates that a ratio exists, which should be written as a fraction. So "*v* out of *w*" means $\frac{v}{w}$.

If 3 out of 4 students walk to school, that means that $\frac{3}{4}$ of the students are walkers. Change a fraction to a percent by dividing it and moving the decimal two places to the right: $\frac{3}{4}$ = 0.75 = **75%**

First, write the ratio of women in Huntington with diplomas to all women in Huntington as a fraction: $\frac{5}{6}$.

Next, turn this fraction into a percent by dividing and moving the decimal two places to the right: $\frac{5}{6} = 0.833\overline{3}$ = **83.$\overline{3}$%**

To change a decimal to a percent, simply multiply by 100 and add a percent symbol. A shortcut for doing this is moving the decimal place two spaces to the right.

1.4 = 1.4 × 100 = **140%**

0.3 = 0.3 × 100 = **30%**

0.0875 = 0.0875 × 100 = **8.75%**

How do you change a percent to a decimal? What is 9% sales tax equivalent to as a decimal?

. . . .

How do you find a given percentage of a number? For example, how would you find 8.5% of $20.00?

. . . .

Lisa bought a climbing rope on sale for 50% off the original price, and then another 25% off the discounted price. If the rope originally cost $188, what was the final sale price that Lisa paid for the rope?

To change a percent into a decimal, simply divide by 100 and remove the percent symbol. A shortcut for this is moving the decimal place two spaces to the left:

$9\% = \frac{9}{100} = \mathbf{0.09}$

First, recall that percentages must be converted into decimals before performing any calculations. Move the decimal point two places to the left and remove the % symbol: 8.5% becomes 0.085. The word "of" in math translates to multiplication, so 8.5% of $20 translates to:

$0.085 \times \$20 = \mathbf{\$1.70}$

The 50% off discounted price of the $188 rope is $94.

25% of $94 = 0.25×94 = $23.50, which is the additional discount.

After taking off another $23.50, the final sale price she paid is **$70.50**.

There are 32 students in the class and 18 of them are girls. What percent of the class is female?

. . . .

The formula used to compute simple interest earned on an investment is $I = PRT$.
What does each of the variables represent?

. . . .

Amara invested $28,000 at 12% simple interest. If she removes all of her original investment plus the interest earned in two and a half years, how much money will she have?

First, write the information as a ratio. If 18 out of 32 students are girls, this is written as $\frac{18}{32}$. Change this fraction to a percent by dividing 18 by 32: $\frac{18}{32} = 0.5625$. Lastly, multiply by 100 and add a percent symbol: $0.5625 \times 100 =$ **56.25%**.

I = the **interest earned**

P = the **principal** (beginning) balance

R = the interest **rate** (written as a decimal)

T = the duration of **time** (in years)

In $I = PRT$, I = interest, P = the principal (beginning) balance, R = the interest rate (written as a decimal), and T = the duration of time (in years). Therefore:

$I = 28{,}000 \times 0.12 \times 2.5 = \$8{,}400$

Amara's interest after 2.5 years will be \$8,400. Add \$8,400 to her initial investment of \$28,000, and the total amount of money she will have is **\$36,400**.

Luke buys Grace a colored pencil set for her birthday. Its retail price is $28 and tax is an additional 8.5%. If he pays the clerk with two $20 bills, how much change will Luke get back?

. . . .

Willa really wants to buy a new power saw for a home renovation project. The saw normally costs $289, but it is now on sale for 15% off. What will the sale price be, before tax?

. . . .

Stan is trying to figure out how much money he needs to leave as a tip for a business luncheon he hosted. If the final bill for the luncheon was $1,240 and he wants to leave a 20% tip, what will the total cost be for the luncheon?

The tax on the colored pencils will be $28 × 0.085 = $2.38. The total price of the colored pencils with tax will be $28 + $2.38 = $30.38. Since Luke gives the clerk $40, he will receive $40 – $30.38 = **$9.62 in change**.

15% of $289 is:

0.15 × $289 = $43.35

So the sale price will be $289 – $43.35 = **$245.65**.

20% of $1,240 = 0.20 × $1,240 = $248, so the total cost will be:

$248 + $1,240 = **$1,488**

Two friends go to a restaurant for lunch and receive a final bill of $24.36. One friend believes they should tip 15%, while the other believes they should tip 20%. To the nearest cent, what is the difference between the two possible tips?

Free My Music pays its sales associates a base rate of $525 per week plus an 8% commission on any sales the employee makes. If an employee makes $4,080 in sales one week, what will his total paycheck be for that week?

A website is selling a printer for $375.00 plus 6.5% state sales tax. A student wishes to purchase two of these printers—one for his sister and one for himself. Including tax, what will be the total cost of his order?

A 20% tip would be: $0.2 \times \$24.36 = \$4.872$

A 15% tip would be: $0.15 \times 24.36 = \$3.654$

To the nearest cent, the difference between these two tips is **$1.22**.

. . . .

An 8% on $4,080 in sales is $0.08 \times \$4{,}080 = \$326.40$

Therefore, the employee's paycheck for the week would be $\$326.40 + \$575 =$ **$851.40**.

. . . .

The student will spend $\$375 \times 2 = \$750$ on the two printers, before tax.

6.5% tax is 0.065 in decimal form, so the tax is $\$750 \times 0.065 = \$48.75$.

The total cost of the student's order is $\$750 + \$48.75 =$ **$798.75**.

How are a *percentage increase* and a *percentage decrease* calculated?

. . . .

Alexis bought a gardening shed for $339. She loved it so much that the next summer she went to buy another one, but the price had gone up to $419. What was the percentage increase in price of her beloved garden shed?

. . . .

Over the last six months, a company's monthly revenue has increased by 28%. If the revenue this month is $246,990, what was the revenue six months ago? Round your answer to the nearest cent.

Both **percentage increase** and **percentage decrease** are calculated with this given formula:

Percentage Increase or Decrease = $\frac{\text{difference of original and new}}{\text{original value}} \times 100$

$\frac{\text{difference of original and new}}{\text{original value}} \times 100 =$

$\frac{419 - 339}{339} =$

$0.2359 \times 100 \approx$ **23.6%**

If x represents the revenue 6 months ago, then x + (28% of x) will equal the current revenue of $246,990. Since 28% of x is $0.28x$, the equation $1x + 0.28x = 246{,}990$ must be true. Solving for x yields:

$x =$ **$192,960.94**

Shirley buys a stock in January, and then it drops 20% in February. By what percent must it now increase in order to be back at its original price?

Doug is an IT consultant who charges $175/hour for consulting. Additionally, he charges a 3% project fee on the base rate of a project plus a 1% telecommunications fee on the cost of his billed hours. If a completed project took Doug 20 hours and the base rate was $5,000, what will be the final amount Doug will charge for this project?

The monthly sales for Mike's Handy Market have dropped 30% over the past two months, since a new competitor opened down the street. If current monthly sales are $6,842, what were the monthly sales two months ago?

The best way to begin problems like this is to choose a starting number of 100 and then solve for the answer. If a stock was \$100 and dropped by 20%, that means that it went down to \$80. It must increase by \$20 to be back at its original price, and since it is now \$80, that percentage increase is: $\frac{20}{80} = \frac{1}{4} = 0.25 =$ **25%**

. . . .

Doug's hourly charges will be \$175 × 20 = \$3,500, and then he will charge 1% on that price: 0.01 × \$3,500 = \$35. Then, 3% of his base rate of \$5,000 is 0.03 × \$5,000 = \$150. In total, he will bill \$3,500 + \$35 + \$5,000 + \$150 = **\$8,685**.

. . . .

If x represents the sales from two months ago, then x – (30% of x) will equal the current revenue of \$6,842. Since 30% of x is $0.30x$, the equation $1x - 0.3x =$ \$6,842 must be true. Solving for x yields $x \approx$ **\$9,774.29**.

The table below indicates the behavior of the price of one share of a given stock over several weeks. If the stock was worth $10.15 a share at the beginning of week 1, what was the value of one share of this stock at the end of week 4?

End of	Change
Week 1	**increased** by $5.00
Week 2	**decreased** by 10%
Week 3	**decreased** by $1.10
Week 4	**doubled** in value

After increasing by $5.00, the share was worth $15.15.

It then decreased in value by 10%, or by 0.1 × 15.15 = 1.515. Therefore, at the end of week 2 it was worth $15.15 – $1.515 = $13.635 a share.

At the end of week 3, it was worth $13.635 – $1.10 = $12.535.

Finally, it doubled in value and was worth 2 × $12.535 = **$25.07**.

How is *unit price* calculated?

. . . .

A 5 lb. bag of organic potatoes costs $6.75. What is the price per pound?

. . . .

A 32-ounce bag of potato chips has a retail cost of $3.45. To the nearest tenth of a cent, what is the price per ounce for this item?

Unit price is calculated by dividing the total cost by the quantity.

• •

Unit price is calculated by dividing the total cost by the quantity.

In this case, the cost is \$6.75 for 5 pounds, so calculate $\frac{\$6.75}{5}$ = **\$1.35 per pound**.

• •

The price per ounce is found by dividing \$3.45 by 32, which yields \$0.1071, or **10.8 cents per ounce**.

Rick's Market is selling 12 lb. turkeys for \$19.50 each, and Mike's Meats is selling 15 lb. turkeys for \$23.85. Which store offers the better price per pound of turkey?

A walking trail is 11,088 feet long. If a mile is 5,280 feet, how many miles long is the walking trail?

Gage typed 150 words in 4.5 minutes. If he continues typing at this rate, how many words can he type in 30 minutes?

The price per pound at Rick's Market is $\frac{\$19.50}{12}$ = \$1.63. The price per pound at Mike's Meats is $\frac{\$23.85}{12}$ = \$1.59. Even though the turkey costs more at **Mike's Meats**, it offers a better price per pound of turkey.

$\frac{11,088}{5,280}$ = **2.1 miles**

Set up a proportion and solve with cross multiplication:

$\frac{150}{4.5} = \frac{g}{30}$

$4.5(g) = 15(30)$

$4.5g = 4,500$

$g =$ **1,000**

A small town has a population of 20,510 and an area of 86.8 square miles. To the nearest tenth, what is the population density as measured by the value "people per square mile"?

Zed bought 9 pounds of lamb. He used a coupon, which saved him $8.37. How much did he save per pound?

What is the formula relating *distance, rate,* and *time*?

Dividing the number of people by the area yields 236.29 ≈ **236.3**.

$\frac{\$8.37}{9}$ = **\$0.93** savings per pound

Distance = Rate × Time, where time is equal to hours in decimal format.

It is important to write the minutes as a decimal. For example, 30 minutes is not 0.3 hours; since it is half an hour, it is written as 0.5 hours.

When using a formula that relates distance, rate, and time, what is the trickiest thing to remember about how time is written?

. . . .

How do you convert minutes into decimal format? Convert 42 minutes into decimal format.

. . . .

It took Terry 1 hour and 45 minutes to walk a 4-mile trail. How many miles per hour did she walk? Round your answer to the nearest tenth.

Distance = Rate × Time, where time is equal to hours in decimal format.

It is important to change the minutes into decimal format by writing them over 60 and converting that fraction to a decimal. For example 15 minutes is not 0.15 hours, but it is $\frac{15}{60} = \frac{1}{4} = 0.25$ hours.

60 minutes comprise 1 hour, so in order to convert minutes into decimal format, write the number of minutes over 60 as a fraction, and then divide. So 42 minutes would be: $\frac{42}{60} = \frac{7}{10} =$ **0.7 hours**.

Distance = Rate × Time

4 = Rate × 1.75

Rate = **2.3 miles per hour**

A remote-controlled vehicle travels at a constant speed around a testing track for a period of 12 hours. In those 12 hours, the vehicle goes around the 4 km track a total of 39 times. In terms of kilometers per hour, at what rate was the vehicle traveling?

An estimated 392,880 people live within the 58 square miles in Minneapolis, Minnesota. Approximately 3.82 million people live within the 503 square miles in Los Angeles, California. What is the difference of people per square mile between these two cities? Round to the nearest whole number.

Since the vehicle went around the 4 km track 39 times, it traveled

$39 \times 4 = 156$ km

Distance = Rate × Time

$156 = \text{Rate} \times 12$

Rate = $\frac{156}{12}$ = **13 kilometers per hour**

• •

First, calculate the number of people per square mile in Minneapolis:

$\frac{392,880}{58}$ = 6,774 people per square mile.

Next, calculate the number of people per square mile in Los Angeles: $\frac{3,820,000}{503}$ = 7,594 people per square mile.

7,594 – 6,774 = **820** more people per square mile in Los Angeles.

• •

What is a *ratio* and what are the correct ways to express a ratio?

What is a *proportion* and how is it written?

How is a proportion solved? For example, what is the easiest way to solve for *w* in this proportion: $\frac{12}{16} = \frac{w}{40}$?

PROPORTIONS

A **ratio** is a comparison of two numbers. There are three different ways to represent a ratio. If there are 12 apples and 17 oranges, the ratio of apples to oranges can be written as 12 to 17, $\frac{12}{17}$, or 12:17.

A **proportion** is two ratios or fractions that are set equal to each other.

$\frac{x}{y} = \frac{c}{d}$ is one example of a proportion. Since these are equivalent fractions, this is an example of another proportion: $\frac{3}{2} = \frac{15}{10}$.

Proportions are solved with cross multiplication. Multiply diagonally and set the two cross products equal to each other. Then, isolate the variable in order to solve.

$\frac{12}{16} = \frac{w}{40}$

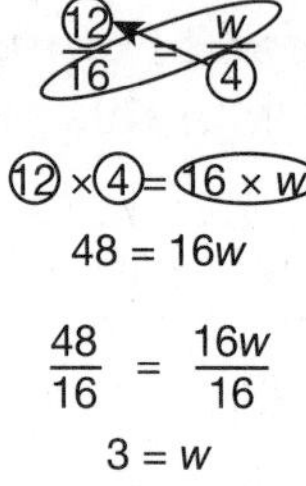

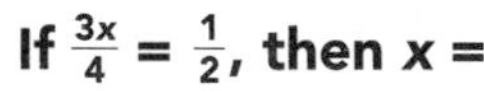

If $\frac{3x}{4} = \frac{1}{2}$, then x =

Of the students in Alton's class, 80% prefer chocolate over vanilla ice cream. If there are 25 students in his class, how many of them prefer vanilla ice cream? How can a proportion be written to model and solve this problem?

A survey of 1,000 registered voters shows that 650 people would choose candidate A in an upcoming election. If 240,000 people vote in the upcoming election, according to the survey, how many votes will candidate A receive?

To isolate the x, use cross multiplication to get rid of the fractions, and then solve for x:

$\frac{3x}{4} = \frac{1}{2}$

$3x(2) = 4(1)$

$6x = 4$

$x = \frac{4}{6} = \mathbf{\frac{2}{3}}$

• •

80% is the same thing as $\frac{80}{100}$, which simplifies to $\frac{8}{10}$ and then $\frac{4}{5}$. If $\frac{4}{5}$ students prefer chocolate, then that means that $\frac{1}{5}$ prefer vanilla. Set $\frac{1}{5}$ equal to $\frac{v}{25}$, where v = the number of students who prefer vanilla. Solve through cross multiplication:

$\frac{1}{5} = \frac{v}{25}$

$5(v) = 1(25)$

$5v = 25$

$v = \mathbf{5}$

• •

$\frac{650}{1{,}000} = \frac{v}{240{,}000}$

$650(240{,}000) = 1{,}000(v)$

$145{,}000{,}000 = 1{,}000v$

$v =$ **156,000 votes**

Miss Molly is making lemonade for a summer picnic. Her recipe calls for 17 tablespoons of sugar for every 2 gallons of lemonade, but she wants to make 7.5 gallons for the neighborhood picnic. Write and solve a proportion to find how many tablespoons of sugar Miss Molly needs to make the lemonade for her picnic.

. . . .

How do you check to see if two ratios are proportional?

. . . .

It takes Peter 51 minutes to make 3 flower arrangements. If he needs to make 20 arrangements for a big event, how many hours and minutes will it take? Solve by using proportions.

Since there are 17 tablespoons of sugar for every 2 gallons of lemonade, that can be represented in the following proportion, which compares tablespoons of sugar to gallons of lemonade:

$\frac{17 \text{ tablespoons}}{2 \text{ gallons}} = \frac{t \text{ tablespoons}}{7.5 \text{ gallons}}$

$17(7.5) = 2(t)$

$127.5 = 2t$

$t = 63.75$

Miss Molly will need **63.75 tablespoons of sugar.**

Two ratios are proportional if their cross products are equal. So, to determine if two ratios are proportional, write them as fractions, multiply diagonally, and compare their cross products.

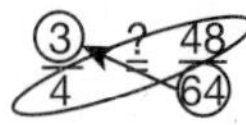

$3 \cdot 64 \stackrel{?}{=} 4 \cdot 48$

$192 = 192$ ✓

So $\frac{3}{4}$ and $\frac{48}{64}$

are proportional.

$\frac{3 \text{ arrangements}}{51 \text{ minutes}} = \frac{20 \text{ arrangements}}{m \text{ minutes}}$

$3(m) = 51(20)$

$3m = 1{,}020$

$m = 340$

340 minutes = **5 hours and 40 minutes**

A map is drawn such that 3 centimeters on the map represents 5 miles. If two cities are 7.8 centimeters apart on the map, then to the nearest tenth of a mile, what is the distance between the two cities?

. . . .

What is the trick to solving word problems that involve ratios of separate parts that make up a whole?

Solve the following: The ratio of boys to girls enrolled at a camp of 145 kids is 2:3. How many boys are enrolled?

. . . .

The ratio of full-time employees to part-time employees in an environmental consulting firm is 3:5. If the firm has 20 more part-time employees than full-time employees, how many employees of each type are there?

$\frac{3 \text{ cm}}{5 \text{ miles}} = \frac{7.8 \text{ cm}}{m \text{ miles}}$

$3(m) = 5(7.8)$

$3m = 39$

$m =$ **13 miles**

• •

The trick to questions like this is attaching a variable, like x, to both of the parts and then writing an equation that represents how the parts relate to each other and the whole. Represent boys as $2x$ and girls as $3x$. Since boys + girls = 145, write and solve the equation $2x + 3x = 145$.

Simplifying yields $x = 29$.

Lastly, plug $x = 29$ into "$2x$" to see that the number of boys is $2 \times 29 =$ **58**.

• •

Write the ratio of full-time to part-time employees as "$3x$ to $5x$." The relationship between part-time and full-time employees is $5x - 3x = 20$. Therefore, $x = 10$. There are $3 \times 10 =$ **30 full-time employees**, and there are $5 \times 10 =$ **50 part-time employees**.

The ratio of bikes to cars in a medium-sized European city is 4:3. If there are a total of 2,000 bikes, how many cars are there in the city?

. . . .

The number of bikes can be expressed as 4x, and the number of bikes is represented as 3x. Since there are 2,000 bikes, write 2,000 = 4x, so x = 500. Substitute 500 in for x to get 3 × 500 = **1,500 cars**.

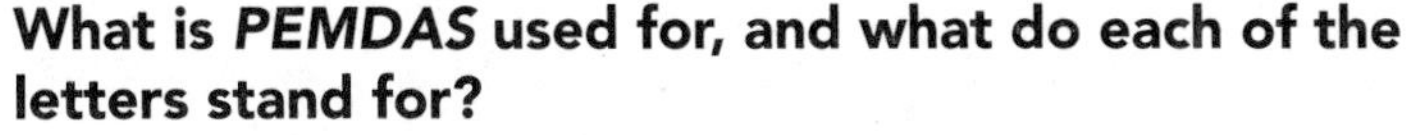

What is *PEMDAS* used for, and what do each of the letters stand for?

What is a common mistake to avoid when using PEMDAS to perform multiplication and division in an expression such as $60 \div 4 \times 3$?

Simplify: $2 \times 24 \div 3$

ORDER OF OPERATIONS

PEMDAS (which you can remember by using the expression *Please Excuse My Dear Aunt Sally*) is used to represent the correct order of operations to follow when evaluating expressions.

P ARENTHESES

E XPONENTS

M ULTIPLY

D IVIDE

A DD

S UBTRACT

It is critical to remember that multiplication and division have equal ranking and must be done from left to right, rather than performing the multiplication first and then division.

$60 \div 4 \times 3 =$

$(60 \div 4) \times 3 =$

$15 \times 3 = 45$

(Note that if 4×3 is incorrectly performed first, the final answer will be $60 \div 12 = 5$.)

Recall that in PEMDAS, multiplication and division are performed in order from left to right.

$2 \times 24 \div 3 =$

$(2 \times 24) \div 3 =$

$48 \div 3 =$ **16**

Simplify: $10 + 30 \div 5$

. . . .

Simplify: $10 + 2(8 - 5)$

. . . .

Simplify: $3 \times 2^3 - 100$

Note that with PEMDAS, division comes before addition:

$10 + 30 \div 5 =$

$10 + 6 =$ **16**

Note that with PEMDAS, the work inside the parentheses comes first:

$10 + 2(8 - 5) =$
$10 + 2(3)$

Then, multiplication comes before addition:

$10 + 2(3) = 10 + 6 =$ **16**

This expression contains multiplication, an exponent, and subtraction. By referring to PEMDAS, see that the exponent comes first:

$3 \times 2^3 - 100 =$

$3 \times 8 - 100$

Then, multiplication comes before addition:

$(3 \times 8) - 100 = 24 - 100 =$ **–76**

Simplify: $2 + 3^2(9 - 6 \div 3)$

Note that with PEMDAS, exponents come before multiplication:

$2 + 3^2(9 - 6 \div 3) =$

$2 + 9(9 - 6 \div 3) =$

$2 + 9(9 - 2) =$

$2 + 9(7) =$

$2 + 63 =$ **65**

Define the term *sum* and translate "the sum of *c* and *d* is 49" into an algebraic equation.

. . . .

Define the term *difference* and translate "the difference of *c* and *d* is 8" into an algebraic equation.

. . . .

The sum of 16 and 60 is how much larger than the absolute value of the difference of 16 and 60?

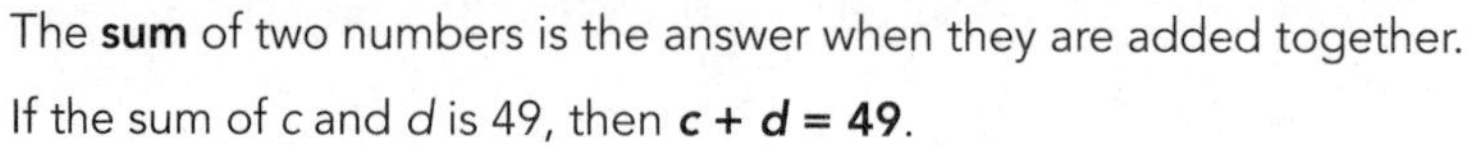

The **sum** of two numbers is the answer when they are added together.

If the sum of c and d is 49, then $\mathbf{c + d = 49}$.

The **difference** of two numbers is the answer when they are subtracted.

If the difference of c and d is 8, then $\mathbf{c - d = 8}$.

The sum of 16 and 60 is $16 + 60 = 76$.

The absolute value of the difference of 16 and 60 is $|16 - 60| = |-44| = 44$.

$76 - 44 =$ **32**, so the sum of 16 and 60 is 32 greater than the absolute value of the difference of 16 and 60.

Define the term *product* and translate "the product of *c* and *d* is 24" into an algebraic equation.

. . . .

Write an expression that represents "5 less than the square of the product of *w* and 5*v* is 95."

. . . .

Define the term *quotient* and translate "the quotient of *c* and *d* is 12" into an algebraic equation.

The **product** of two numbers is the answer when they are multiplied.

If the product of c and d is 24, then $\mathbf{c \times d = 24}$.

. . . .

The product of w and $5v$ is $w \times 5v = 5wv$.

The square of this product is $(5wv)^2$.

5 less than this square is $(5wv)^2 - 5$.

Since this expression is 95, set it equal to 95:

$\mathbf{(5wv)^2 - 5 = 95}$

. . . .

The **quotient** of two numbers is the answer when they are divided.

If the quotient of c and d is 12, then $\mathbf{\frac{c}{d} = 12}$.

What is a *coefficient*? In the term $76v^4w$, what is the coefficient?

. . . .

What is the answer when the sum of the coefficients is divided by the leading power in the expression $4x^2 + 3x - 5$?

. . . .

What is the trick for correctly translating into math the terms "quantity of" or "sum of" in word problems? For example, how is the following expressed: "6 times the quantity of 5 plus *x*"?

A **coefficient** is a number that comes before the variable or variables in an expression. In $76v^4w$, the coefficient is **76**.

• •

The coefficients are 4 and 3 and the leading power is 2, so the answer is $\frac{7}{2}$. (Since 5 does not have any variables, it is called a *constant* and not a coefficient.)

• •

When you see "quantity of" or "sum of" in a word problem, it is an indication that two or more items need to be grouped within a set of parentheses.

"6 times the quantity of 5 plus *x*" is correctly written as **6(5 + *x*)**.

Translate the following into an algebraic expression: "6 times the sum of 8 and x^2"

. . . .

Consider the phrases "5 less than *x*" and "5 fewer than *x*." What operation do "less than" and "fewer than" represent?

What is the tricky thing to remember when translating these expressions into a mathematical expression?

. . . .

Translate the following into an algebraic equation: "*x* less than 7 is 13."

$6(8 + x^2)$

. . . .

"Less than" and "fewer than" both mean subtraction.

The tricky thing about these two phrases is that *you* must reverse the order of the items as they are presented. For example, "5 less than x" is written as $x - 5$, not $5 - x$.

. . . .

"Less than" means subtraction. The equation "x less than 7 is 13" is written **$7 - x = 13$**.

Pete has 6 fewer than 3 times the number of cookbooks that Celia has. If Celia has *c* cookbooks, write an expression, in terms of *c*, for how many cookbooks Pete has.

In word problems, what does the term "twice" represent?
Translate the following into an equation: "James is twice as tall as Erin."

Bob has 10 fewer tools than Erica. Erica has 2 fewer than twice the number of tools as Juan. Juan has 13 tools. How many tools does Bob have?

$p = 3c - 6$

"Twice" represents multiplication by 2.

"James is twice as tall as Erin" is written as **James's height = Erin's height × 2**.

If Juan has 13, then twice that would be 26. "Two fewer than twice" would be 24, so Erica has 24 tools. Since Bob has 10 fewer tools than Erica, he has **14 tools**.

In word problems, what operation does the word "of" represent? (Think about how many pencils would be purchased if Sam bought 5 packages of 8 pencils each.)

. . . .

What is the difference between "14 is less than 2*y*" and "14 less than 2*y*"?

. . . .

Tina owns *c* fish. Beth owns 10 fewer than twice the number of fish that Tina owns. Write an expression that represents the number of fish that Beth owns in terms of *c*.

The word "of" translates to multiplication. 5 packages of 8 pencils each would be 5×8 = **40 pencils**.

• •

The key difference here is the word "is." "Is" translates to an equal sign, and "is less than" (or "is greater than") translates to an inequality symbol such as $<$ or $>$. "14 is less than $2y$" is written as $\mathbf{14 < 2y}$.

If there is no "is" with the "less than," then "less than" is referring to subtraction: "14 less than $2y$" is written as $\mathbf{2y - 14}$.

• •

$\mathbf{b = 2c - 10}$

As part of a game, Gil uses special procedures to come up with a new number. To come up with his new number, Gil takes the original number, cubes it, adds 5 to it, and finally multiplies it by 2. If the original number is represented by *g*, write an expression that represents Gil's new number.

. . . .

A real estate agent found that the asking price of a home in his area can be estimated by multiplying the square footage of the house by $154 and adding $8,065. If *S* represents the square footage and *P* represents the asking price, write a formula to represent this estimation method.

. . . .

$2(g^3 + 5)$

Multiplying *S* by \$154 is represented by \$154*S*. Then \$8,065 is added to this term, which gives the final equation ***P* = \$154*S* + \$8,065**.

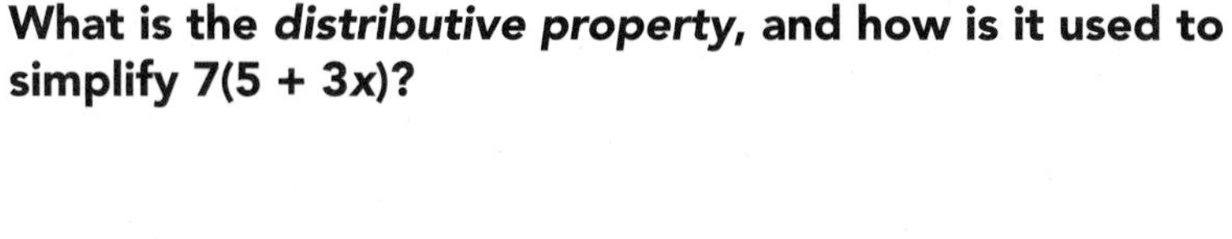

What is the *distributive property,* and how is it used to simplify $7(5 + 3x)$?

. . . .

Simplify: $-9(-5x + 3y - 2)$

. . . .

What is a common mistake to avoid when simplifying expressions that have a number being added to the factor outside a set of parentheses?

Perform the following:

$5 + 3(4 + x)$

The **distributive property** is used when a number is to be multiplied to two or more expressions inside parentheses. When a number is directly touching a parenthesis, it means that this is a factor that must be multiplied to every number within the parentheses:

$7(5 + 3x) =$

$7(5) + 7(3x) =$ $\mathbf{35 + 21x}$

. . . .

$-9(-5x + 3y - 2) =$

$-9(-5x) + (-9)(3y) - (-9)(2) =$

$\mathbf{45x - 27y + 18}$

. . . .

Since PEMDAS states that multiplication comes before addition, you cannot add the 5 to the 3 as the initial step. The 3 must first be multiplied to all of the items in the parentheses:

$5 + 3(4 + x) =$

$5 + 3(4) + 3(x) =$

$5 + 12 + 3x =$

$\mathbf{17 + 3x}$

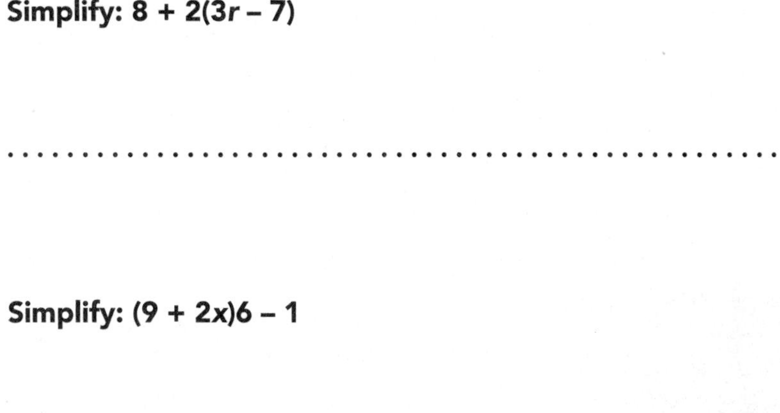

Simplify: $8 + 2(3r - 7)$

Simplify: $(9 + 2x)6 - 1$

How do you rewrite an expression such as $42x + 18$ using the greatest common factor and the distributive property?

$8 + 2(3r - 7) =$

$8 + 2(3r) - 2(7) =$

$8 + 6r - 14 =$

$\mathbf{6r - 6}$

Even though the factor of 6 is on the right-hand side of the parentheses, this expression still requires the distributive property:

$(9 + 2x)6 - 1 =$

$(9)6 + (2x)6 - 1 =$

$54 + 12x - 1 =$

$\mathbf{53 + 12x}$

First, identify that the GCF of 42*x* and 18 is 6. Then, write that GCF outside a set of parentheses and divide both 42*x* and 12 by the factor (6) in order to calculate the numbers that will fill the parentheses:

$42x + 18 =$

6(___ + ___) =

6(7x + 3) since $(6)(7x) + (6)(3) = 42x + 18$.

Factor out the greatest common factor:
$16g^2 - 40g$

What is a common mistake to avoid when simplifying expressions that have a negative sign preceding the number being distributed?
Simplify: $4y - 2(y - 9)$

Simplify: $12 - (4x - 8)^3$

The greatest common factor of $16g^2 - 40g$ is $\mathbf{8g}$.

$16g^2 - 40g = 8g(\_\_\_ - \_\_\_) =$

$8g(2g - 5)$

. . . .

Since subtraction is the same as adding a negative, the "$4y - 2$" before the parentheses is equivalent to "$4y + (-2)$." This means that the negative sign must get distributed along with the 2.

$4y - 2(y - 9) =$

$4y + (-2)(y - 9) =$

$4y + (-2)(y) - (-2)(9) =$

$4y - 2y - (-18) =$

$\mathbf{2y + 18}$

. . . .

Even though the factor of 3 is on the right-hand side of the parentheses, this expression still requires the distributive property:

$12 - (4x - 8)3 =$

$12 - [(4x)(3) - (8)(3)] =$

$12 - [12x - 24]$

Now, distribute the negative sign before the parentheses:

$12 - 12x + 24 =$

$\mathbf{-12x + 36}$

Simplify: $10 - 2(-6 + 3x)$

What are the two linear factors of the polynomial $2x^2 - x$?

What are "like" terms?

This expression requires that the distributive property be used to distribute the –2:

$10 - 2(-6 + 3x) =$
$10 + (-2)(-6 + 3x) =$
$10 + (-2)(-6) + (-2)(3x) =$
$10 + 12 + (-6x) =$
$\mathbf{-6x + 22}$

. . . .

Both terms only share x as a factor. When this term is factored out, the resulting expression is $x(2x - 1)$, so the two linear factors are **x** and **2x – 1**.

. . . .

Two terms are said to be "like" if they contain identical variables and exponents.

$5x^3y^2z$ and $-13x^3y^2z$ are like terms since they both contain x^3, y^2, and z. (The coefficients do not need to be the same and are normally different.)

What are "unlike" terms?

. . . .

Identify which pairs of terms are like and which are unlike:

A. $8jkg$ and $-8jk$
B. $13dn^3$ and $-81dn^3$
C. $7v^2w^5z^3$ and $7v^2w^4z^3$

. . . .

Which can be added and subtracted?

A. Only unlike terms
B. Only like terms
C. Both unlike and like terms

OPERATIONS ON ALGEBRAIC EXPRESSIONS

Two terms are said to be "unlike" either if they contain different variables or if any of their matching variables have different exponents. $10x^3y^2z$ and $10x^2y^2z$ are unlike terms because $10x^3y^2z$ has x^3 and $10x^2y^2z$ has x^2.

A. $8jkg$ and $-8jk$ are **unlike**.

B. $13dn^3$ and $-81dn^3$ are **like**.

C. $7v^2w^5z^3$ and $7v^2w^4z^3$ are **unlike**.

Only **like terms** may be added and subtracted. If any of the variables or exponents are not identical, then the terms are unlike and cannot be combined through addition or subtraction.

How are the following like terms added?
$7a^5b^2 + 70a^5b^2$

. . . .

Write and simplify an expression that is equivalent to the sum of $\frac{1}{2}x$ and $\frac{3}{4}x - 5$.

. . . .

What types of terms can be multiplied?
A. Only unlike terms
B. Only like terms
C. Both unlike and like terms

To add or subtract like terms, add or subtract the coefficients and keep the variables and their exponents the same.

$7a^5b^2 + 70a^5b^2 =$

$(70 + 7)(a^5b^2) =$

$\mathbf{77a^5b^2}$

$\frac{1}{2}x + \frac{3}{4}x - 5 =$

$\frac{2}{4}x + \frac{3}{4}x - 5 =$

$\mathbf{\frac{5}{4}x - 5}$

Although only like terms can be added and subtracted, **both unlike and like terms** may be multiplied.

How do you simplify $4a^2b \times 10a^3b^2c$?

Simplify: $6x^2y^3 \times -4x^5y^{-2}$

What types of terms can be divided?

A. Only unlike terms

B. Only like terms

C. Both unlike and like terms

Simplify: $\frac{24a^7b^4}{6a^3b^3}$

Unlike terms may be multiplied. In order to multiply terms, follow these steps:

1. Multiply their coefficients.
2. Add the exponents of like variables.
3. Write the coefficient and variables as a single–term product.

Multiply: $4a^2b \times 10a^3b^2c$

$(4 \times 10) \times a^{(2+3)} \times b^{(1+2)} \times c$

$\mathbf{40a^5b^3c}$

$6x^2y^3 \times -4x^5y^{-2} =$

$(6 \times -4) \times x^{(2+5)} \times y^{(3+-2)} =$

$\mathbf{-24x^7y}$

Both unlike and like terms may be divided. In order to divide terms, follow these steps:

1. Divide the coefficients.
2. Subtract the exponents of like variables in the denominator from the exponents of the like variables in the numerator.
3. Write the new coefficient quotient and variables as a single term.

$\frac{24a^7b^4}{6a^3b^3} =$

$(\frac{24}{6})(a^{7-3})(b^{4-3}) =$

$\mathbf{4a^4b}$

Simplify: $\frac{10x^8y^3}{-4x^7y^{-3}}$

. . . .

How do you add and subtract polynomial expressions like $(5x^3 + 2x^2 - 14x) + (10x^3 + 8x^2 - 7x)$?

. . . .

Simplify: $(6x^2 + 2xy - 9) - (4x^3 + 2x^2 - 5xy + 8)$

$\frac{10x^8y^3}{-4x^7y^{-3}} =$

$\left(\frac{10}{-4}\right)(x^{8-7})(y^{3-(-3)}) =$

$\mathbf{-\frac{5}{2}xy^6}$

· ·

$(5x^3 + 2x^2 - 14x) + (10x^3 + 8x^2 - 7x)$

Since these polynomials do not have any factors, and there is no negative sign that needs to be distributed, eliminate the parentheses and regroup the like terms together as follows:

$\underline{5x^3 + 10x^3} + \underline{2x^2 + 8x^2} + \underline{(-14x) - 7x}$

Combine like terms:

$\mathbf{15x^3 + 10x^2 - 21x}$

· ·

Since there is a subtraction sign between the two sets of parentheses, you need to distribute that negative to all the terms inside the second set of parentheses:

$(6x^2 + 2xy - 9) - (4x^3 + 2x^2 - 5xy + 8) =$

$6x^2 + 2xy - 9 - 4x^3 - 2x^2 + 5xy - 8$

Then, group like terms together:

$\underline{-4x^3} - \underline{2x^2 + 6x^2} + \underline{2xy + 5xy} - \underline{9 - 8} =$

Then, combine like terms:

$\mathbf{-4x^3 + 4x^2 + 7xy - 17}$

$(x^2 + 5) - (x^2 - x) =$

. . . .

$2w(w - 1) - (w - 1) =$

. . . .

Simplify: $-2(-3x^2 - 8x + 4) + 3(4x^2 + 9x - 5)$

These expressions are being subtracted and not multiplied. Distribute the negative sign and combine like terms:

$x^2 + 5 - x^2 + x =$

$\underline{x^2 - x^2} + 5 + x =$

$\mathbf{5 + x}$

Distribute the $2w$ to the first set of parentheses and the negative sign to the second set:

$2w(w - 1) - (w - 1) =$

$2w^2 - 2w - w + 1 =$

$\mathbf{2w^2 - 3w + 1}$

First, distribute the –2 and the 3:

$(-2)(-3x^2) - (-2)(8x) + (-2)(4) + (3)(4x^2) + (3)(9x) - (3)(5) =$

$6x^2 + 16x - 8 + 12x^2 + 27x - 15$

Then, group like terms and combine:

$\underline{6x^2 + 12x^2} + \underline{16x + 27x} - \underline{8 - 15} =$

$\mathbf{18x^2 + 43x - 23}$

$-x^2(x + 1) - (x^3 + 4x^2) =$

. . . .

What does FOIL stand for when multiplying binomials? How do you use FOIL to multiply $(x + 3)(x - 2)$?

. . . .

$(3x - 5)(4x - 1) =$

$-x^2(x + 1) - (x^3 + 4x^2) =$

$-x^3 - x^2 - x^3 - 4x^2 =$

$-x^3 - x^3 - x^2 - 4x^2 =$

$\mathbf{-2x^3 - 5x^2}$

FOIL stands for First, Outer, Inner, and Last. These terms designate each pair of numbers that gets multiplied when finding the product of two binomials:

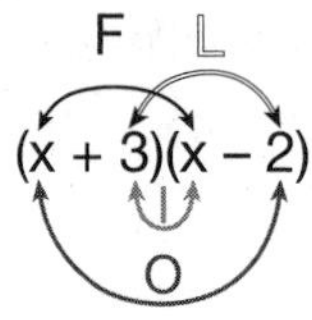

First Outer Inner Last

$x \cdot x + x \cdot (-2) + 3 \cdot x + 3 \cdot (-2)$

$= x^2 - 2x + 3x - 6$

$= x^2 + x - 6$

Using FOIL,

$(3x - 5)(4x - 1) =$

$12x^2 - 3x - 20x + 5 =$

$\mathbf{12x^2 - 23x + 5}$

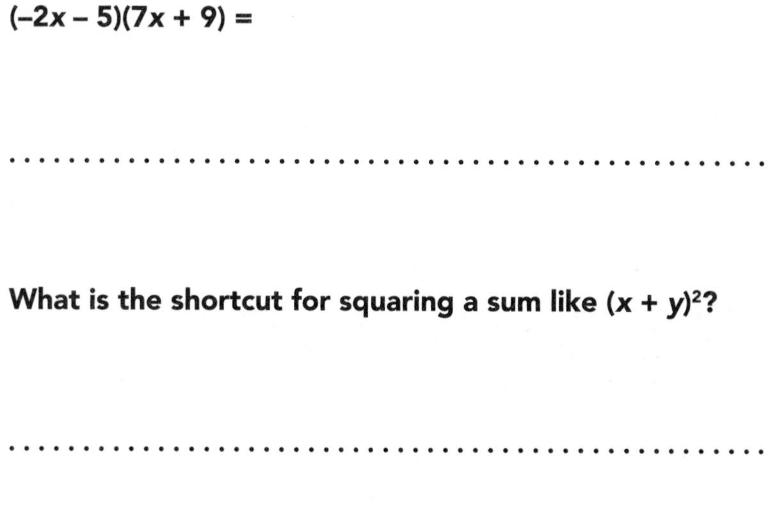

$(-2x - 5)(7x + 9) =$

. . . .

What is the shortcut for squaring a sum like $(x + y)^2$?

. . . .

Simplify: $(v + 4w)^2$

Using FOIL,

$(-2x - 5)(7x + 9) =$

$-14x^2 - 18x - 35x - 45 =$

$\mathbf{-14x^2 - 53x - 45}$

$(x + y)^2 =$

$(x + y)(x + y) =$

$\mathbf{x^2 + 2xy + y^2}$

The shortcut for squaring a sum like $(x + y)^2$ is to square the first term, add twice the product of the terms, and add the square of the second term.

This is the square of a sum:

$(v + 4w)^2 =$

$v^2 + 2(4wv) + (4w)^2 =$

$\mathbf{v^2 + 8wv + 16w^2}$

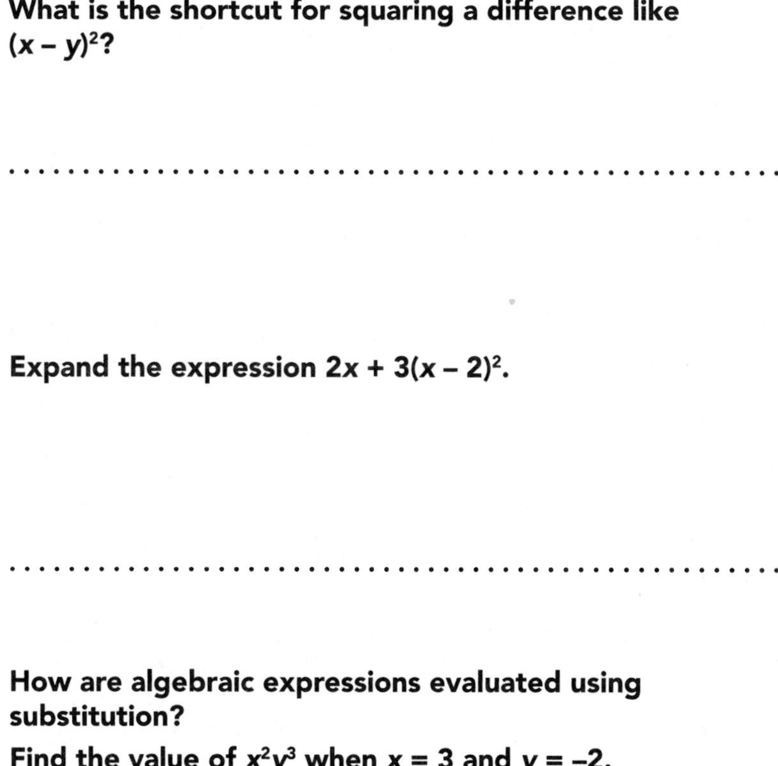

What is the shortcut for squaring a difference like $(x - y)^2$?

Expand the expression $2x + 3(x - 2)^2$.

How are algebraic expressions evaluated using substitution?
Find the value of x^2y^3 when $x = 3$ and $y = -2$.

$(x - y)^2 =$

$(x - y)(x - y) =$

$\mathbf{x^2 - 2xy + y^2}$

The shortcut for squaring a difference like $(x - y)^2$ is to square the first term, subtract twice the product of the terms, and add the square of the second term.

. . . .

Following the order of operations, the binomial $(x - 2)$ must first be squared, then the 3 needs to be distributed, and then like terms combined:

$2x + 3(x - 2)^2 =$

$2x + 3(x^2 - 4x + 4) =$

$2x + 3(x^2) - 3(4x) + 3(4) =$

$2x + 3x^2 - 12x + 12 =$

$\mathbf{3x^2 - 10x + 12}$

. . . .

In order to evaluate expressions, carefully substitute the values of the given variables into the equation and follow PEMDAS. Be especially careful when substituting negative numbers!

$x^2y^3 =$

$(3)^2(-2)^3 =$

$9 \times (-8) = \mathbf{-72}$

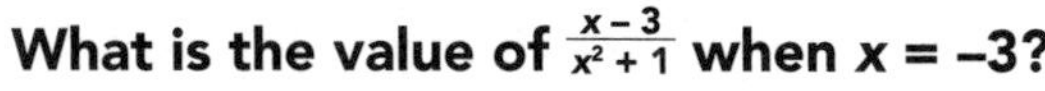

What is the value of $\frac{x-3}{x^2+1}$ when $x = -3$?

. . . .

Evaluate the expression $4x^2 + 3(1 - x)$ when $x = -2$.

. . . .

What is $2x^2 + x - 4$ when $x = -3$?

$\frac{x-3}{x^2+1} =$

$\frac{(-3)-3}{(-3)^2+1} =$

$\frac{-6}{9+1} =$

$\frac{-6}{10} = \mathbf{\frac{-3}{5}}$

You cannot multiply 4×-2 and then square the answer because exponents come before multiplication in the order of operations. Plus, there are parentheses in the second half of the problem, and PEMDAS indicates you solve those first.

$4x^2 + 3(1 - x) =$

$4(-2)^2 + 3(1 - (-2)) =$

$4(-2)^2 + 3(3) =$

$4(-2)(-2) + 3(3) =$

$4 \times 4 + 3(3) =$

$16 + 9 = \mathbf{25}$

Replace every x with the given value of -3:

$2(-3)^2 + (-3) - 4 =$

$2 \times 9 + -3 - 4 =$

$18 - 3 - 4 =$

$15 - 4 = \mathbf{11}$

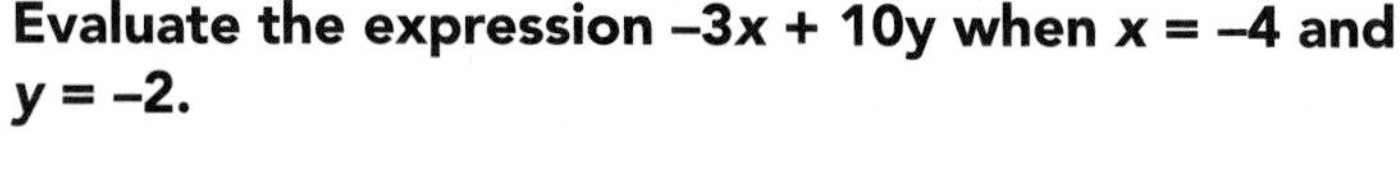

Evaluate the expression $-3x + 10y$ when $x = -4$ and $y = -2$.

Simplify the expression $5x + 3(x - 4)^2$.

Simplify the expression $\frac{3}{x} \div \frac{5x}{2}$.

$-3(-4) + 10(-2) =$

$12 - 20 =$ **-8**

$5x + 3(x - 4)^2$

$5x + 3(x - 4)(x - 4)$

$5x + 3(x^2 - 8x + 16)$

$5x + 3x^2 - 24x + 48$

$3x^2 - 19x + 48$

$\frac{3}{x} \div \frac{5x}{2} =$

$\frac{3}{x} \times \frac{2}{5x} =$

$\frac{6}{5x^2}$

$\frac{2}{x(x-1)} + \frac{1}{x-1} =$

Simplify the following expression:
$4x + 5 + 2(6x - 7) - (5x^2 + 3x)$

When given $\frac{2}{x(x-1)} + \frac{1}{x-1}$, it is first necessary to find a common denominator. Multiply the second fraction by $\frac{x}{x}$ to create the common denominator of $x(x - 1)$: $\frac{1}{x-1} \times \frac{x}{x} = \frac{x}{x(x-1)}$. Now add the numerators and keep the denominators the same: $\mathbf{\frac{2}{x(x-1)} + \frac{x}{x(x-1)} = \frac{2x}{x(x-1)}}$

$4x + 5 + 2(6x - 7) - (5x^2 + 3x) =$

$4x + 5 + 12x - 14 - 5x^2 - 3x =$

$-5x^2 - \underline{3x + 4x + 12x} + \underline{5 - 14} =$

$\mathbf{-5x^2 + 13x - 9}$

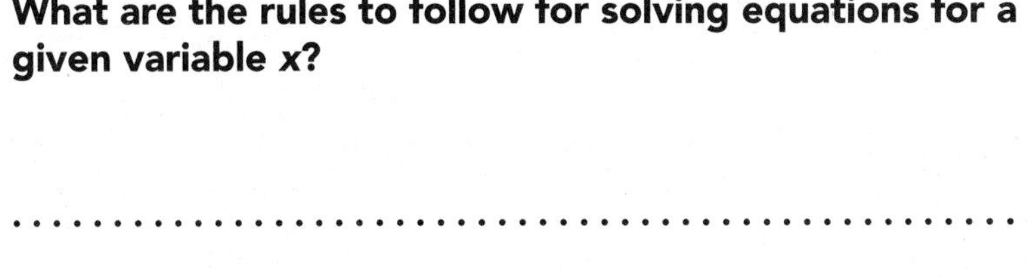

What are the rules to follow for solving equations for a given variable *x*?

What are the required steps to isolate *x* in the equation below?
$-8x + 1 = -23$

Solve for *y*:
$2y - 4 = 21$

SOLVING EQUATIONS

1. Whatever is done to one side of the equation must be done to the other.
2. Use opposite operations to isolate x (addition undoes subtraction, subtraction undoes addition, division undoes multiplication, multiplication undoes division, taking the square root undoes an exponent of 2).
3. When isolating x, reverse the order of PEMDAS and begin with addition/subtraction, then move onto division/multiplication, and if necessary, save taking the square root until the end.

. . . .

When solving equations for a variable, the order of operations is reversed. In order to get x alone, first subtract 1 from both sides and then divide both sides by –8:

$-8x + 1 = -23$

$\underline{\quad -1 \quad -1}$

$-8x = -24$

$\frac{-8x}{-8} = \frac{-24}{-8}$

$\mathbf{x = 3}$

. . . .

Remember, reverse PEMDAS and use opposite operations to get the variable alone. To move the – 4 away from y, add 4 to each side of the equation:

$2y - 4 = 21$

$\underline{\quad +4 \quad +4}$

$2y + 0 = 25$

Next, divide each side of the equation by 2 to isolate y.

$\frac{2y}{2} = \frac{25}{2}$

$\mathbf{y = 12.5}$

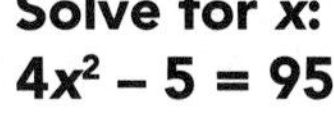

Solve for *x*:
$4x^2 - 5 = 95$

Solve for *x*:
$10x - 4y = 2$

Solve for *x* in terms of *y*, *w*, and *v*: $xy + w = v$

$$\begin{array}{l} 4x^2 - 5 = 95 \\ \underline{+5 \quad +5} \\ 4x^2 = 100 \end{array}$$

$\frac{4x^2}{4} = \frac{100}{4}$

$x^2 = 25$

$\mathbf{\sqrt{x^2} = \pm 5}$

$10x - 4y = 2$

$10x = 2 + 4y$

$x = \frac{2 + 4y}{10}$

$\mathbf{x = \frac{1 + 2y}{5}}$

$xy + w = v$

$\underline{\quad -w \quad -w}$

$xy = v - w$

$\frac{xy}{y} = \frac{v - w}{y}$

$\mathbf{x = \frac{v - w}{y}}$

If $\frac{3}{4}x = 72$, then $x =$

A customer uses two coupons to purchase a product at a grocery store, where the original price of the product was $8.30. If the final price paid by the customer was $7.00 and each coupon gave the same discount in money off (not percentage discount), what was the value of the discount provided by a single coupon?

Twice the sum of a number and 10 is 42. What is the number?

Multiply both sides by $\frac{4}{3}$ to get x alone:

$(\frac{3}{4}x) \times \frac{4}{3} = 72 \times \frac{4}{3}$

$x = \frac{72}{1} \times \frac{4}{3} = \mathbf{96}$

. . . .

If x represents the discount provided by a single coupon, then $2x$ represents the combined discount provided by both. Given the prices before and after, the following equation can be written and solved:

$8.3 - 2x = 7$

$-2x = -1.3$

$\mathbf{x = \$0.65}$

. . . .

Let the number = n. Twice the sum of this number and 10 is represented as $2(n + 10)$. Set this equal to 42 and solve for n:

$2(n + 10) = 42$

$2n + 20 = 42$

$2n = 22$

$\mathbf{n = 11}$

How is it determined if a given coordinate pair is a solution to a linear equation? Is (5,–2) a solution to the equation $-3x + 4y = -23$?

. . . .

What is the *slope-intercept form* of a linear equation, and what is it useful for?

. . . .

What is the equation $y = mx + b$ and what does m represent?

Given the point (5,–2) and the equation $-3x + 4y = -23$, substitute $x = 5$ and $y = -2$ into the linear equation to see if it results in a true or false statement. If it is a true statement, like 7 = 7, then the point is a solution. If it is a false statement, such as 1 + 1 = 5, then the point is not a solution.

$-3x + 4y = -23$
$-3(5) + 4(-2) = -23$
$-15 + -8 = -23$, which is a true statement, so **(5,–2) is a solution**.

. . . .

$\boldsymbol{y = mx + b}$ is the slope-intercept form of linear equations. This is a useful form because at a single glance, you can see what the y-intercept and the slope are.

. . . .

$y = mx + b$ is the **slope-intercept form** of a linear equation, and m represents the **slope**. The slope is a measure of how quickly a line rises or falls. Slope is the ratio of $\frac{\text{rise}}{\text{run}}$ where "rise" is the change in y values compared to "run," which is the change in x values between any two points.

What does *b* stand for in the equation $y = mx + b$?

. . . .

What do *x* and *y* represent in the slope-intercept form of a linear equation, $y = mx + b$?

. . . .

What is the *x-intercept* of a linear equation and how is it found?

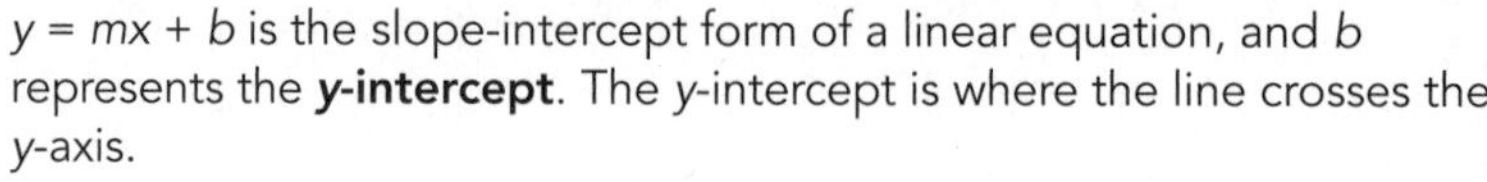

$y = mx + b$ is the slope-intercept form of a linear equation, and b represents the **y-intercept**. The y-intercept is where the line crosses the y-axis.

---

x and y represent all **coordinate pairs (x,y)** that are points on the line. The numerical values of (x,y) coordinate points that are on the line will also make a true arithmetic statement when substituted into the equation $y = mx + b$.

The x-intercept is **where the line crosses the x-axis**. Regardless of what form a linear equation is presented in, the x-intercept can always be found by replacing the y with 0 and then solving for x.

What is the *y-intercept* of a linear equation and how is it found?

. . . .

Find the x-intercept and y-intercept of the line $y = 3x + 4$.

. . . .

What is the *slope* of a line? How is the slope found when given two points, (x_1,y_1) and (x_2,y_2)?

The *y*-intercept is **where a line crosses the *y*-axis**. Regardless of what form a linear equation is presented in, the *y*-intercept can always be found by replacing the *x* with 0 and then solving for *y*. (If the line is represented in $y = mx + b$ form, then the *y*-intercept is *b*.)

. . . .

Since this line is in the form $y = mx + b$, where *b* is the *y*-intercept, it is evident that the *y*-intercept is 4. In order to find the *x*-intercept, replace *y* with 0 and solve for *x*:

$y = 3x + 4$

$0 = 3x + 4$

$-3x = 4$

$\mathbf{x = \frac{-4}{3}}$

. . . .

The slope is the **rate of change** of a line, which shows how quickly a line rises or falls as *x* increases. Slope is the ratio of the vertical change, $y_2 - y_1$ = rise, to the horizontal change, $x_2 - x_1$ = run.

The formula for finding slope between any two points, (x_1,y_1) and (x_2,y_2), is:

$\mathbf{m = \frac{rise}{run} = \frac{y_2 - y_1}{x_2 - x_1}}$

What is the slope of the line that goes through the points (8,–3) and (–2,2)?

. . . .

The slope of line *v* is $\frac{2}{5}$. If line *v* goes through points (–4,7) and (6,*x*), find the value of *x*.

. . . .

How can you find the rate of change from the data in the table below?

x	*y*
3	6
4	8
5	10
6	12

$m = \frac{2-(-3)}{-2-8} = \frac{5}{-10} = \mathbf{\frac{-1}{2}}$

$m = \frac{2}{5} = \frac{y_2 - y_1}{x_2 - x_1} = \frac{x-7}{6-(-4)}$

$\frac{2}{5} = \frac{x-7}{10}$

$5(x-7) = 2(10)$

$5x - 35 = 20$

$5x = 55$

$x = \frac{55}{5} = \mathbf{11}$

Regardless of whether a table is presented vertically or horizontally, all that is needed to find the rate of change of a linear relationship are two (x,y) coordinate pairs. In this case, use (3,6) and (4,8) to substitute into the equation for m:

$m = \frac{\text{rise}}{\text{run}} = \frac{y_2 - y_1}{x_2 - x_1}$

$m = \frac{\text{rise}}{\text{run}} = \frac{y_2 - y_1}{x_2 - x_1} = \frac{8-6}{4-3} = \frac{2}{1} = \mathbf{2}$

x	0	2	4	6
y	1	4	7	10

The table above shows four points in the *x-y* coordinate plane that lie on the graph of a line *y* = *mx* + *b*. Based on this information, what is the value of *m*?

Examine each of the proportional relationships below. Which athlete, A or B, ran faster?

A.

Time (seconds)	Distance (meters)
2	5
3	7.5
4	10
5	12.5

B.

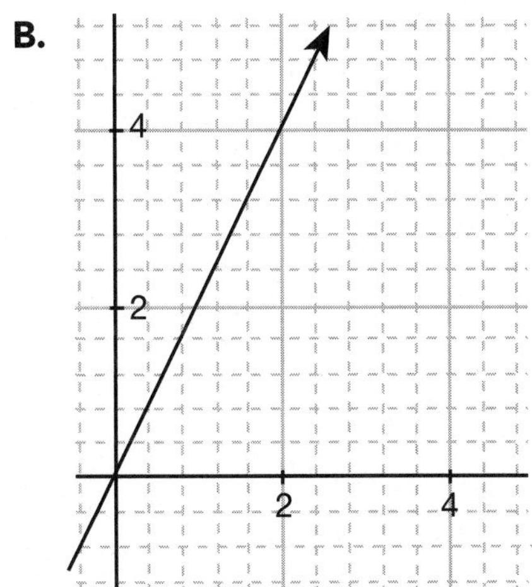

Use the first two points (0,1) and (2,4) in the equation $m = \frac{y_2 - y_1}{x_2 - x_1}$:

$m = \frac{y_2 - y_1}{x_2 - x_1} = \frac{4-1}{2-0} = \mathbf{\frac{3}{2}}$

To determine which athlete ran faster, we have to find the rate of change for each runner. This will give us the slope, which in this case is the speed.

Athlete A = $\frac{\text{change in distance}}{\text{change in time}}$ = 2.5 m/s

Athlete B = $\frac{\text{change in distance}}{\text{change in time}}$ = 2 m/s

So **Athlete B** was faster by **0.5 m/s**.

The figure below represents the cumulative number of packages loaded onto trucks in one day at a small warehouse. When the day began, there were already 50 packages loaded. Based on this graph, how many packages were loaded each hour?

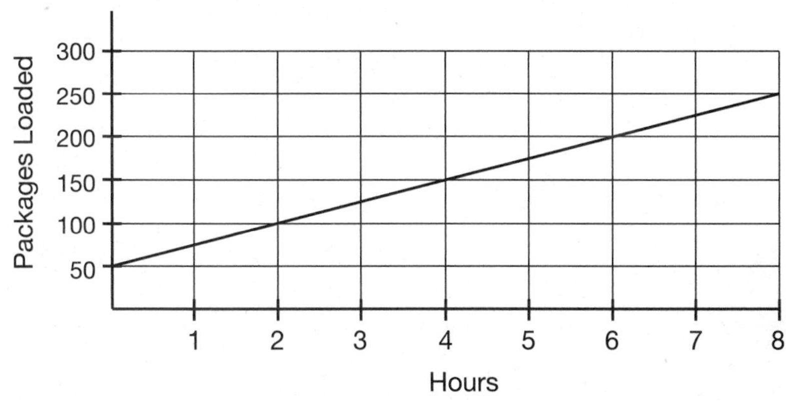

What is the slope of a vertical line?

What is the slope of a horizontal line?

The slope of the line represents the unit rate. Use the start point (0,50) and the end point (8,250) in the slope formula:

$m = \frac{y_2 - y_1}{x_2 - x_1}$

$m = \frac{250 - 50}{8 - 0} = \frac{200}{8} =$ **25 packages per hour**

All vertical lines have a run of 0, since they have only vertical change and no horizontal change. Since any fraction that has a zero in the denominator is undefined, **the slope of all vertical lines is undefined**. (A trick to remember this is that it is impossible to walk on a vertical line, so its slope is undefined.)

All horizontal lines have a rise of 0, since they have only horizontal change and no vertical change. Since any fraction that has a 0 in the numerator is 0, **the slope of all horizontal lines is 0**. (A trick to remember this is if you were to walk on a horizontal line, you would not be walking uphill or downhill because it has a slope of 0.)

A line passes through the point (4,0) and has a slope of $\frac{3}{4}$. What is the equation of this line in slope-intercept form?

What is the equation of the line graphed on the coordinate plane below?

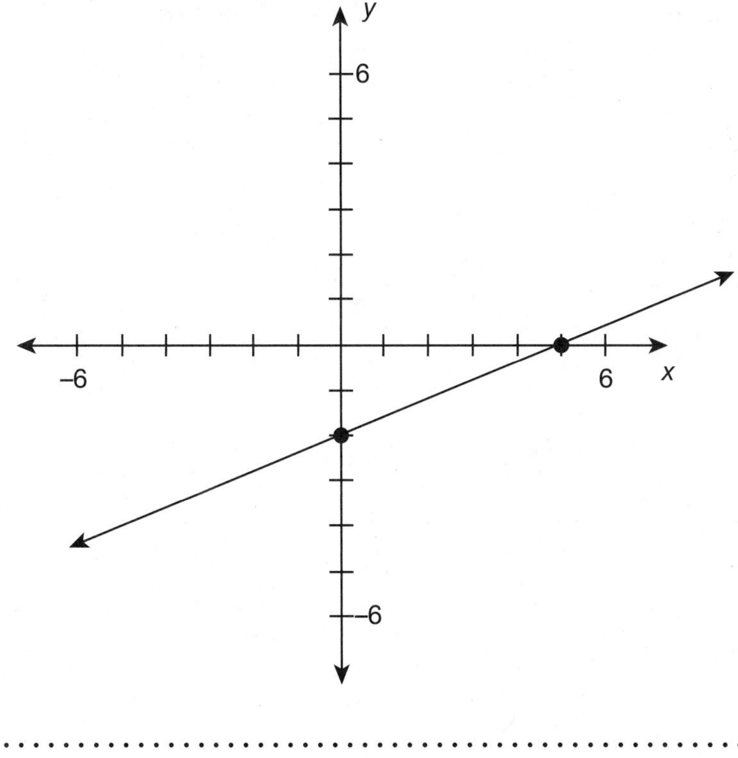

Using the given information, put $x = 4$, $y = 0$, and $m = \frac{3}{4}$ into the slope-intercept equation, $y = mx + b$:

$y = mx + b$

$0 = \frac{3}{4}(4) + b$

$0 = 3 + b$

$b = -3$

Put m and b back into the equation to get $\mathbf{y = \frac{3}{4}x - 3}$ as the final answer.

. . . .

Using the two given points, when y increases by 2 units, x increases by 5 units. This means the slope must be $m = \frac{2}{5}$. Furthermore, the y-intercept is at -2, so $b = -2$. Using the equation $y = mx + b$, we have $\mathbf{y = \frac{2}{5}x - 2}$.

. . . .

How is the slope determined in a line that is in the form $ax + by = c$?

. . . .

What is the slope of the line represented by the equation $10x - 4y = 2$?

. . . .

If given a line in the form $y = \frac{3}{4}x - 2$ how could it be written in $ax + by = c$ form?

A line in the form $ax + by = c$ must be algebraically manipulated so that it is in $y = mx + b$ form. Then, the slope will be m.

. . . .

To find the slope of the line with this equation, isolate the y-variable and put the equation in the form $y = mx + b$, where m is the slope.

$10x - 4y = 2$

$\underline{-10x \qquad -10x}$

$-4y = -10x + 2$

$\frac{-4y}{-4} = \frac{-10x + 2}{-4}$

$\mathbf{y = \frac{5}{2}x - \frac{1}{2}}$

. . . .

First, multiply all terms by 4 in order to get rid of the fraction, and then move the x term and y term to the left side of the equation:

$y = \frac{3}{4}x - 2$

$(4)y = (4)\frac{3}{4}x - (4)2$

$4y = 3x - 8$

$\mathbf{-3x + 4y = -8}$

Find the equation of the line that passes through the points (–8,1) and (4,9) in the *x*-*y* coordinate plane. Write your answer in slope-intercept form.

. . . .

Find the equation of the line that passes through (9,–5) and has a slope of 0.5.

. . . .

The *point-slope form* of a linear equation is a form that represents a line with a slope of *m* that passes through a given point (x_1,y_1). What is the point-slope formula of a line?

First find the slope, *m*:

$m = \frac{y_2 - y_1}{x_2 - x_1} = \frac{9 - 1}{4 - (-8)} = \frac{8}{12} = \frac{2}{3}$

Then, plug the slope and the point (4,9) into $y = mx + b$ to solve for b:

$\mathbf{y = \frac{2}{3}x + \frac{19}{3}}$

• •

Substitute the known values into the equation $y = mx + b$ and solve for b.

$y = mx + b$

$-5 = 0.5(9) + b$
$-5 = 4.5 + b$
$\underline{-4.5 \; -4.5}$
$-9.5 = b$

The equation of this line is $\mathbf{y = 0.5x - 9.5}$.

• •

The point-slope formula of a line with a slope of m that passes through a point (x_1,y_1) is $\mathbf{(y - y_1) = m(x - x_1)}$.

A line passes through the point (6,–7) and has a slope of $-\frac{1}{2}$. What is the equation of this line in point-slope form?

How is a coordinate axis set up? Where is the origin, *x*-axis, and *y*-axis?

The point-slope form of a line is $(y - y_1) = m(x - x_1)$.

$(y - (-7)) = -\frac{1}{2}(x - 6)$

$\mathbf{(y + 7) = -\frac{1}{2}(x - 6)}$

• •

The *x*-axis is the **horizontal axis**, the *y*-axis is the **vertical axis**, and the point at which they intersect is called the origin. The origin has the coordinate pair value of **(0,0)**.

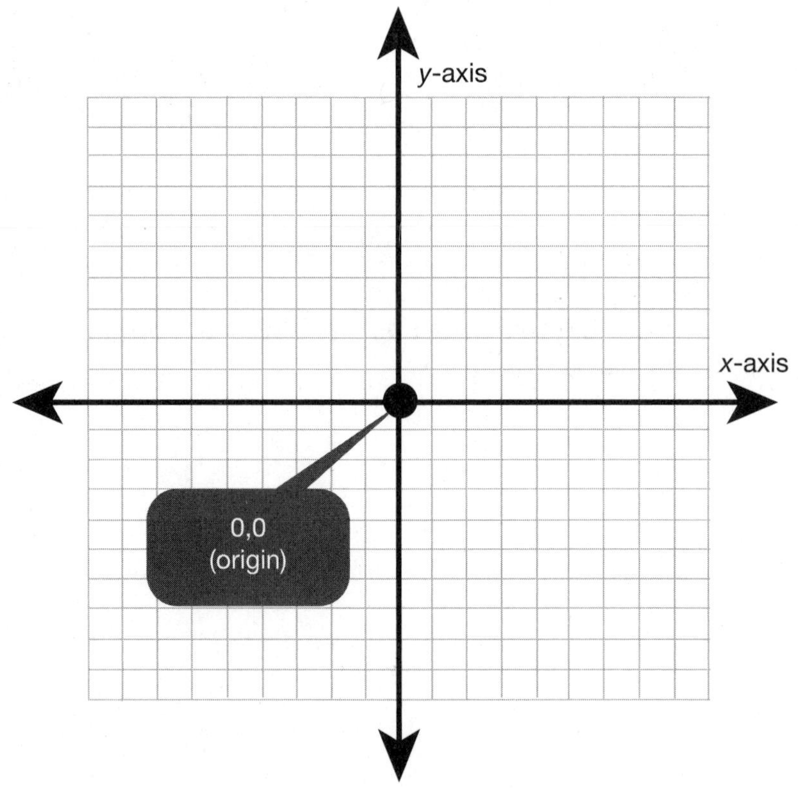

• •

Where do all points in the form (0,*y*) fall in the coordinate plane for all real number values of *y*?

. . . .

Where do all points in the form (*x*,0) fall in the coordinate plane for all real number values of *x*?

. . . .

What are the correct steps for graphing a point (*x*,*y*) in the coordinate plane?

Coordinate points that have a value of 0 for *x* will fall on the *y*-axis. This is the case because there is no horizontal (left or right) movement from the starting point (0,0) at the origin.

. . . .

Coordinate points that have a value of 0 for *y* will fall on the *x*-axis. This is the case because there is no vertical (up or down) movement from the starting point (0,0) at the origin.

. . . .

To graph a coordinate point (*x*,*y*), begin at the origin, (0,0). Move *x* units to the right if *x* is positive, or *x* units to the left if *x* is negative. Next, from that position, move *y* units up if *y* is positive, or *y* units down if *y* is negative. Then, plot the point.

Draw a dot on the coordinate grid to plot the point indicated by the ordered pair (–2,1).

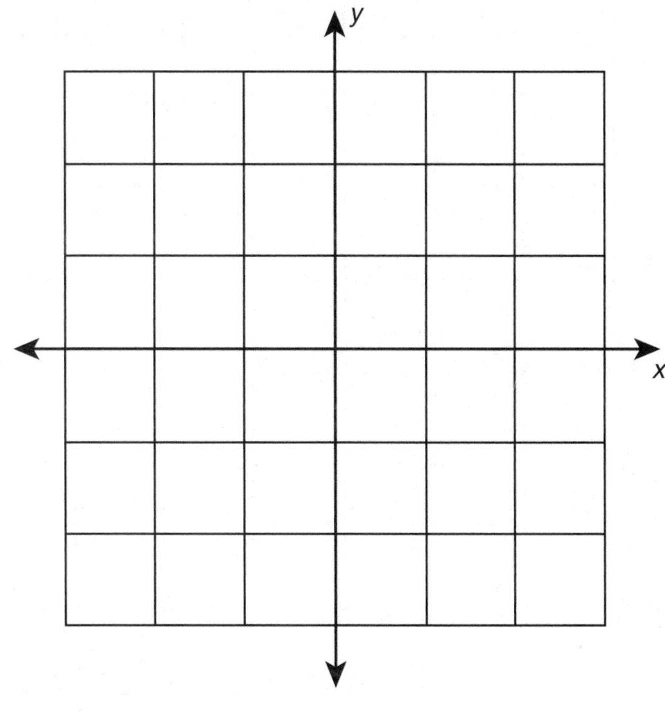

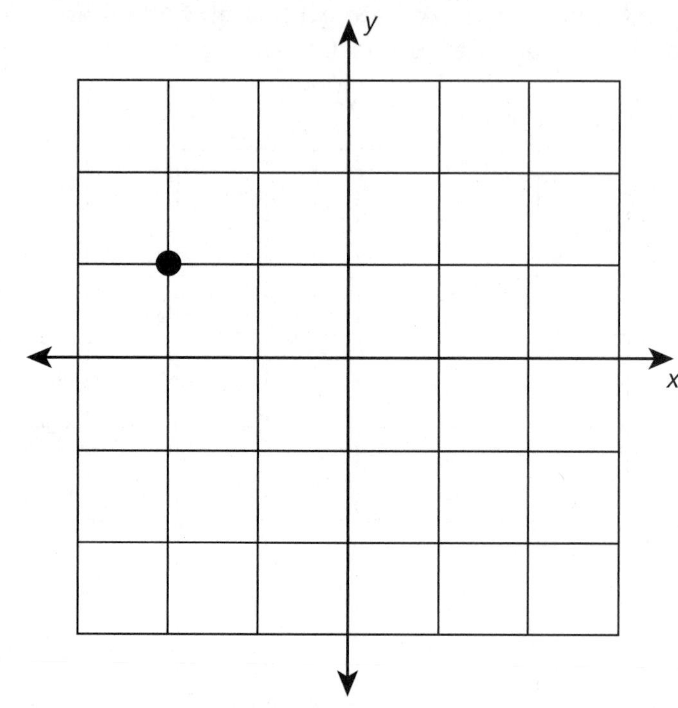
y
x

On the *x*-*y* coordinate plane below, plot the ordered pair (4,–2).

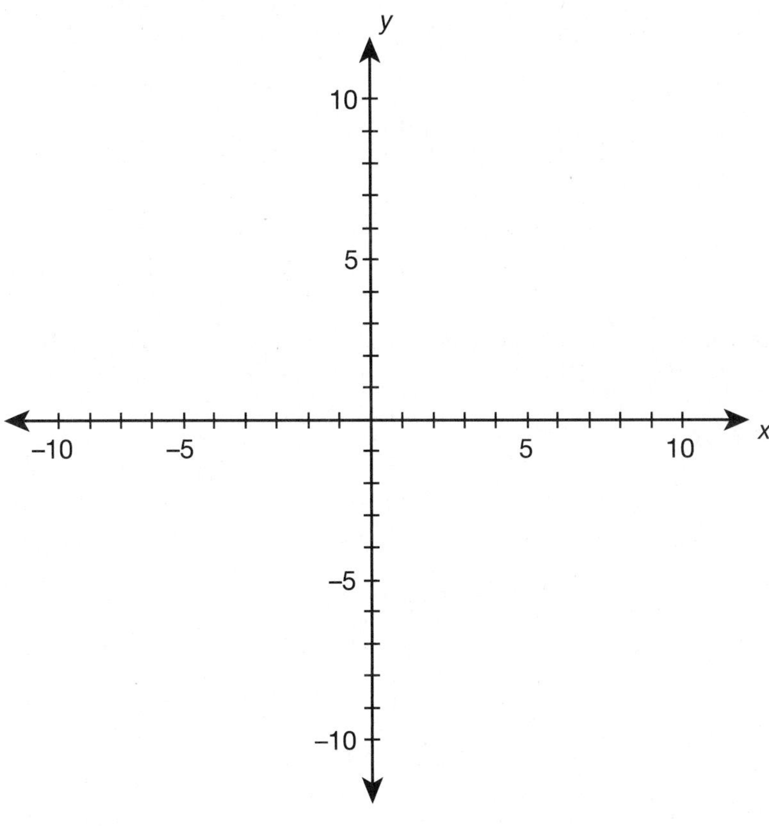

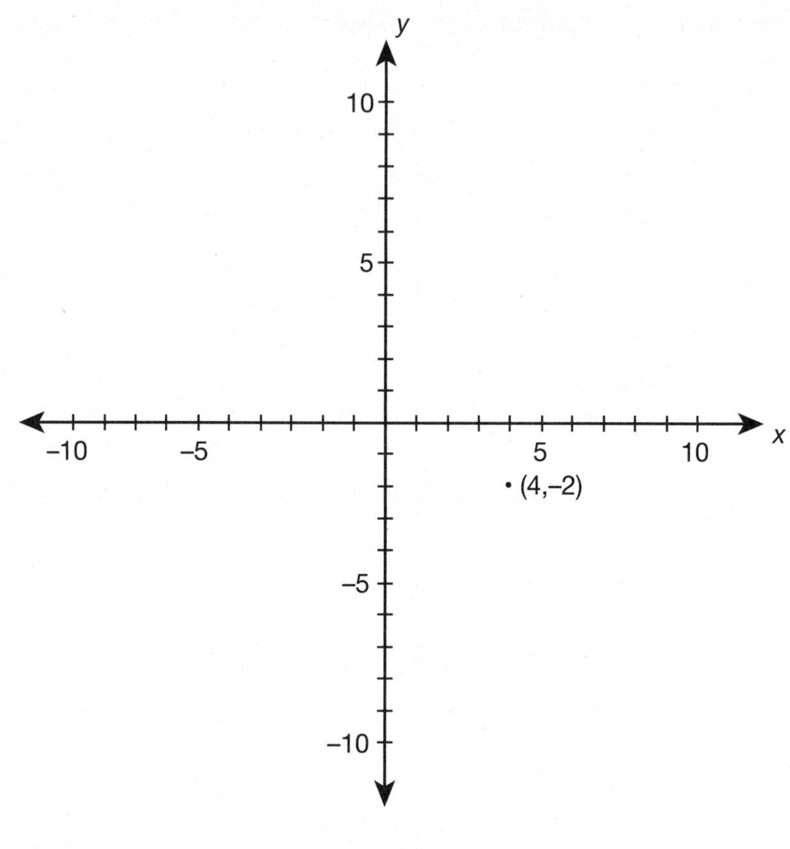
y
10
5
-5
-10
x
-10
-5
5
10
• (4,-2)

What is the ordered pair for point B?

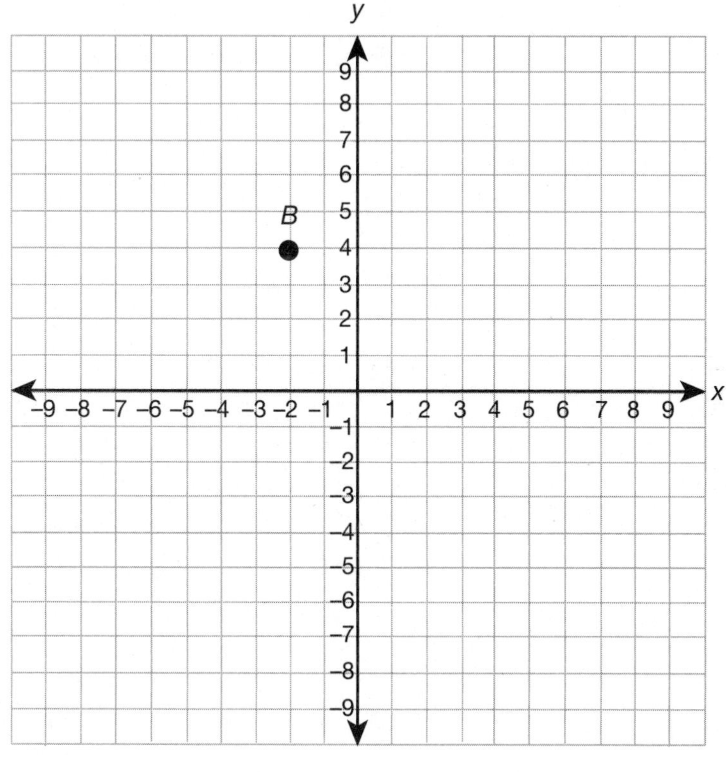

(–2,4)

What are the coordinate pairs for each of the points on the *x*-*y* coordinate grid below?

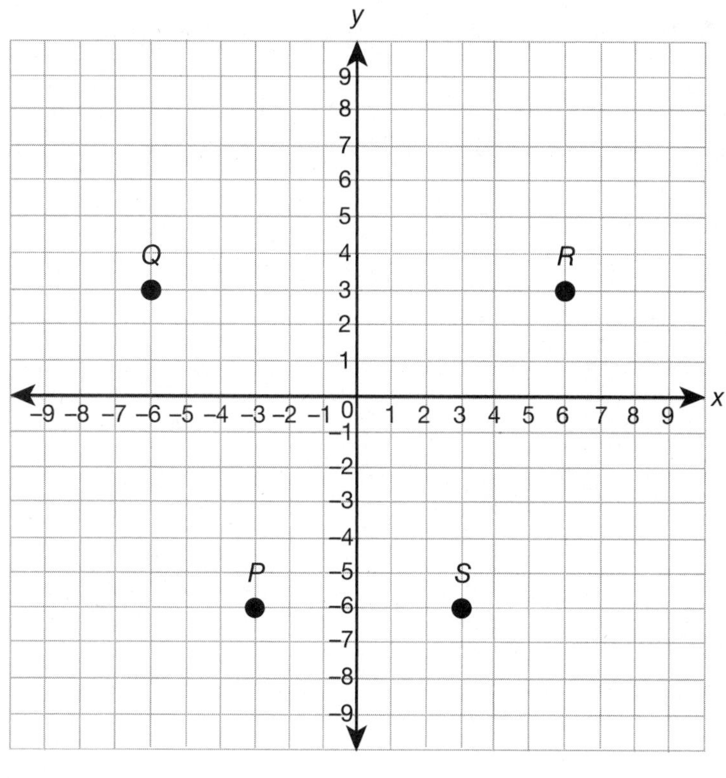

R **(6,3)**

Q **(–6,3)**

P **(–3,–6)**

S **(3,–6)**

How are linear equations in the form $y = mx + b$ graphed?

. . . .

How is it possible to find the equation of a line from its graph?

. . . .

Since *b* is the *y*-intercept, first plot that point on the *y*-axis. Then, write *m* in fraction form and recall that *m* is the slope and it stands for $\frac{\text{rise}}{\text{run}}$. For a positive slope, start at the *y*-intercept and move up the number of units in your rise and move right the number of units in your run. Connect the two points. (For a negative slope, you will move up and left instead of up and right.)

First, select any two points on the line and find the slope by using $m = \frac{y_2 - y_1}{x_2 - x_1}$. Then, select any coordinate pair on the line and substitute it in for (x_1, y_1) into the point-slope form, $(y - y_1) = m(x - x_1)$.

Write the equation of the line graphed below in slope-intercept form.

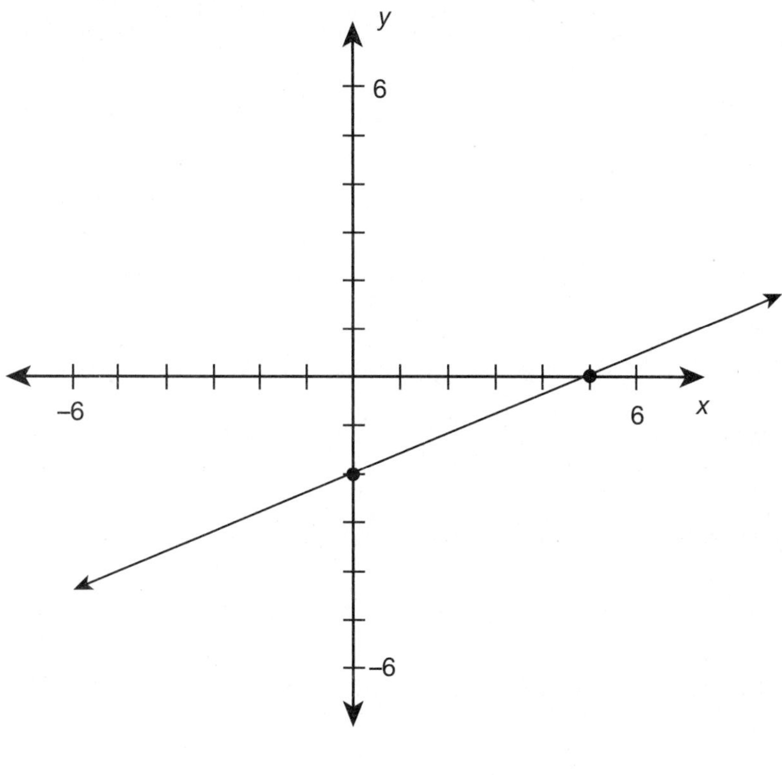

What is the equation of the line that passes through the points (–2,1) and (4,5)?

Use the points (0,–2) and (5,0) to find that the slope is $\frac{2}{5}$. The *y*-intercept is at –2, so the equation of the line is $\mathbf{y = \frac{2}{5}x - 2}$.

$m = \frac{y_2 - y_1}{x_2 - x_1} = \frac{5 - 1}{4 - (-2)} = \frac{4}{6} = \frac{2}{3}$

$y = \frac{2}{3}x + b$

$5 = \frac{2}{3}(4) + b$

$b = 5 - \frac{8}{3} = \frac{7}{3}$

$\mathbf{y = \frac{2}{3}x + \frac{7}{3}}$

All horizontal lines on a coordinate grid have the same general form. What is the general form for horizontal lines?

. . . .

All vertical lines on a coordinate grid have the same general form. What is the general form for vertical lines?

. . . .

For the graph of the equation $3x - 2y = 1$, what is the value at which the line intersects the *y*-axis?

$y = k$, where k = any real number, is the form for horizontal lines. All the points on a horizontal line have the same y-value, but the x-values are changing, which is why the general form of a horizontal line is $y = k$.

$x = k$, where k = any real number, is the form for vertical lines. All the points on a vertical line have the same x-value, but the y-values are changing, which is why the general form of a vertical line is $x = k$.

Put the equation into $y = mx + b$ form to get $y = -\frac{3}{2}x - \frac{1}{2}$. The y-intercept is $-\frac{1}{2}$.

What is the equation of line *m*?

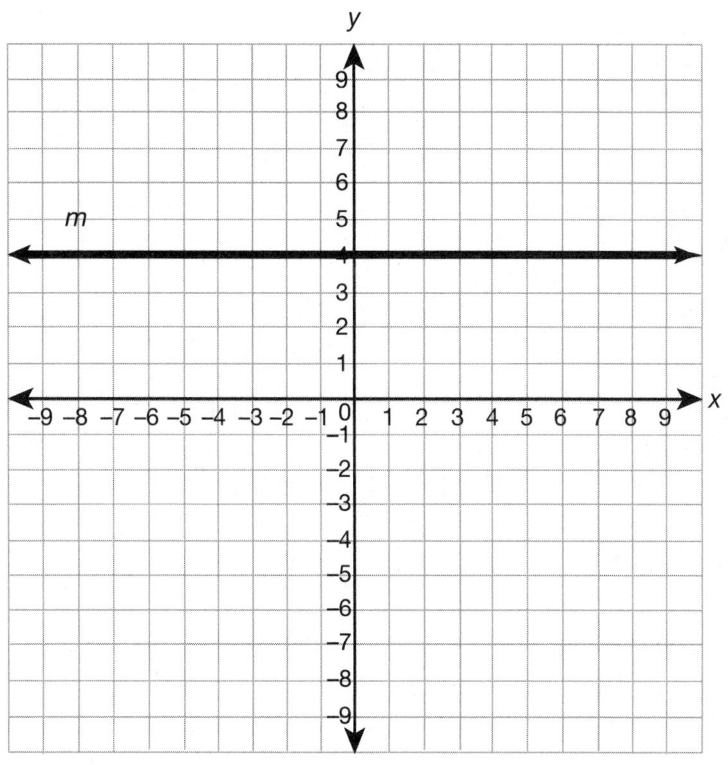

Horizontal lines always have the equation y = k, so line *m* is **y = 4**.

A line *P* graphed in the *x*-*y* coordinate plane crosses the *x*-axis at (–5,0). If another line Q has an equation of $y = 3x - 2$, then which of the following statements is true?

A. The *x*-intercept of line *P* is closer from the origin than the *x*-intercept of line Q.

B. The *x*-coordinate of the *x*-intercept of line *P* is smaller than the *x*-coordinate of the *x*-intercept of line Q.

C. The *x*-intercepts of both lines lie to the right of the *y*-axis.

D. The *x*-intercept of line Q cannot be determined from the given information.

Choice B is correct. The *x*-intercept of line *P* is –5. By subbing $y = 0$ into the equation for line Q, it is found that the *x*-intercept of line Q is $\frac{2}{3}$. So, the *x*-intercept of line *P* is smaller than the *x*-intercept of line Q.

The graph represents the rate of cooling for a particular material after it was placed in a super-cooled bath. If the temperature, in Fahrenheit, is represented by *T* and the number of hours elapsed is represented by *H*, then which expression represents a situation where the rate of cooling was faster than the rate indicated in the graph?

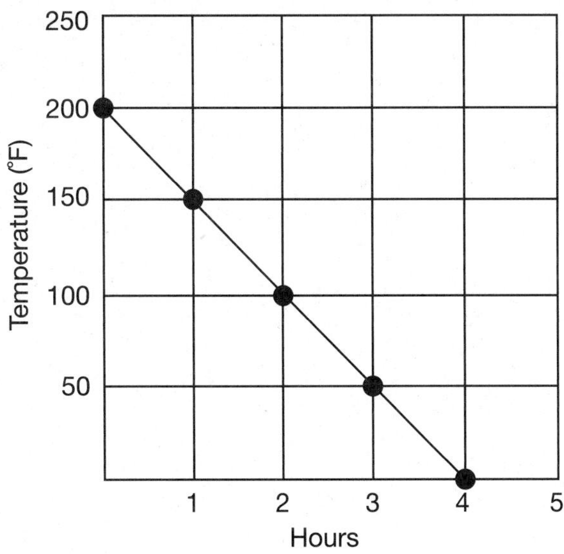

A. $T = -25H + 150$
B. $T = -60H + 300$
C. $T = -10H + 200$
D. $T = -50H + 250$

What does it mean if a function is "increasing" or "decreasing" over a certain interval?

Choice B is correct. The rate of cooling indicated in the graph is the slope of the line passing through the points (0,200) and (4,0). This slope is –50, which implies the material is losing 50 degrees every hour. The slope of the equation in choice **B** is –60, which implies the material is losing 60 degrees every hour for a faster rate of cooling.

An **increasing** function will have a positive slope and will be going upward toward the right (as *x* increases, *y* increases). A **decreasing** function will have a negative slope and will be moving down toward the right (as *x* increases, *y* decreases).

What does it mean if a function is "positive" or "negative" over a certain interval?

Which line in the coordinate plane below represents the graph of the equation $3x - 2y = 1$?

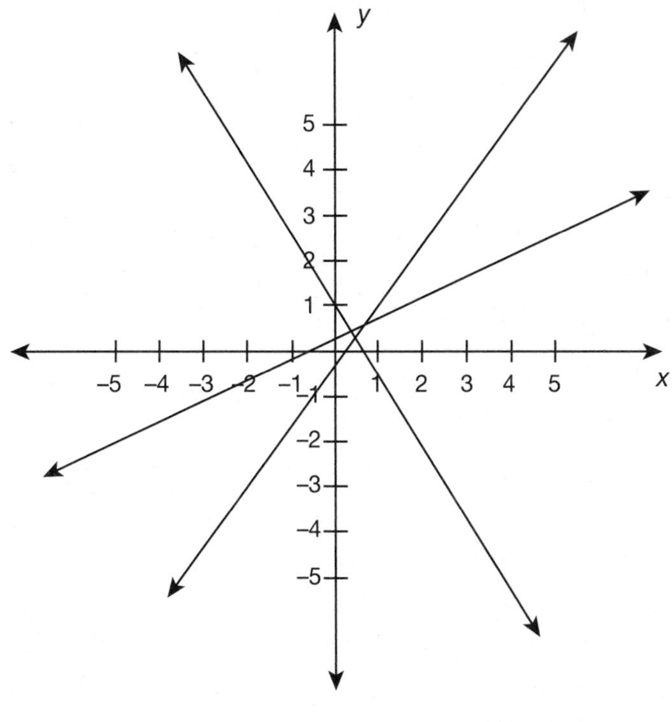

The *y*-value determines whether a function is positive or negative. A function is **positive** over a certain interval if the *y*-values over that interval are positive. A function is **negative** over a certain interval if the *y*-values over that interval are negative.

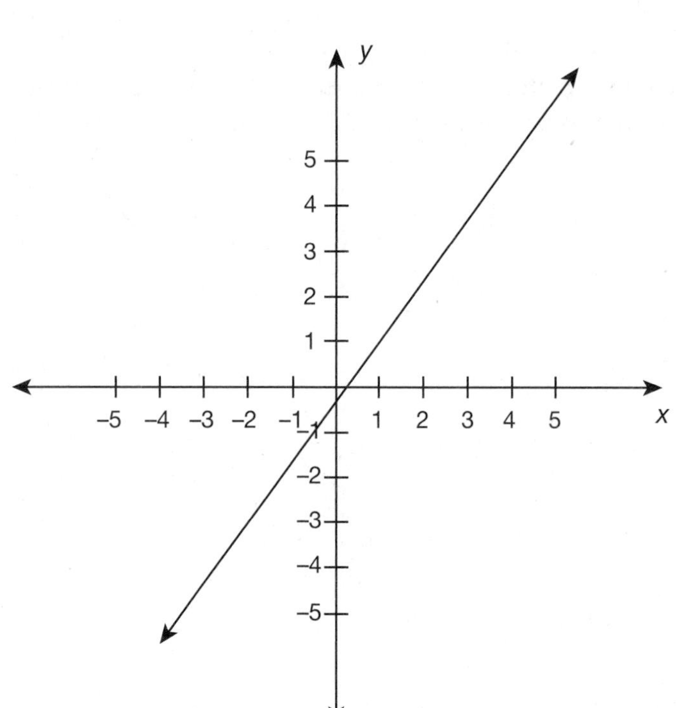

Each of the given lines has a different *y*-intercept. Solving for *y* in the given equation yields the $y = mx + b$ form, where *b* is the *y*-intercept. In this case, that equation is $y = \frac{2}{3}x - \frac{1}{2}$. The line given in the image above is the only line with a *y*-intercept of $\frac{1}{2}$.

What is a *system of linear equations,* and what does it mean if an (x,y) coordinate pair is a solution to a given system of linear equations? For example, explain the significance of $(-1,7)$ being the solution to the system $y = 2x - 5$ and $y = 3x - 4$.

. . . .

How many different cases are possible when solving a system of equations? How many solutions can a system of equations have?

. . . .

How many solutions are there to the following systems of linear equations?

A. $4x + 8y = 10$ and $y = -\frac{1}{2}x + \frac{5}{4}$

B. $y = \frac{3}{4}x + 2$ and $-3x + 4y = 5$

A **system of linear equations** is a pairing of two equations that are being solved simultaneously. A solution to a system of linear equations is a coordinate pair (x,y) that is a solution to each of the individual equations. This (x,y) pair will be the point where the two lines intersect. If the point $(-1,7)$ is a solution to $y = 2x - 5$ and $y = 3x - 4$, then it works in both of the given equations and is the point of intersection of the two lines.

There are **3 cases**:

1. If the lines intersect just once, there will be one solution.
2. If the lines are parallel, there will be no solutions.
3. If the lines are on top of one another (i.e., the same line but written in different forms), then there are infinite solutions.

A. The system $4x + 8y = 10$ and $y = -\frac{1}{2}x + \frac{5}{4}$ has **infinite solutions** because these are the same lines written in different formats. (If you divide all of the terms by 8 in the equation $4x + 8y = 10$, then it is equivalent to $y = -\frac{1}{2}x + \frac{5}{4}$.)

B. The system $y = \frac{3}{4}x + 2$ and $-3x + 4y = 5$ has **no solutions** because these lines are parallel with different y-intercepts, so they will never intersect. (We know they are parallel because when the second equation is divided by 4 and solved for y, both lines have the same slope of $\frac{3}{4}$.)

For which of the following systems of equations is (2,–3) a solution? (There may be more than one answer.)

A. $4x - 3y = 17$ and $x - y = -1$

B. $-5x - y = 7$ and $y = 7x - 17$

C. $(y + 5) = \frac{1}{2}(x + 2)$ and $4x - 2y = 14$

How is a system of linear equations solved through *substitution*? For example, how would the following system of equations be solved using substitution?
$4x + 2y = 20$ and $x = 2 + y$

Solve the following system of equations using substitution:
$y = 3x - 5$ and $2y + 2x = 14$

A. (2,–3) is a solution for $4x - 3y = 17$, but it does not work in $x - y = -1$, so it is not a solution for this system of equations.
B. (2,–3) is not a solution for $-5x - y = 7$, but it is a solution for $y = 7x - 17$, so it is not a solution for this system of equations.
C. (2,–3) is a solution to both $(y + 5) = \frac{1}{2}(x + 2)$ and $4x - 2y = 14$, so it is a solution to this system of equations.

The **substitution method** isolates one variable in one of the equations and substitutes its equivalent value into the other equation. When this is done, only one variable exists in the new equation, and it can be solved for that variable.

$4\underline{\mathbf{x}} + 2y = 20$ and $x = \underline{\mathbf{2 + y}}$

1. Replace the x in the first equation with $(2 + y)$ from the second equation: $4(\underline{\mathbf{2 + y}}) + 2y = 20$
2. Solve $4(2 + y) + 2y = 20$ for y: $8 + 4y + 2y = 20$, so $6y = 12$ and $y = 2$.
3. Solve for x by substituting $y = 2$ into one of the original equations: $x = 2 + y$, so $x = 2 + 2 = 4$.

The solution to this system of equations is (**4,2**).

$y = \underline{\mathbf{3x - 5}}$ and $2\mathbf{y} + 2x = 14$

1. Replace the y in the second equation with $(3x - 5)$ from the first equation: $2(\underline{\mathbf{3x - 5}}) + 2x = 14$
2. Solve $2(3x - 5) + 2x = 14$ for x: $6x - 10 + 2x = 14$, so $8x = 24$ and $x = 3$.
3. Solve for y by substituting $x = 3$ into one of the original equations: $y = 3x - 5$, so $y = 3(3) - 5 = 4$.

(**3,4**) is the solution to the system of equations.

How is a system of linear equations solved through *combination*? For example, how would the following system of equations be solved using combination?
$y = 2x + 6$ and $y = x + 8$

Solve the following system of equations through combination:
$x - 2y = 8$ and $x + 2y = 14$

How is a system of linear equations solved through graphing?

The **combination method** is easiest to use when both equations are in the same form and when either x or y have the opposite coefficient in both equations, like $5x$ and $-5x$.

$y = 2x + 6$ and $y = x + 8$

1. If necessary, multiply one of the equations by –1 so that either x or y have the opposite coefficients. $-1(y) = -1(2x + 6)$, so $-y = -2x - 6$.
2. Add both of the equations together, so that one of their variables cancels out:

$$\begin{array}{rcl} -y &=& -2x - 6 \\ y &=& x + 8 \\ \hline 0 &=& -x + 2 \end{array}$$

3. Solve for the remaining variable: $0 = -x + 2$, so $x = 2$.
4. Plug the answer from step 3 back into one of the equations to solve for the other variable: $y = 2 + 8 = 10$.

(2,10) is the solution to the system of equations.

. . . .

Using the combination method, adding the two equations yields the equation $2x = 22$, which has a solution of $x = 11$. Substitute $x = 11$ back into the equation $x + 2y = 14$ to solve for y: $11 + 2y = 14$, so $2y = 3$ and $y = \frac{3}{2}$. The solution to this system is $\mathbf{(11,\frac{3}{2})}$.

. . . .

Graph both of the equations on the same coordinate plane, and the point of intersection will be the solution to the system.

Drew's school is having a raffle contest. People can buy a red ticket for $10 for a chance to win a TV or a blue ticket for $5 for a chance to win a bicycle. Drew sold a record high of 130 tickets for a total of $1,100. How many tickets of each color did Drew sell?

Use r for the number of red tickets and b for the number of blue tickets.

The first equation showing the number of tickets Drew sold is $r + b = 130$.

The second equation showing ticket prices and money collected is

$10r + 5b = 1{,}100$.

So, solve the system of equations, $r + b = 130$ and $10r + 5b = 1{,}100$, by using combination or substitution. **Drew sold 40 blue tickets at $5 each and 90 red tickets at $10 each.**

What does it mean when two lines are *parallel*? Be sure to discuss their slopes.

. . . .

What is the slope of a line parallel to $y = 5x - 3$?

. . . .

Which of the following lines is parallel to the line $y = \frac{2}{9}x - \frac{1}{5}$?

A. $y = -\frac{9}{2}x + 1$

B. $y = \frac{3}{4}x + 1$

C. $y = \frac{2}{9}x - 8$

D. $y = \frac{3}{4}x - \frac{1}{5}$

Parallel lines are lines that never intersect. Parallel lines are increasing or decreasing at the same rate, so they have **identical slopes**.

Parallel lines have identical slopes. Any line that has a slope of **5** will be parallel to $y = 5x - 3$.

Parallel lines have the same slope, and m is the slope in $y = mx + b$. Choice **C** is the correct answer because $y = \frac{2}{9}x - \frac{1}{5}$ and $y = \frac{2}{9}x - 8$ both have a slope of $\frac{2}{9}$.

Line *m* is parallel to line *n*. If line *n* has the equation $5x - 7y = 13$, what is the slope of line *m*?

....

What does it mean when two lines are *perpendicular*? Be sure to discuss their slopes.

....

Parallel lines have the same slope. Put the equation $5x - 7y = 13$ into $y = mx + b$ form by subtracting $5x$ from both sides and then dividing by -7. This yields $y = \frac{5}{7}x + \frac{13}{7}$. So, the slope of line m is $\mathbf{\frac{5}{7}}$.

Perpendicular lines intersect at a 90° angle, forming four right angles. Perpendicular lines have slopes that are **opposite reciprocals**. This means that they are opposite signs and are flipped versions of one another. If one line has a slope of $\frac{5}{7}$, then a line perpendicular to it will have a slope of $-\frac{7}{5}$.

What kind of angles do perpendicular lines form? What symbol is used to demonstrate that two lines are perpendicular?

Perpendicular lines form right angles, which are angles that measure 90°. In order to demonstrate that two lines are perpendicular, a small square is drawn in the angle. Another way to show that two lines are perpendicular is to use the symbol ⊥ written between two line names, such as $m \perp n$.

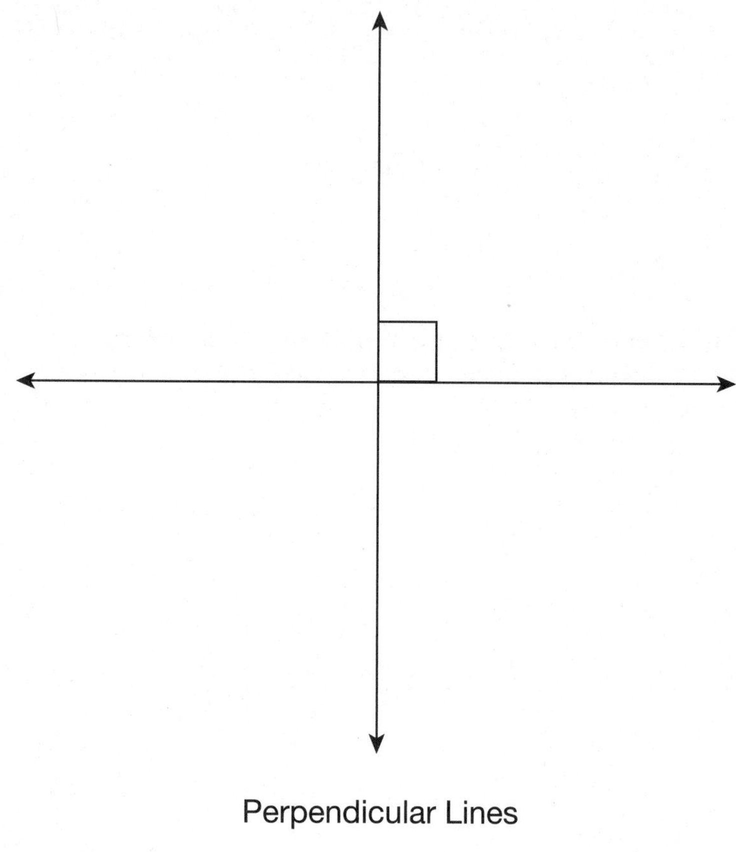

Perpendicular Lines

What is the slope of a line perpendicular to $y = 5x - 3$?

. . . .

How do you find the equation of a line that is parallel to a given line and passes through a given point?

. . . .

The line *n* is parallel to the line $y = 3x - 7$ and passes through the point (5,1). At what point does the line *n* cross the *y*-axis?

Perpendicular lines have opposite reciprocal slopes. Since the slope of the given line is 5, or $\frac{5}{1}$, any line that has a slope of $-\frac{1}{5}$ will be perpendicular to it.

. . . .

1. First, identify the slope of the given line by looking for m in either slope-intercept form ($y = mx + b$) or point-slope form $(y - y_1) = m(x - x_1)$. The parallel line will have the same slope.
2. Then, plug the given point and the slope into the point-slope formula $(y - y_1) = m(x - x_1)$.

. . . .

Since line n is parallel to $y = 3x - 7$, it is known that line n has a slope of 3. Put $m = 3$ along with the point (5,1) into the equation $y = mx + b$ to solve for b:

$1 = 3(5) + b$, so $b = -14$.

Line n will cross the y-axis at $\mathbf{y = -14}$.

A line z is perpendicular to the line $y = -x + 5$. If z passes through the points $(0,-2)$ and $(x,5)$, what is the value of x?

A line is perpendicular to the line $-5x + 6y = 6$ and has a y-intercept of $(0,-4)$. What is the equation of this line?

Since z is perpendicular to $y = -x + 5$, it must have a slope of 1 (since 1 is the opposite reciprocal of –1). The given point (0,–2) is the y-intercept, so the equation of line z must be $y = x - 2$. Plugging in the given y-value of 5 in the point $(x,5)$ yields the equation $5 = x - 2$, which has the solution $\mathbf{x = 7}$.

First, rewrite the equation in slope-intercept form so that the slope can be identified:

$y = \frac{5}{6}x + 1$. The slope will be the negative reciprocal of the given slope of $\frac{5}{6}$, and b in the equation $y = mx + b$ must be equal to –4. Therefore, the equation of the perpendicular line is $\mathbf{y = -\frac{6}{5}x - 4}$.

What do the following symbols and statements mean?
$x > 2$
$x \geq 2$
$x < 2$
$x \leq 2$

How is $x < 5$ graphed on a number line?

How is $x \geq -3$ graphed on a number line?

LINEAR INEQUALITIES

$x > 2$ means that x is **greater than** 2, but does not equal 2.

$x \geq 2$ means that x is **greater than or equal** to 2.

$x < 2$ means that x is **less than** 2, but does not equal 2.

$x \leq 2$ means that x is **less than or equal** to 2.

$x < 5$ means "x is less than 5." Make a number line with 5 in the middle of it and add increasing integers to the right and decreasing integers to the left. Draw an open circle around the hash mark at 5 and shade the number line to the left of 5 since x is less than 5. The circle will not be shaded in because 5 is not part of the solution set.

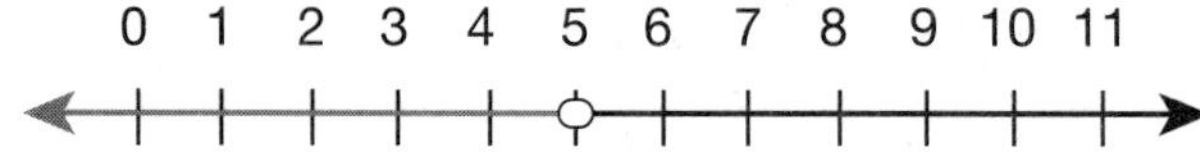

$x \geq -3$ means "x is greater than or equal to -3." Make a number line with -3 in the middle. Draw a circle around the hash mark at -3 and shade both the circle and the number line to the right of -3. The circle is shaded to indicate that -3 is part of the solution set.

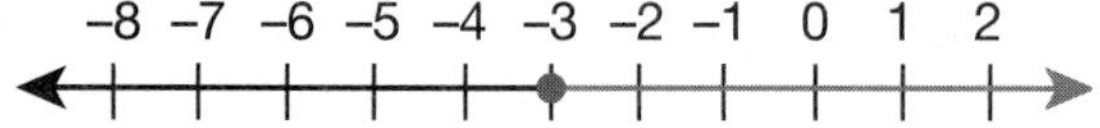

Which of the following shows the solution set represented by $2 < x$?

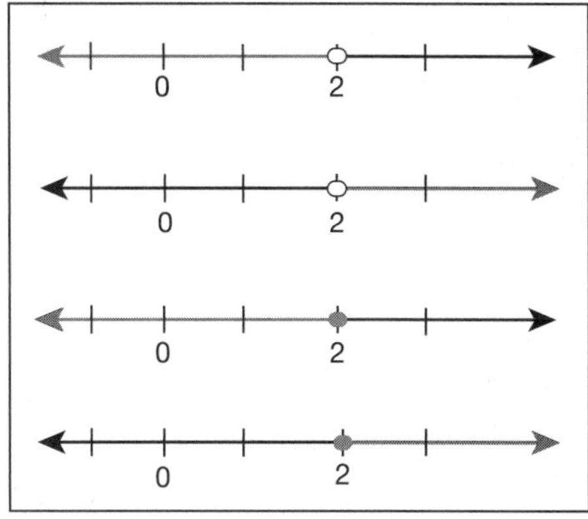

How do you solve the following inequality? Interpret and explain what the final answer means.
$8x - 10 < 62$

What is the trickiest concept to remember when solving inequalities? (Hint: You will need to remember this trick when the variable has a negative coefficient, such as in the following inequality: $-7x + 6 > 41$.)

$2 < x$ is the same as $x > 2$, which is read "x is greater than 2." (It is usually easier to understand the context of the inequality when the variable is written first.) Since 2 is not part of the solution set, the circle on the hash mark of 2 on the number line must remain open, and number line should be shaded to the right. The second answer choice represents $2 < x$.

. . . .

Inequalities are solved similarly to regular equations. Isolate x by using opposite operations in the reverse order of PEMDAS.

$8x - 10 < 62$

$8x < 72$

$\mathbf{x < 9}$

This answer means that all values of x that are less than 9 will be a solution to the original equation, $8x - 10 < 62$.

. . . .

In inequalities, whenever *dividing or multiplying by a negative number*, the direction of the inequality symbol must be reversed. This ONLY holds true if the number that is being multiplied or divided is negative, and not in cases when only the final answer is negative!

$-7x + 6 > 41$

$-7x > 35$

$\frac{-7x}{-7} > \frac{35}{-7}$

$\mathbf{x < -5}$

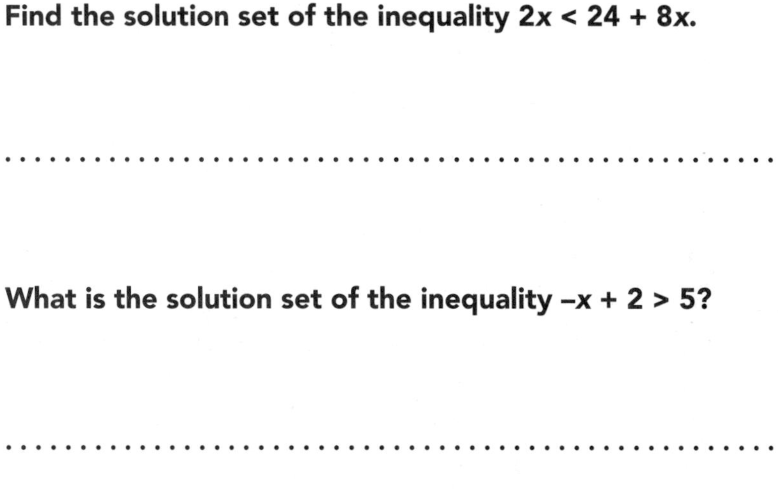

Find the solution set of the inequality $2x < 24 + 8x$.

What is the solution set of the inequality $-x + 2 > 5$?

How do you solve compound inequalities in the form $3 < 4x - 9 < 23$?

$2x < 24 + 8x$

Subtract 8x from both sides to move all the *x* terms to the left:

$-6x < 24$

Divide by –6 to get *x* alone, and switch the direction of the inequality sign:

$\mathbf{x > -4}$

. . . .

$-x + 2 > 5$

$-x > 3$ (divide by –1)

$\mathbf{x < -3}$

. . . .

The goal is to isolate *x* in the middle of the two inequalities. What you do to the middle of the inequality, you must do to the left and right sides as well:

$$\begin{array}{l} 3 < 4x - 9 < 23 \\ \underline{+9 \quad\;\; +9 \quad +9} \\ 12 < 4x < 32 \end{array}$$

$\frac{12}{4} < \frac{4x}{4} < \frac{32}{4}$

$\mathbf{3 < x < 8}$

x is the set of all numbers greater than 3 and less than 8.

How are compound inequalities graphed on a number line?
Graph $-5 < x \leq 3$ on a number line.

. . . .

Solve the compound inequality below and graph the solution set on a number line:
$-15 < 3x - 6 < 18$

. . . .

How is the following compound inequality solved and graphed on a number line?
$\frac{h}{2} < 3$ or $\frac{h}{4} > 3$

$-5 < x \leq 3$ means that x is all real numbers that are greater than –5 but less than or equal to 3.

First, draw a number line that spans from –6 to 4. Draw an open circle around the –5, a shaded circle around 3, and shade the number line between these two circles. 3 is shaded since it is part of the solution set, and –5 is not shaded since it is not part of the solution set.

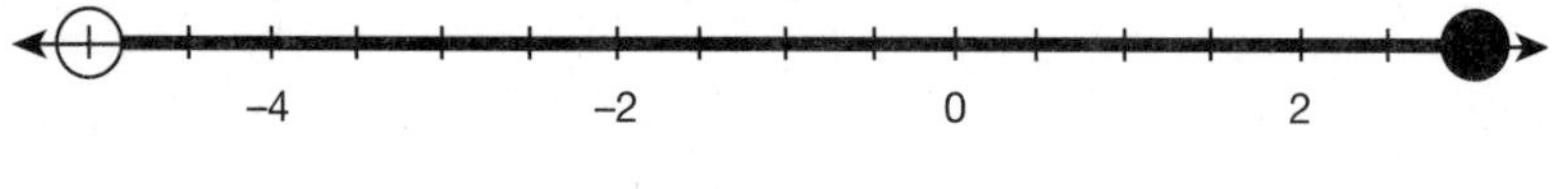

The goal is to isolate x in the middle of the two inequalities.

$$\begin{array}{rcl} -15 < & 3x - 6 & < 18 \\ +6 & +6 & +6 \\ \hline -9 < & 3x & < 24 \end{array}$$

$$-\frac{9}{3} < \frac{3x}{3} < \frac{24}{3}$$

$$-3 < x < 8$$

x is all real numbers between –3 and 8.

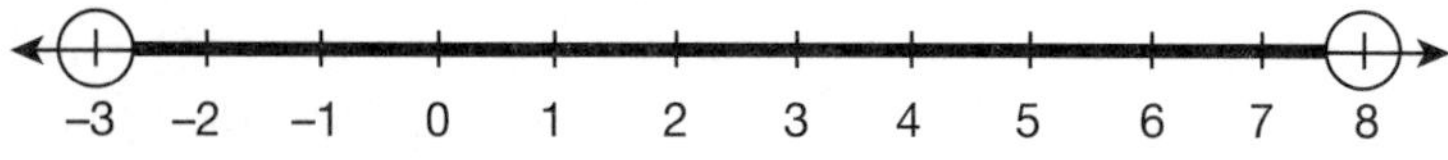

$\frac{h}{2} < 3$ or $\frac{h}{4} > 3$

In this type of compound inequality, when there is an "or," there are two distinct solution sets that both satisfy the inequality even though they have no overlap. Each equation is solved separately, and the two different solution sets are graphed on the same number line. To solve $\frac{h}{2} < 3$, multiply both sides by 2 to get $h < 6$. Next, to solve $\frac{h}{4} > 3$, multiply both sides by 4 to get $h > 12$.

Graph both solutions on the same number line:

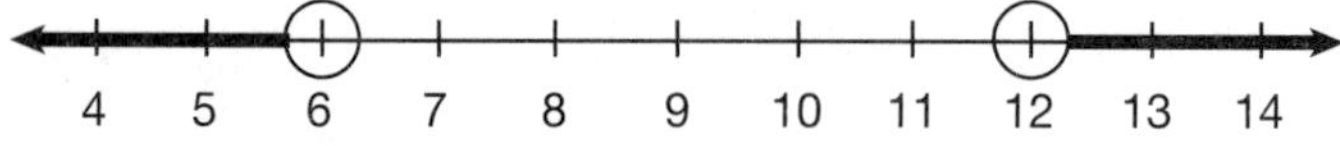

Solve the compound inequality and graph the solution set on a number line: $3d \leq 15$ or $\frac{d}{5} > 3$

. . . .

The sum of 10 and a number *r* is less than 8 times a number *b*. If *b* is 5, then use an inequality to find the solution set for *r*.

. . . .

A factory is able to produce at least 16 items, but no more than 20 items, for every hour the factory is open. If the factory is open for 8 hours a day, write an inequality to represent the possible range of numbers of items produced by the factory over a seven-day work period.

There are two distinct solution sets that satisfy the inequality:

$3d \leq 15$ gives the solution $\mathbf{d \leq 5}$.

$\frac{d}{5} > 3$ gives the solution $\mathbf{d > 15}$.

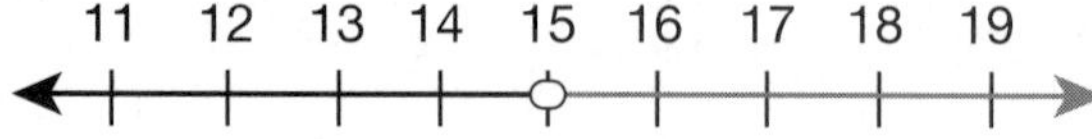

$10 + r < 8b$, where $b = 5$

$10 + r < 8 \times 5$

$10 + r < 40$

$\mathbf{r < 30}$

The inequality that would represent the number of items produced in 1 hour would be $16 \leq h < 20$, where h = hours. Since the factory is open for 8 hours each day, this would become $(8)16 \leq (8)h \leq (8)20$, which simplifies to $128 \leq d \leq 160$, where d = days. Over 7 days, the inequality becomes $(7)128 \leq (7)d \leq (7)160$.

This translates to $\mathbf{896 \leq w \leq 1{,}120}$, where w is the production per week. The factory will produce anywhere from 896 to 1,120 items in a 7-day week of 8 hours per day.

Richard has a T-shirt company. He needs to make at least $2,500 this month to meet his sales goal. If each T-shirt sells for $16.50, write an inequality that models the number of T-shirts Richard must sell to reach his sales goal. Let *t* represent the number of T-shirts.

. . . .

You make $1,500 a month after taxes. You have $1,000 of expenses, including rent, utilities, and food. You want to put at least $325 in savings each month so that you can buy a used car in a year or two. How much spending money could you potentially have each month? Model this situation with an inequality using *m* to represent your spending money.

. . . .

Richard needs to make at least \$2,500, but the words "at least" show that he'd like to earn more. The words "at least" indicate that this will be an inequality. The total amount Richard earns should be equal to OR greater than \$2,500.

$\$16.50t \geq \$2,500$

Solving this equation shows that Richard needs to sell at least **152 T-shirts**. Go Richard!

. . . .

$\$1,500 - \$1,000 - m > \$325$, where m = spending money

$\$500 - m > \$325$

$\$175 > m$, which means your spending money must be **less than \$175** per month in order to meet your long-term goal of saving enough money to purchase a car.

. . . .

What is a *quadratic equation*, and what does the graph of a quadratic equation look like?

. . . .

What is the standard form of a quadratic equation, and what does *a* represent?

. . . .

What is the standard form of a quadratic equation, and what does *c* represent?

QUADRATIC EQUATIONS

A **quadratic equation** is an equation in the form $ax^2 + bx + c = y$, where a, b, and c are coefficients.

The x^2 in the first term is what differentiates this from a linear equation and makes it a quadratic equation. When graphed, quadratics are in the shape of a parabola, which is a bell-shaped curve.

The standard form of a quadratic equation is $ax^2 + bx + c = y$, where a determines the direction and steepness of the parabola. When a is positive, the parabola opens upward and looks like a smile. When a is negative, the parabola opens downward and looks like a frown. When a is a large number, the parabola has a steep and narrow curve. When a has a smaller value, the parabola has a wider curve.

The standard form of a quadratic equation is $ax^2 + bx + c = y$. c will always be the y-intercept of the parabola, or where the parabola crosses the y-axis.

What is the *vertex* of a parabola, and what does it represent?

. . . .

What are the *roots* of a quadratic equation? Name three different methods for finding them.

. . . .

What is the *quadratic formula*, and what is it used for?

The **vertex** of a parabola is where the slope of a parabola changes from negative to positive or vice versa. The vertex is where the parabola has either a minimum value if the parabola is upward facing or a maximum value if the parabola is downward facing.

The **roots** of a quadratic are the *x*-intercepts, which are very useful for graphing an equation. The roots can be calculated by using the quadratic formula, by factoring, or by completing the square.

The **quadratic formula** is used to solve for the roots, or *x*-intercepts, of a quadratic equation that is in the form $y = ax^2 + bx + c$.

The quadratic formula is:

$$x = -b \pm \frac{\sqrt{b^2 - 4ac}}{2a}$$

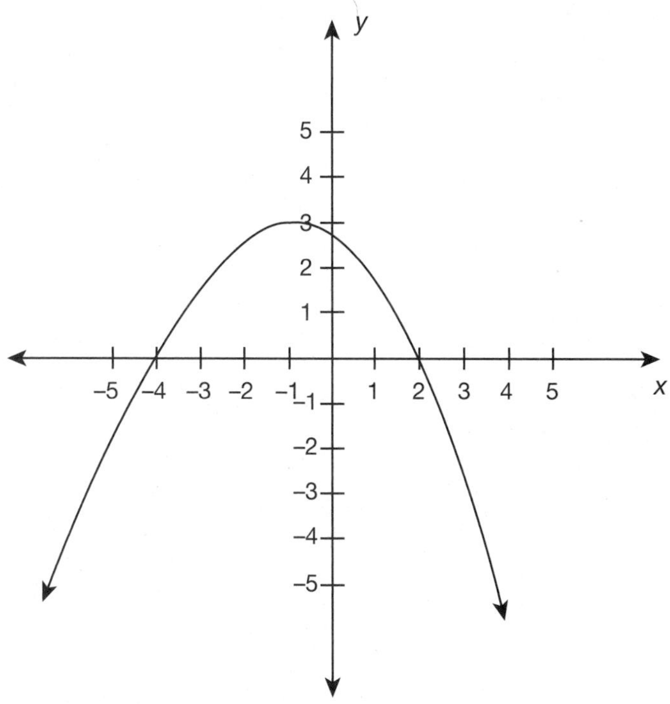

The graph shown here represents a function $y = g(x)$. Find the minimum or maximum value of the function, the roots, the interval on which $g(x)$ is increasing, and the interval on which $g(x)$ is decreasing.

How do you graph a quadratic equation?

The function has a maximum value of 3 when $x = -1$, so that is written as $(-1,3)$. The roots of the equation are at $x = -4$ and $x = 2$. The interval on which $g(x)$ is increasing is $(-\infty,-1)$, and the interval on which $g(x)$ is decreasing is $(-1,\infty)$.

. . . .

In order to graph a quadratic equation, first find the vertex by using the equation $x = \frac{-b}{2a}$. After finding x, substitute it back into the equation to solve for y. This (x,y) pair is the vertex and can now be plotted on a coordinate graph. Solve for the roots through the quadratic equation or factoring and plot those. Lastly, plot the y-intercept, which is c, and then sketch the parabola through these points.

. . . .

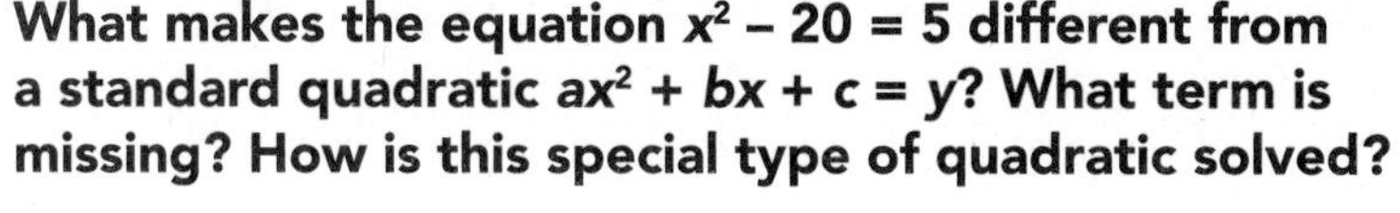

What makes the equation $x^2 - 20 = 5$ different from a standard quadratic $ax^2 + bx + c = y$? What term is missing? How is this special type of quadratic solved?

. . . .

Solve: $x^2 + 40 = 45$

. . . .

What is the *zero product property* and what is it used for?

When a quadratic has an x^2 and a constant, but not an x term, it is easily solved by isolating the x^2 and taking the square root of both sides. In this case, $x^2 - 20 = 5$ becomes $x^2 = 25$, and after the square root is taken of both sides, $x = \pm 5$. Make sure that when solving an equation by taking a square root, you include both answers—the negative and the positive.

Since this equation only has an x^2 and does not have an x term, isolate the x^2 and take the square root of both sides:

$x^2 + 40 = 45$

$x^2 = 5$

$\sqrt{x^2} = \sqrt{5}$

$x = \sqrt{5}$ and $-\sqrt{5}$

The **zero product property** states that the equation $A \times B = 0$ has two solutions: $A = 0$ and $B = 0$. It is most commonly used in the final step of solving quadratic equations that have been factored into a form $(x + m)(x + n) = 0$. In this case, it is true that $(x + m) = 0$ and $(x + n) = 0$ would both produce correct answers to the quadratic, thus giving two solutions.

What makes the equation $4x^2 - 20x = 0$ different from a standard quadratic $ax^2 + bx + c = y$? What term is missing? How is this special type of quadratic solved?

When factoring a quadratic in the form $x^2 + bx + c$, the quadratic will be broken down into the product $(x + m)(x + n)$ for two real numbers m and n. There are two tricks to finding the values of m and n:

1. **m and n must multiply to ____.**
2. **m and n must add to ____.**

Factor the following expression: $x^2 + 6x + 5$

$4x^2 - 20x = 0$ is a quadratic where $c = 0$. When there is only an x^2 and an x term in a quadratic that is set equal to 0, the equation can be solved by factoring out the greatest common factor and then applying the zero product property.

$4x^2 - 20x = 4x(x - 5)$

$4x(x - 5) = 0$

The zero product property holds that $4x = 0$ and $x - 5 = 0$ are both solutions.

So, **$x = 0$ and $x = 5$**.

. . . .

When factoring a quadratic in the form $x^2 + bx + c$ into the product $(x + m)(x + n)$,

1. *m* and *n* must multiply to ***c***.
2. *m* and *n* must add to ***b***.

. . . .

When factoring a quadratic in the form $x^2 + bx + c$, it will be broken down into the product of factors $(x + m)(x + n)$.

1. *m* and *n* must multiply to *c*.
2. *m* and *n* must add to *b*.

So, with $x^2 + 6x + 5$, since $5 \times 1 = 5$ and $5 + 1 = 6$, the factors are

$(x + 5)(x + 1)$.

By what methods can the equation $x^2 + 7x + 12 = 0$ be solved? Find the solutions.

. . . .

What is a positive solution to the equation $x^2 - 5x = 14$?

. . . .

What are the two solutions to the equation $x^2 - 2x - 3 = 0$?

When a quadratic equation has an x^2, an x, and a constant, it cannot be solved like a linear equation by isolating the x^2 and x. The equation must be solved by factoring, completing the square, or graphing. Since 4 and 3 multiply to 12 and add to 7, $x^2 + 7x + 12 = 0$ can be factored into $(x + 4)(x + 3) = 0$. The zero product property shows that **$x = -4$** and **$x = -3$**.

. . . .

Rewriting the equation by subtracting 14 from both sides yields the quadratic equation $x^2 - 5x - 14 = 0$. Since -7 and 2 multiply to -14 and add to -5, this equation can be factored into $(x - 7)(x + 2) = 0$. The solutions to $(x - 7)(x + 2) = 0$ are $x = 7$ and $x = -2$, so the positive solution is **7**.

. . . .

$x^2 - 2x - 3 = 0$ can be factored into $(x - 3)(x + 1) = 0$ because -3 and 1 multiply to -3 and add to -2. Using the zero product property, this results in the equations $x - 3 = 0$ and $x + 1 = 0$. The solutions to these equations are **$x = 3$ and -1**, respectively.

What is the largest possible value of x if $x^2 - 14x + 35 = -10$?

. . . .

For what values of x is the function $f(x)$ undefined?
$f(x) = \frac{3}{x^2 - 3x + 2}$

. . . .

What does it mean to factor a "difference of perfect squares"?
What is the shortcut for factoring this generic difference of perfect squares: $x^2 - y^2$?

Adding 10 to both sides yields the equation $x^2 - 14x + 45 = 0$. This quadratic can be factored into $(x - 5)(x - 9) = 0$, resulting in solutions of 5 and 9. **Nine** is the larger of the two solutions to the equation.

. . . .

For an expression or function to be undefined, the denominator must equal zero. In this case, there is a quadratic in the denominator. To find the values of x where $f(x)$ is undefined, we must factor the quadratic and set it equal to 0. When factored, $x^2 - 3x + 2 = (x - 2)(x - 1)$, so $f(x)$ is undefined when $\mathbf{x = 2}$ **and** $\mathbf{x = 1}$.

. . . .

Factoring a "difference of perfect squares" means that two perfect squares are being subtracted, such as in $x^2 - 4$. $x^2 - y^2$ will always break down to the sum of the square roots of x^2 and y^2 times the difference of the square roots of x^2 and y^2:

$$\mathbf{x^2 - y^2 = (x - y)(x + y)}$$

The example $x^2 - 4$ factors into $(x - 2)(x + 2)$.

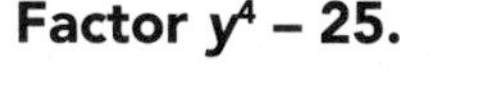

Factor $y^4 - 25$.

What are the steps to solving quadratics in the general form $x^2 + bx + c = 0$ by completing the square?
Solve $x^2 + 6x - 16 = 0$ by completing the square.

Solve the following quadratic by completing the square: $x^2 + 6x - 16 = 0$.

y^4 and 25 are both perfect squares, and the trick for factoring two perfect squares that are being subtracted is $x^2 - y^2 = (x - y)(x + y)$. Following this technique:

$y^4 - 25 = \mathbf{(y^2 + 5)(y^2 - 5)}$.

. . . .

When completing the square, first get the x^2 and bx terms alone on one side with the constant on the other side:

$x^2 + bx - c = 0$ becomes $x^2 + bx = c$.

Then find half of b and square it: $(\frac{1}{2}b)^2$

Add $(\frac{1}{2}b)^2$ to both sides:

$x^2 + bx + (\frac{1}{2}b)^2 = c + (\frac{1}{2}b)^2$

Now the left side will factor into a sum squared:

$(x + \frac{1}{2}b)(x + \frac{1}{2}b) = c + (\frac{1}{2}b)^2$

$(x + \frac{1}{2}b)^2 = c + (\frac{1}{2}b)^2$

At this point, it will be possible to take the square root of both sides and solve for x.

. . . .

When completing the square, first get the x^2 and bx terms alone on one side with the constant on the other side:

$x^2 + 6x - 16 = 0$ becomes $x^2 + 6x = 16$.

Then find half of b and square it: $(\frac{1}{2}b)^2$

Here, $(\frac{1}{2}b)^2$ is $(3)^2 =$ ___.

Add 9 to both sides:

$x^2 + 6x + \underline{9} = 16 + \underline{9}$

Next, factor the left side of the equation, which is now a sum squared:

$(x + 3)^2 = 25$

Take the square root of both sides: $(x + 3) = \pm 5$

Finally, solve for $x + 3 = 5$ and $x + 3 = -5$ to get $\mathbf{x = 2}$ **and** $\mathbf{-8}$.

Can a quadratic equation have no roots? If that is possible, what would its graph look like?

Terry is given instructions to lay stone tiles for a rectangular patio. The dimensions of the patio will have a length that is twice as long as the width. He only has a budget to pay for 72 ft^2 of tile. How can Terry figure out the dimensions of the largest possible tiled area to stay within his budget? Use a quadratic to model and solve.

The roots of a quadratic are the x-intercepts of the parabola. A parabola could be an upward facing parabola with a vertex that sits above the x-axis. It could also be a downward facing parabola with a vertex that sits below the x-axis. Both of these situations are cases where a quadratic will have no roots.

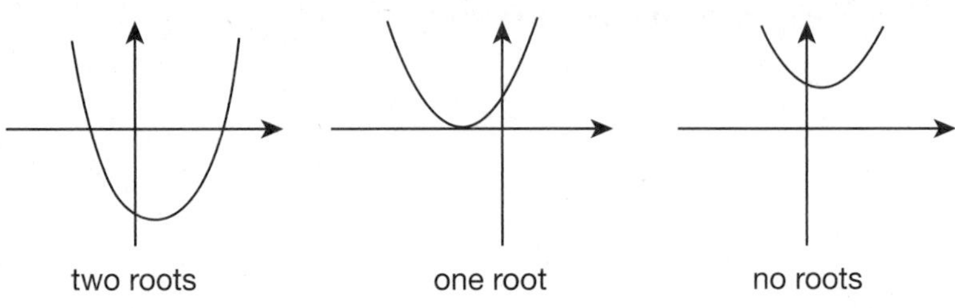

• •

width = w

length = $2 \times$ width = $2w$

area = (length)(width) = $(2w)(w)$ = $\mathbf{2w^2}$

Since this area of $2w^2$ must equal 72:

$2w^2 = 72$

$\frac{2w^2}{2} = \frac{72}{2}$

$w^2 = 36$

$w = \pm 6$

Only the positive solution of $w = 6$ is possible, so the width is **6** and the length is **12**.

• •

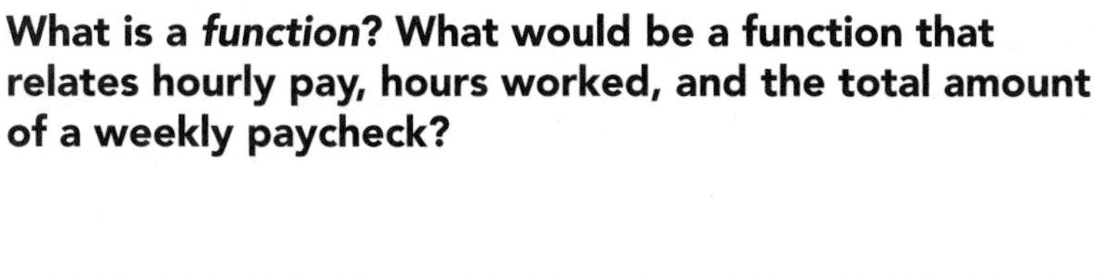

What is a *function*? What would be a function that relates hourly pay, hours worked, and the total amount of a weekly paycheck?

. . . .

When is a relation NOT a function?
Choose a value or values for the unknown *y* that would cause this relation to NOT be a function:
{(1,5), (2, 5), (3,–5), (1,__)}

. . . .

How can the *vertical line test* be used to see if a relation is a function?

FUNCTIONS

A **function** is a mathematic relationship where every *x* input corresponds to a unique *y* output. A function that relates hourly pay, hours worked, and the total amount of a weekly paycheck would be:

(Hours worked) × (Hourly Pay) = (Paycheck)

So if a job pays $12/hour, this would be written Pay = $12*h*, where *h* is the hours worked.

• •

A relation is not a function when one of its *x* inputs has two different *y* output values. Therefore, given the values {(1,5), (2,7), (3,8), (1,__)}, if the last coordinate pair is anything other than (1,5), then this relation will NOT be a function. Note: It is permitted for a function to have two different *x*-values with the same *y*-value, such as with points (1,5) and (2,5). However, a function cannot have two different *y*-values for the same *x*-value.

• •

Recall that a relation is not a function when there is an *x*-input that has two different *y*-outputs. If a relation is a function, it will pass the **vertical line test**: A vertical line should be able to pass over the relation from left to right without touching more than one point at a time. If a vertical line would intersect two points at the same time, then the relation fails the vertical line test and is not a function.

Which of the following graphs shows *n* as a function of *m*?

A.

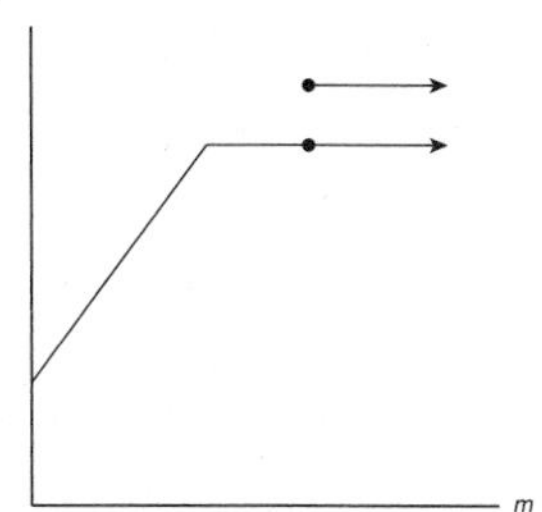

B.

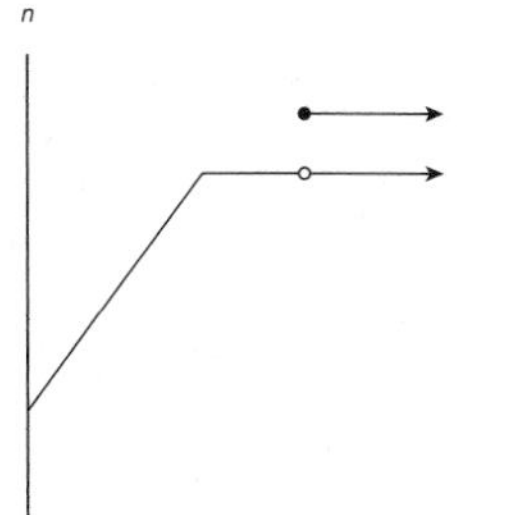

C.

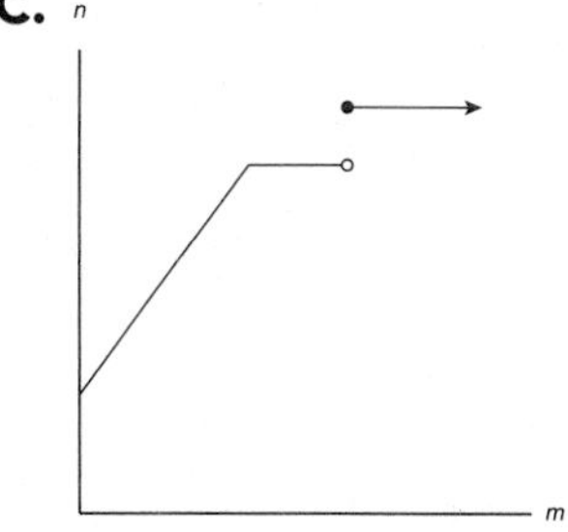

D.

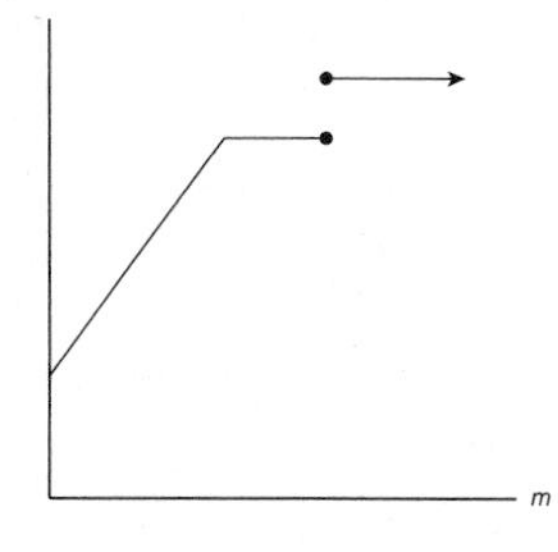

Choice C is correct. For each possible value of *m*, there is only one possible value of *n*. This is the only graph that passes the vertical line test.

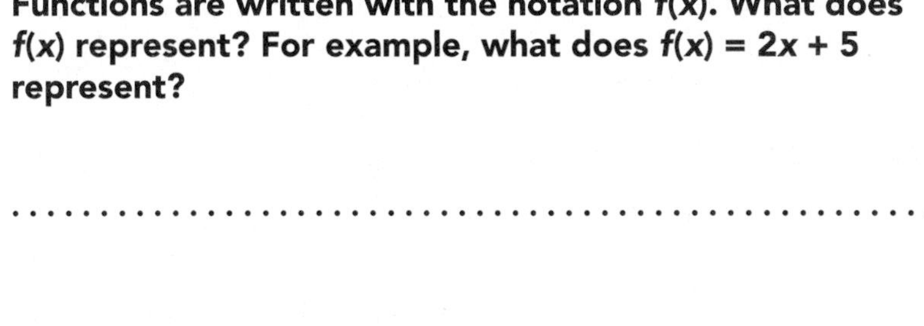

Functions are written with the notation $f(x)$. What does $f(x)$ represent? For example, what does $f(x) = 2x + 5$ represent?

. . . .

If given the function $f(x) = 4x + 10$, what does $f(5)$ mean and how would you solve for it?

. . . .

For input k, the function f is defined as $f(k) = -2k^2 + 1$. What is the value of $f(-8)$?

FUNCTIONS

$f(x)$ is read "f of x," and this notation represents the y-value of a function for a given x-value. $f(x) = 2x + 5$ is another way to write $y = 2x + 5$. $f(x)$ is used to show that the input values for x determine the output values for y. $f(4)$ is the y-value of a function when $x = 4$. In order to use this notation, replace all of the x-values in an equation with the value inside $f(x)$:

If $f(x) = 2x + 5$, then $f(\mathbf{4}) = 2(\mathbf{4}) + 5 = 13$.

Given the function $f(x) = 4x + 10$, $f(5)$ means the y-value of the function when $x = 5$.

$f(5) = 4(5) + 10 = 30$, so $\mathbf{f(5) = 30}$.

Remember that when subbing a negative value in for a squared variable, the negative is also squared:

$f(k) = -2k^2 + 1$

$f(-8) = -2(-8)^2 + 1$

$f(-8) = -2(64) + 1$

$f(-8) = -128 + 1 = \mathbf{-127}$

What is the value of $f(-1)$ if $f(x) = 3x^2 - 6x + 8$?

. . . .

$f(x) = 3x^3 - 12$
Complete the table below:

x	$f(x)$
–2	
–1	
3	
5	

. . . .

Evaluate the function $f(x) = 2x^2 + 5x$ when $x = 3v$.

In order to find $f(-1)$ if $f(x) = 3x^2 - 6x + 8$, both of the x variables must be replaced with –1:

$f(-1) = 3(-1)^2 - 6(-1) + 8$

$f(-1) = 3(1) + 6 + 8$

$\mathbf{f(-1) = 17}$

. . . .

To find the output values, substitute the given x-values into the function $f(x) = 3x^3 - 12$:

x	$f(x)$
–2	**–36**
–1	**–15**
3	**69**
5	**363**

. . . .

$f(x) = 2x^2 + 5x$

$f(3v) = 2(3v)^2 + 5(3v)$

$f(3v) = 2(9v^2) + 15v$

$f(3v) = 18v^2 + 15v$

$\mathbf{f(3v) = 3v(6v + 5)}$

What is the *domain* of a function?
What are two situations to be careful of when considering the domain of a function?

. . . .

How can fractions restrict the domain of a function? Consider the function $f(x) = \frac{8}{2 + x}$.

. . . .

Find the domain of $f(x) = \frac{5}{3 - x}$.

The **domain** consists of all the possible x input values that can be substituted into a function.

The two situations to be aware of when considering the domain are fractions and square roots. A fraction cannot have zero in the denominator, and it is not possible to take the square root of a negative number, so any values that would make a denominator 0 or the radicand negative will not be part of the domain of a function.

The domain consists of all the possible x inputs, so it is important to look for anything that restricts possible x-values. Fractional functions that have x in the denominator are something to look out for, since the denominator is never allowed to equal zero in fractions. For example, if $f(x) = \frac{8}{2+x}$, then x cannot equal –2, since that would result in a zero denominator. Therefore, the domain is **all real numbers except –2**.

$f(x) = \frac{5}{3-x}$

$(3 - x) \neq 0$, since a zero in the denominator would make this fraction undefined. Therefore, $x \neq 3$. All other values of x would not be problematic. Therefore, the domain is **all real numbers other than 3**.

How can square roots restrict the domain of a function? Consider $f(x) = \sqrt{2 + x}$.

Find the domain of the equation graphed on the coordinate plane below:

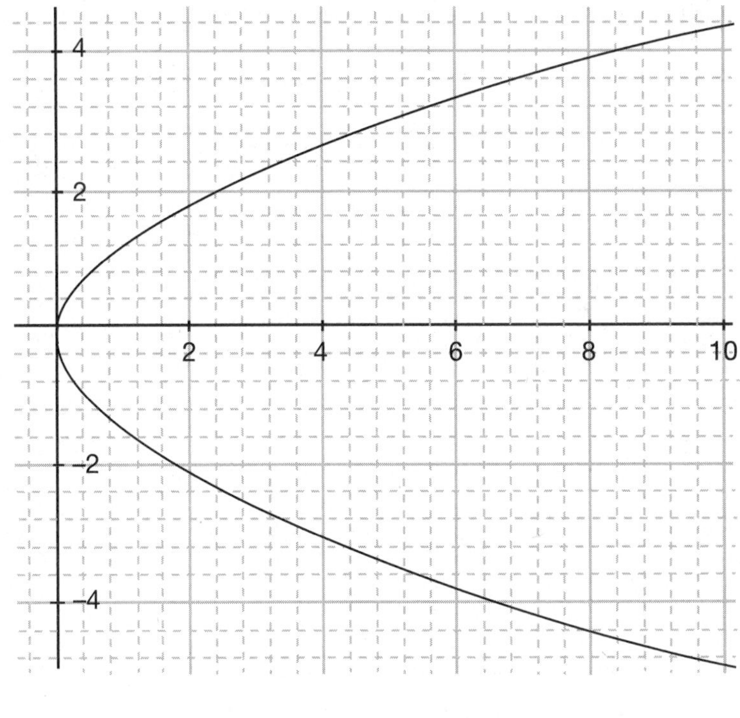

The domain consists of all the possible x inputs, so it is important to look for anything that restricts possible x-values. When x is part of a radicand, special care must be taken since it is not possible to take the square root of a negative number.

For example, if $f(x) = \sqrt{2 + x}$, the $(2 + x)$ cannot be negative in order for $\sqrt{2 + x}$ to be a real number. Set up and solve:

$2 + x \geq 0$
$\mathbf{x \geq -2}$ is the domain.

The graph illustrated does not have any coordinate pairs with x-values that are less than 0, so the domain of this graph is **$[0,\infty)$**.

Greg gets paid through an hourly rate as well as a flat commission for the number of refrigerators he sells each day. He gets $13/hour and works 8-hour days. For every refrigerator he sells, he gets $40. Write a function that represents the amount of money Greg earns on a day when he sells *n* refrigerators.

Since \$13/hour times 8 hours equals \$104, Greg will earn \$104 plus \$40 for each refrigerator he sells:

G* = \$104 + \$40*n

What are *bar graphs* best used for?

. . . .

How is a *vertical bar graph* set up?

. . . .

On average, how many more children did households have in the first generation displayed than in the current Dexter generation?

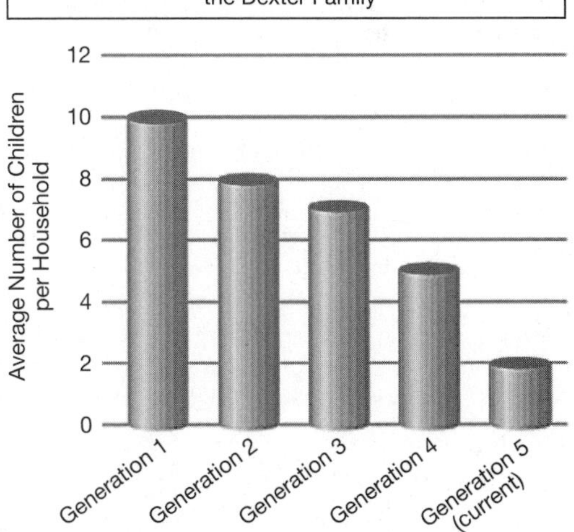

Bar graphs are used to display data with differing values for each category. The differing heights of the bars offer a quick comparison of data. A great example of data that would be well represented in a bar graph is the average number of inches of rain a city gets over the 12 months of the year.

Vertical bar graphs display the categories along the *x*-axis and the numerical values along the *y*-axis. If a bar graph was to show the average number of inches of rain a city gets over the 12 months of the year, the months would go along the *x*-axis and the number of inches of rain would go along the *y*-axis.

The bar graph shows the average number of children per household for the Dexter family. The data includes the past five generations. The height of the bar for Generation 1 is 10, which means each household had an average of 10 children. The height of the bar for the current generation, Generation 5, is 2, which means that each household in the Dexter family today has an average of 2 children. On average, the first generation of the Dexter family had **8 more children** than the current generation.

How is a *horizontal bar graph* set up?

. . . .

A survey of elite runners' favorite brands of running shoes was conducted at the Boston Marathon. The researcher collecting the data wishes to display the results as categories, without displaying individual results or percentages. Which data display should the researcher choose?

A. line graph
B. bar graph
C. circle graph
D. stem-and-leaf plot

. . . .

Horizontal bar graphs display the categories along the *y*-axis and the data values along the *x*-axis. This bar graph shows the average number of children per household for the Dexter family over five generations.

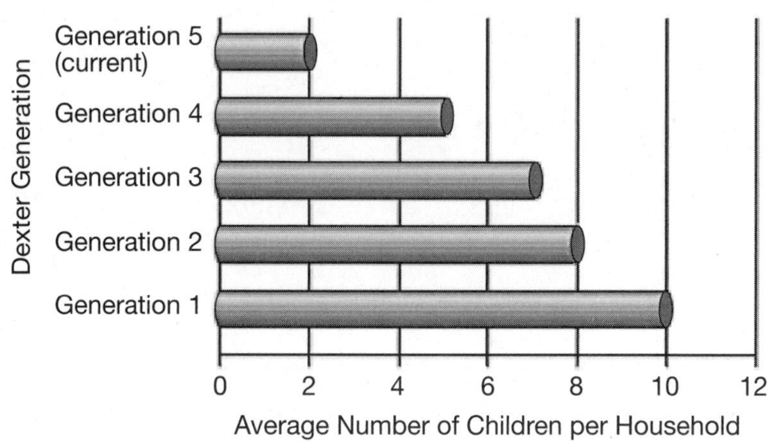

Choice B, a bar graph, is the best way to display categorical data that is not broken down into percentages or quantified into individual scores. For a vertical bar graph, the name brands would go on the *x*-axis and the number of runners who selected each brand would be represented on the *y*-axis and by the heights of the columns.

The bar chart below represents the total dollar value of sales for four different versions of a product in July. Which two versions of the product had combined sales of approximately $50,000 in July?

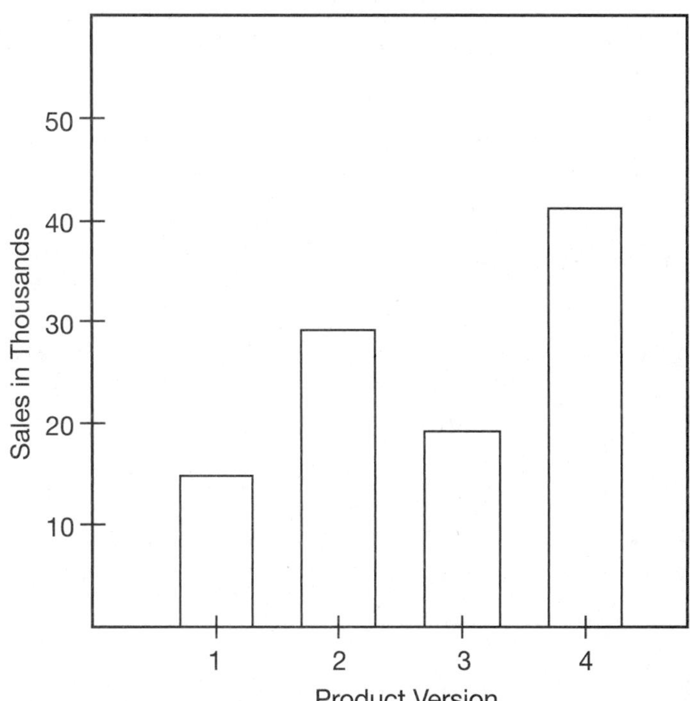

Product versions 2 and 3 have combined sales of approximately **$50,000**.

What type of data is displayed in *circle graphs*? (Circle graphs are also called pie charts.)

Circle graphs, or pie charts, are used to express a set of data that collectively make up a whole. The data is represented not as numbers, but as percentages of the whole. Consider children under 5 years of age in developing countries: if a study finds that 80% are malnourished and 20% are nourished, then the pie chart here represents this survey.

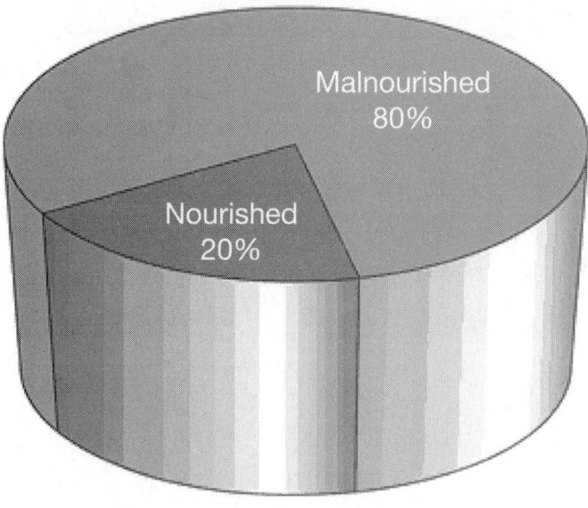

The following pie chart shows the percentage of the different forms of transportation that are involved in road accidents during one December in South Africa. What percentage of accidents involved bakkies?

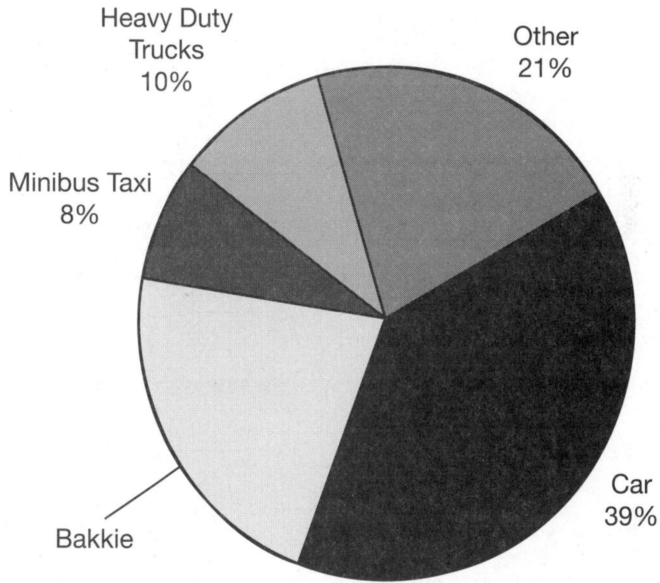

*** Image adapted from http://cnx.org/content/m35761/1.1/**

Only the category representing accidents involving bakkies is not labeled. Therefore, add up all of the other percentages and subtract that subtotal from 100%:

100% – 78% = 22%

So **22%** of the accidents involved bakkies that December.

Use the following pie chart to estimate the percentage of each transportation category.

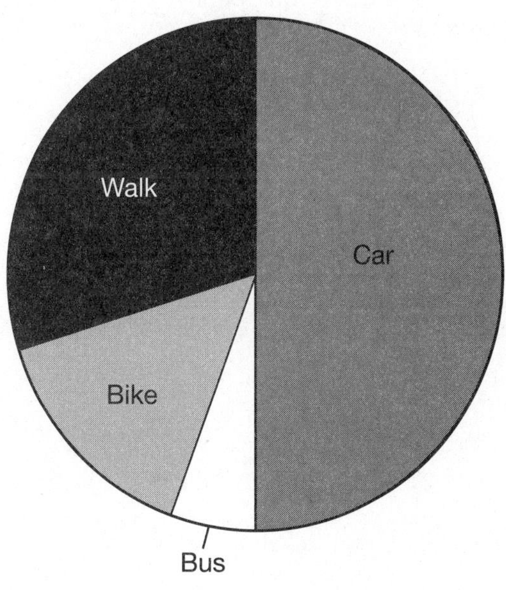

All the percentages must add to 100%. Cars take up half of the pie chart, so they account for **50%**. Walkers make up more than one-quarter of the graph, so a good estimate for walkers is **28%**. The remaining 22% is made up of bikes and buses. Buses account for around $\frac{1}{4}$ of this 22%, so estimate that buses represent around **5%**, which would leave bikes at **17%** (since 22% – 5% = 17%).

Create a circle graph that accurately represents this data.

U.S. Census Bureau Statistics, 2012

Single Mothers with Children Under 18	Single Fathers with Children Under 18
10.322 million	1.956 million

Source of data: http://singlemotherguide.com/single–mother–statistics/*

. . . .

What are *dot plots* best used for?

. . . .

To represent information in a circle graph, find the percentage of the whole for each statistic. First, find the total number of single parents by adding 10.322 million and 1.956 million to get 12.278 million. Now, find the percentage of single mother families and single father families by dividing each category by the whole: $\frac{10.322}{12.278}$ = 84.1% single mothers and $\frac{1.956}{12.278}$ = 15.9% single fathers. The circle graph below represents this data:

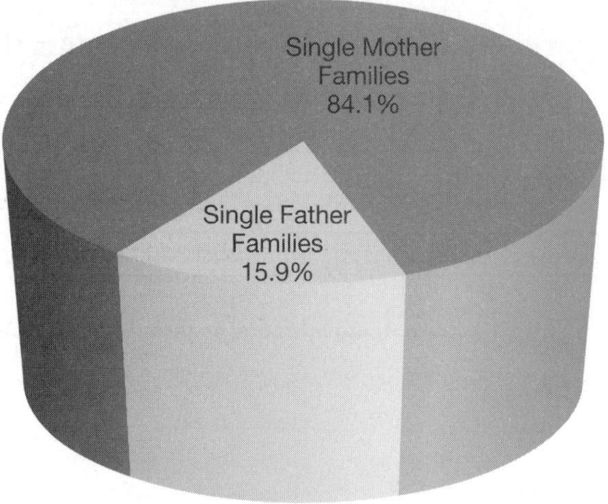

Dot plots are used to display categorical data on a number line. They are what they sound like: dots plotted above a number line. The frequency of the dots plotted above each number helps give a quick visual of how the data is distributed.

The students in Ms. Ono's class reported how many hours they practiced their musical instruments each week. Each dot represents one student. How many students are in Ms. Ono's class, and which category of practice hours has the most number of students?

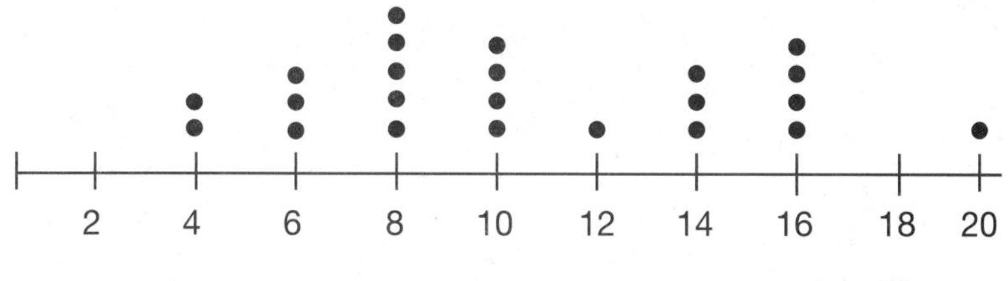

The dot plot below shows test scores for seven out of the eight students in Mr. Kissam's Latin class. The eighth student's score is between 84 and 92. Plot the missing score on the dot plot if the median of all eight scores is 90.

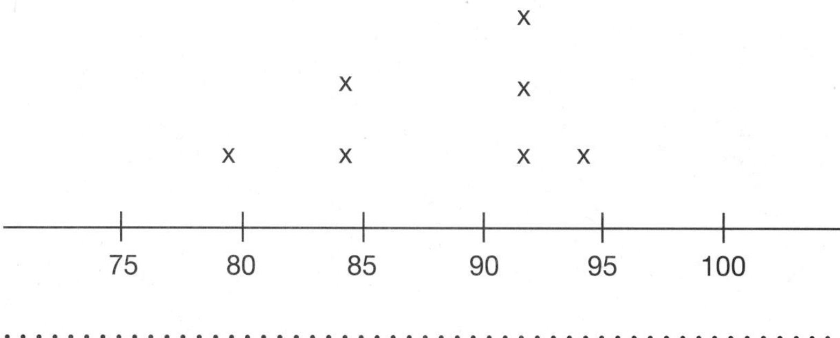

What is a *box plot* and what kind of data does it best represent?

There are **23 students** in her class, and **8 hours** is the category with the most number of students. Five students reported practicing 8 hours per week.

The median score is the middle score when the data is listed from least to greatest. The problem states that the missing point in the data set is between 84 and 92. So, let *x* represent the missing score added to the chronological list: 79, 84, 84, **x, 92**, 92, 92, 94. The middle two numbers are *x* and 92, so the average of *x* and 92 must be 90, which means the eighth student's score must be **88**.

Box plots are similar to dot plots in that they are also organized on a number line, but individual data points are not represented in a box plot. Box plots are useful for summarizing large amounts of data by breaking a set down into five different measures: the minimum, maximum, median, and medians of the upper and lower halves of data points.

What are the five different number values that are represented in a box plot, and how are they illustrated in the box plot?

. . . .

What do the *lower and upper quartiles* represent in a box plot?

How are they calculated?

. . . .

What do the *lower and upper extremes* represent in a box plot?

1. The **median** of the entire data set is the line drawn inside the box.
2. The **lower quartile** is the left-side edge of the box.
3. The **upper quartile** is the right-side edge of the box.
4. The **lower extreme** is the left-most point of the plot.
5. The **upper extreme** is the right-most point of the plot.

The **lower quartile** is the median of the lower half of the data set. The **upper quartile** is the median of the upper half of the data set.

Organize the data in chronological order, and after this list is split in half, the lower half is used to find the lower quartile and the upper half is used to find the upper quartile.

The **lower extreme** is the lowest point of the data set, and the **upper extreme** is the highest point of the data set.

Looking at the given box plots, which destination has a more consistent temperature in the fall?

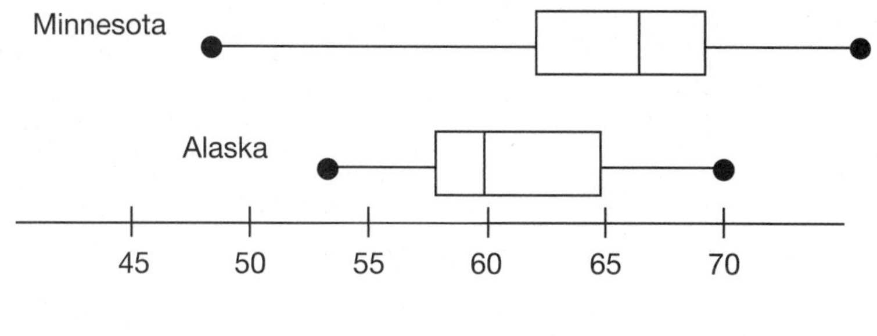

. . . .

What is necessary about how the data must be arranged before the five critical numbers for a box plot can be determined?

. . . .

Find the five critical numbers needed to make a box plot for the following set of numbers: 84, 91, 85, 100, 91, 67, 78, 93, 79, 83, 86, 76, 93, 87, 69, 87, 75, 89, 90, 91, 82, 92, 55, 65, 93

The span of the extreme temperatures is not quite as wide in Alaska as the span of the extreme temperatures in Minnesota, so Alaska has more consistent temperatures in the fall.

. . . .

Since three of the five measures of box plots are medians, it is critical that the data be sorted in order of least to greatest.

. . . .

First, put the data in order of least to greatest: 55, 65, 67, 69, 75, <u>76, 78</u>, 79, 82, 83, 84, 85, <u>86</u>, 87, 87, 89, 90, 91, <u>91, 91</u>, 92, 93, 93, 93, <u>100</u>

86 is the median because there are an even 12 numbers on each side of it in the data set.

There are an even number of data points below the median, so for the lower quartile, find the average of 76 and 78, which is 77. The lower quartile is **77**.

There are an even number of data points above the median, so for the upper quartile find the average of 91 and 91, which gives an upper quartile of **91**.

The lower extreme is **55**, and the upper extreme is **100**.

Use the following data to make a box plot:
Lower extreme: 55
Lower quartile: 77
Median: 86
Upper quartile: 91
Upper extreme: 100

. . . .

What does the box represent in a box plot?

. . . .

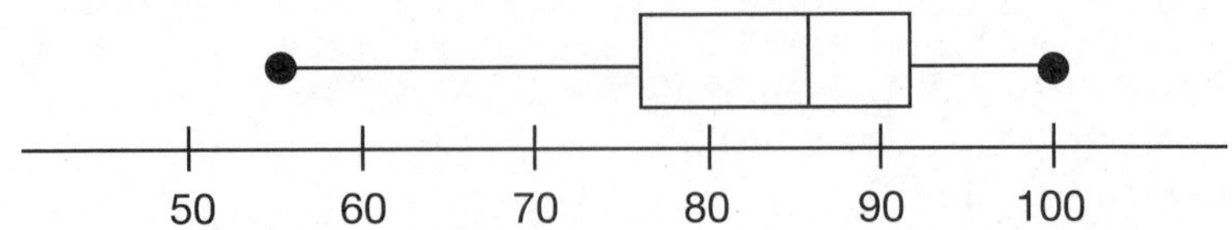

Since the box begins at the lower quartile and ends at the upper quartile, it represents the **middle 50%** of the data.

In a study of its employees, a company found that about 50% of employees spent more than 2 hours a day composing or reading emails. The overall distribution of time employees spent on these activities was skewed to the right, with a mean time of about 2.5 hours. Draw as many vertical lines as needed on the graph to complete the box plot so it represents the data.

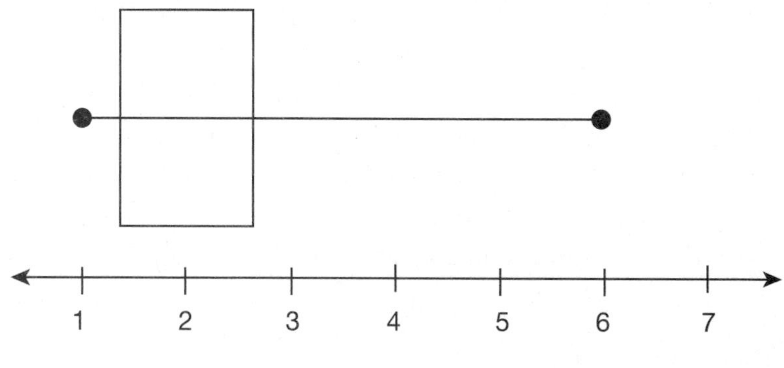

What are *histograms* used for?

Although the mean is 2.5, this is not a measure that is represented on a box plot. The critical piece of information is that "about 50% spent more than 2 hours a day composing or reading emails." This implies that the median is 2 hours, which is illustrated in the box plot below:

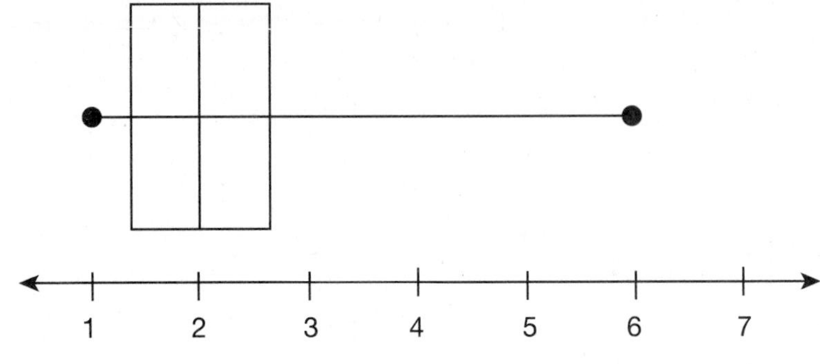

Histograms are similar to bar graphs, except the bottom of a histogram contains numbers, rather than categories. Histograms are the best tools to graph continuous sets of data that are measured in intervals. Ranges of salaries, populations, or temperatures are all great illustrations of data that are best displayed in histograms. Unlike bar graphs, there are no gaps between the bars.

The following table shows the distribution of salaries of the Woodlawn Conservation Group. Approximately how many employees earn over $66,000?

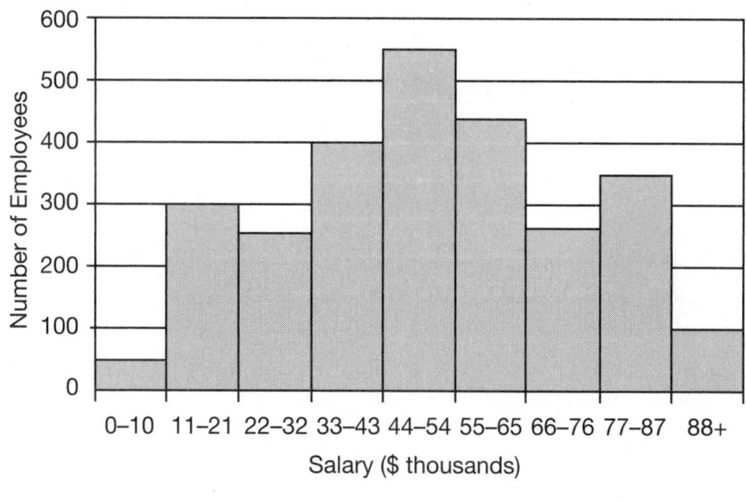

There are three columns that represent earning over $66,000. The number of employees in these three columns is approximately 250 + 350 + 100 = **700**.

According to the histogram below, how many students are in Mr. Duvall's class?

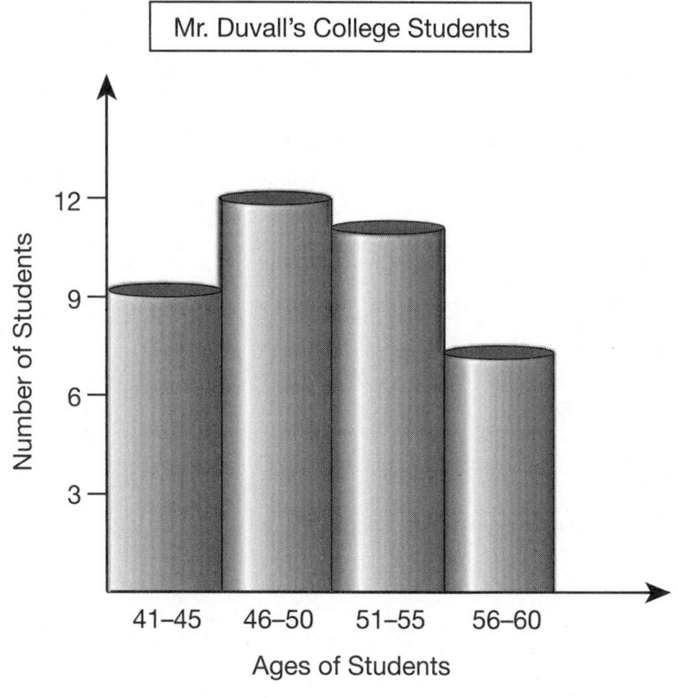

Add up the number of students in each of the age ranges: 9 are 41–45 *years* old, 12 are 46–50 *years* old, 11 are 51–55 *years* old, and 7 are 56–60 *years* old. In total, there are **39 students**.

According to the histogram below, what percentage of Mr. Duvall's students are 46–50 years old?

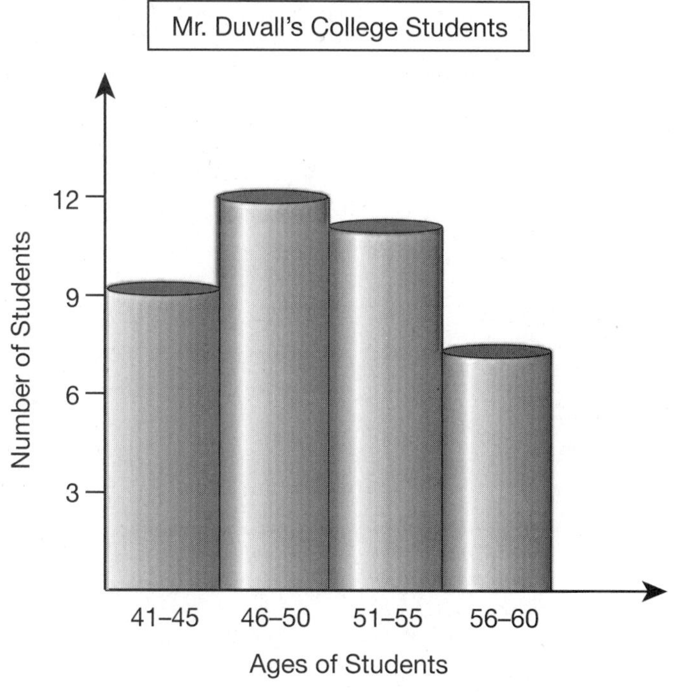

To find the percentage of students between 46 and 50 years old, first find the total number of students, which is 39. The number of students between 46 and 50 years old is 12. To find the percentage of students between 46 and 50, divide 12 by 39 and then move the decimal point two spaces to the right: $\frac{21}{39}$ = **31%**.

The histogram below represents the data collected through a survey of students at a large commuter college. Each student surveyed provided the one-way distance he or she travels to campus.

1. **How many students are represented in the histogram?**
2. **How many students travel less than 20 miles, round trip?**
3. **How many students travel more than 19 miles, one way?**

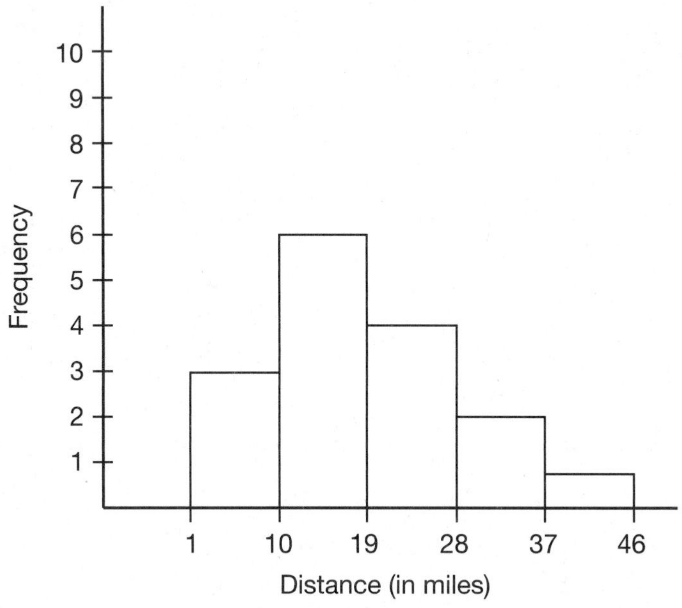

1. Add the height of all the columns to see the total number of students represented: 3 + 6 + 4 + 2 + 1 = **16 students**.
2. The first column shows that **3 students** travel less than 10 miles one way, which is 20 miles round trip.
3. 4 + 2 + 1 = **7 students** travel more than 19 miles, one way.

What kind of data do *scatterplots* best display?

. . . .

When is it useful to plot data in a scatterplot?

. . . .

When looking at a data set, what is an *outlier*?

Scatterplots display data that have two different variables and are presented as coordinate pairs. This type of data is referred to as bivariate.

Scatterplots are useful for identifying the relationship between two variables so that trends can be recognized. It is possible to make an equation that models the data in the scatterplot, and then predictions can be made.

An **outlier** is a point that is not within the cluster. It is either significantly larger or smaller than the rest of the data or is a point that does not correlate with the rest of the data.

Looking at the scatterplot below, identify the outlier and explain what line of reasoning might account for it.

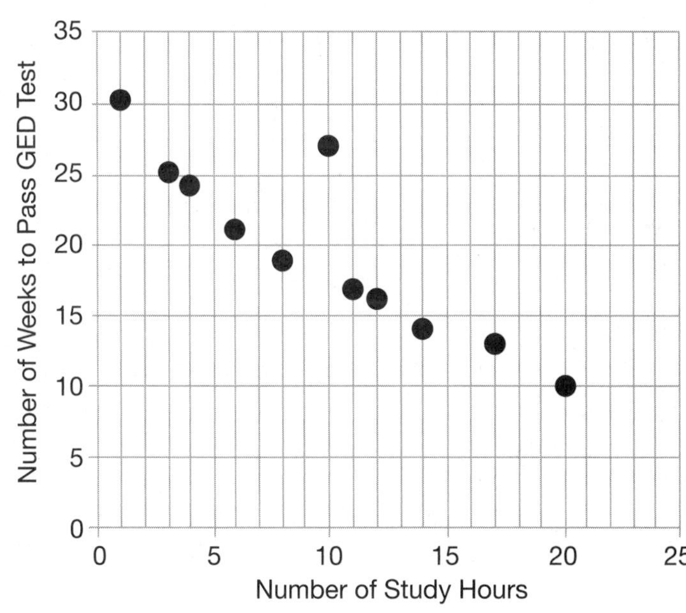

. . . .

What does it mean if the bivariate data in a scatterplot has a *linear association*?

. . . .

The outlier is the point that is most outside the cluster. In this graph, it is the student that spent 10 hours a week studying and took 27 weeks to pass the GED® test. Perhaps this student had poor study habits while studying, so his or her study time was not as effective as that of the other students represented in the scatterplot.

A scatterplot has a **linear association** if the plotted points resemble a line.

What does it mean if the bivariate data in a scatterplot has a *nonlinear association*?

. . . .

Which statement is NOT true about the scatterplot?

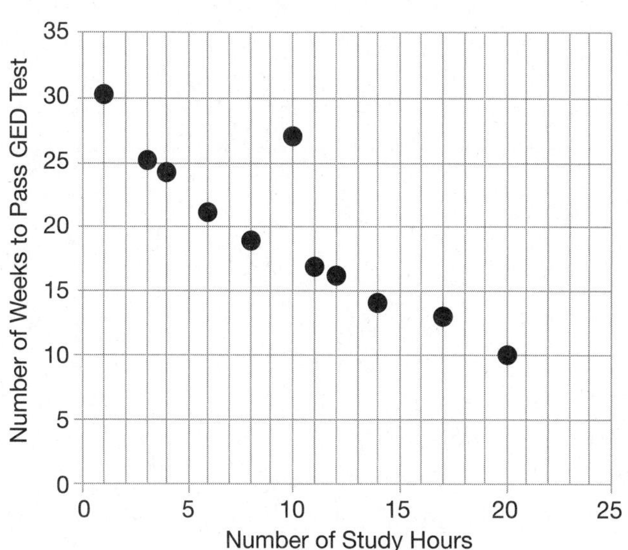

A. The data shows a negative, linear association.
B. The greater amount of hours one studies each week, the quicker one passes his/her GED® test.
C. The data shows a nonlinear association.
D. One can confidently predict that a student who studies 19 hours a week will pass his/her GED® test in roughly 11 weeks.

. . . .

A scatterplot has a **nonlinear association** if the plotted points resemble a curve.

The graph does show a linear association, so **choice C** is not true. The graph has a negative linear association: As the number of hours of studying increases, the number of weeks it takes to pass the GED® test decreases.

What does it mean if the bivariate data in a scatterplot has a *positive association*?

What does it mean if the bivariate data in a scatterplot has a *negative association*?

When there is a **positive association** in a scatterplot, as the independent data on the *x*-axis increases, the data on the *y*-axis increases as well.

When there is a **negative association** in a scatterplot, as the independent data on the *x*-axis increases, the data on the *y*-axis decreases.

The following scatterplot shows the relationship between the number of hours spent studying per week as this relates to the number of weeks it takes to pass the GED® test. Does this data show a positive or negative association?

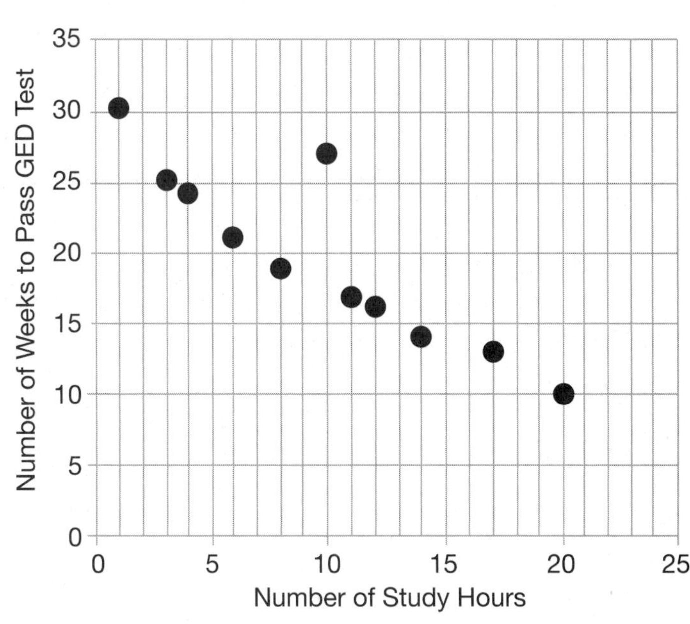

As the number of hours studying per week increases, the number of weeks it takes to pass the GED® test decreases, so this data shows a **negative association**.

A beauty product manufacturer collected the data shown in the scatterplot below, which shows the time participants spend on their morning beauty routines versus the amount of money the participants spend per month on beauty products.

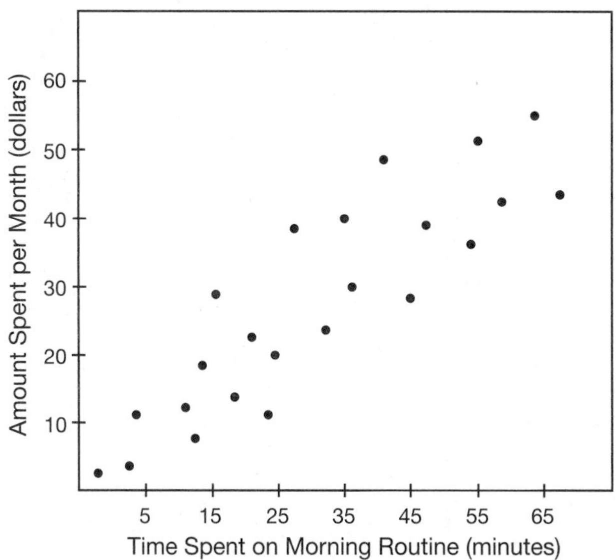

Given this plot, make a conclusion about the type of association there is between the data, and discuss how the amount of time spent on a morning routine relates to the amount of money spent on beauty products.

The pattern in the scatterplot has a general upward trend from left to right. This indicates a **positive association**—as the time spent on the morning routine increases, the amount spent on beauty products also increases.

Amber has been rehearsing for a soliloquy she has in King Lear. On what day of practice did she have $\frac{3}{4}$ of her soliloquy memorized?

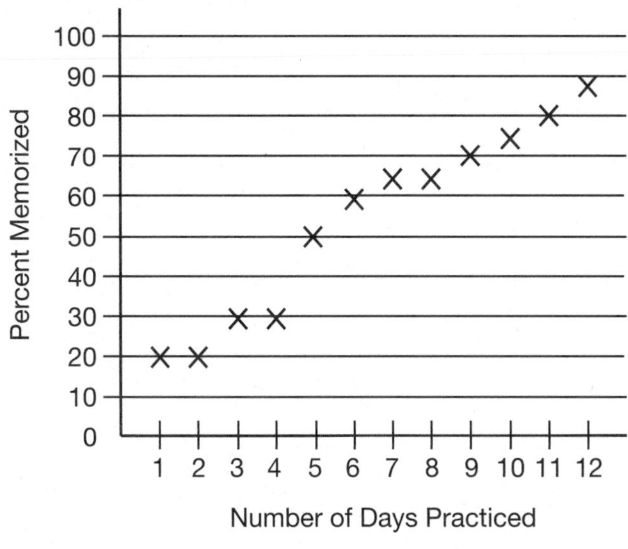

Which type of graph or table would be best to show the number of families that live in different income brackets in the state of Oregon?

Which type of graph or table would be best to show the percentage breakdown of how the average college student spends his or her time during the day?

$\frac{3}{4}$ is equal to 75%, and Amber had 75% memorized on **day 10**.

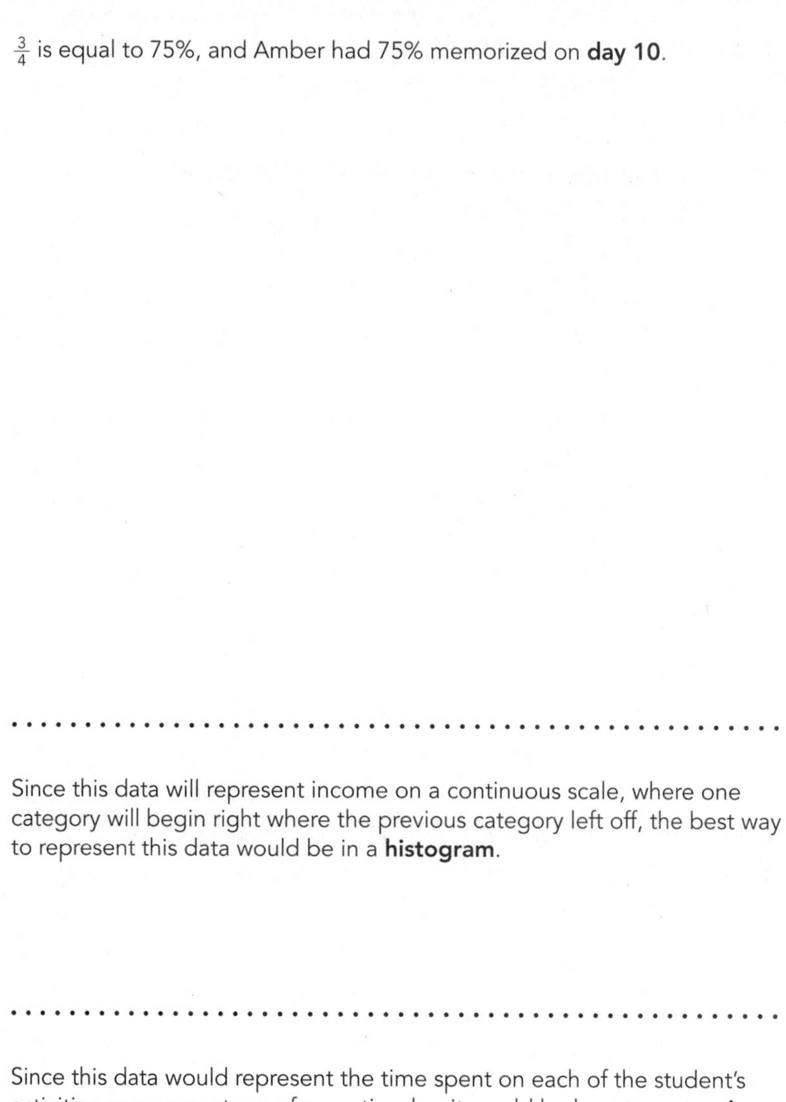

Since this data will represent income on a continuous scale, where one category will begin right where the previous category left off, the best way to represent this data would be in a **histogram**.

Since this data would represent the time spent on each of the student's activities as a percentage of an entire day, it would be best to use a **pie chart**.

Which type of graph or table would be best to compare the number of students that are enrolled in ten different summer programs at a given camp?

The chart below represents the number of households in selected cities that have subscribed to a new company's Internet service. Based on this data, how many households have subscribed to the service in San Diego?

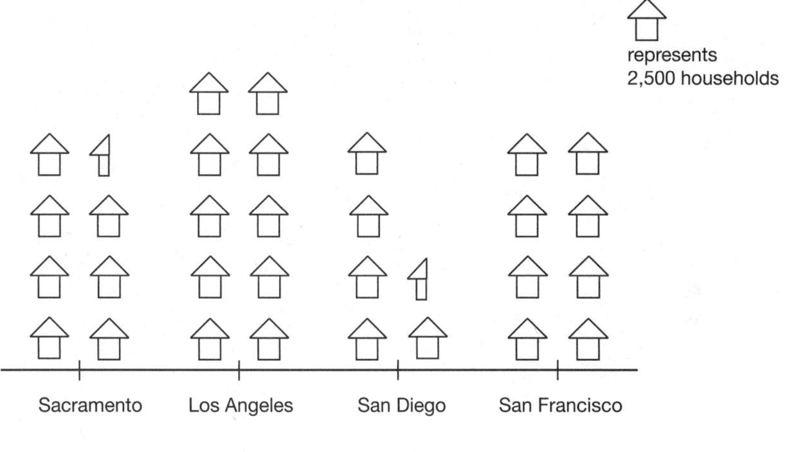

It would be best to use a **bar graph** where the names of the ten summer programs are the independent variables and the frequency of students involved in each summer program would be the dependent variable.

• •

There are 5.5 house symbols used in the chart for San Diego. Since each house represents 2,500 subscribers, there are $5.5 \times 2{,}500$ = **13,750** subscribing households in San Diego.

• •

How many x-intercepts does the graph of a quadratic equation have?

. . . .

How is the slope described of a function where y increases as x increases?

. . . .

How is the slope described of a function where y decreases as x increases?

KEY FEATURES OF GRAPHS

1. A quadratic equation can have **one** *x*-intercept if the vertex of the parabola is on the *x*-axis.
2. A quadratic equation can have **two** *x*-intercepts if the parabola is upward facing with a vertex below the *x*-axis or if the parabola is downward facing with a vertex above the *x*-axis.
3. A quadratic equation can have **zero** *x*-intercepts if the parabola is upward facing with a vertex above the *x*-axis or if the parabola is downward facing with a vertex below the *x*-axis.

The slope of a function where *y* increases as *x* increases is said to be **positive** or **nonnegative**. These functions go up toward the right.

The slope of a function where *y* decreases as *x* increases is said to be **negative** or **nonpositive**. These functions go down toward the right.

Can a function be increasing, but also negative, over the same interval? Similarly, can a function be decreasing and positive over the same interval?

The graph shown here represents the total weekly revenue for a company over several weeks. Over which two weeks did the revenue increase the most, and over which weeks did revenue remain the same?

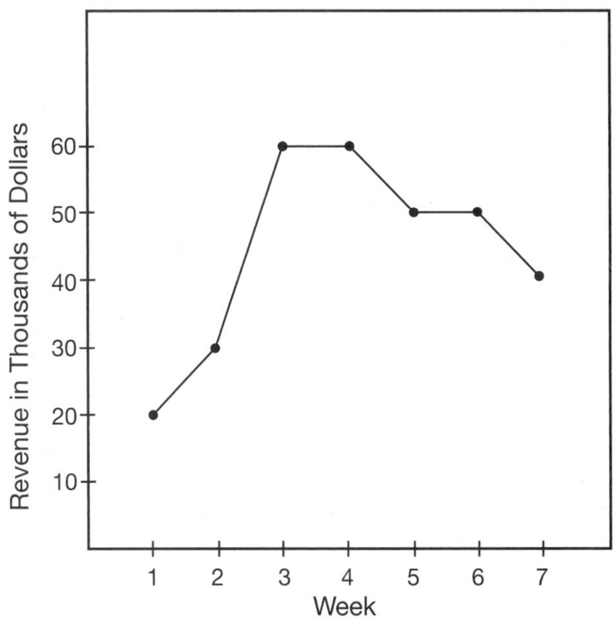

The terms "increasing" and "decreasing" refer to the slope, or rate of change, of a function as *x* increases. The terms "negative" and "positive" refer to *y*-values of a function over an *x*-interval. Both of the scenarios are possible: Think of a company that has decreasing profits, but it is still making money; this is an example of a model that has a negative slope with a positive value. Think of the temperature rising during the course of the day, but it is still below zero (negative); this is an example of a model that has a positive slope with a negative value.

The revenue increased the most from **week 2 to 3**. The revenue remained the same from **week 3 to 4** and again from **week 5 to 6**.

The following line graph shows the sales of a company from 2008 to 2012.

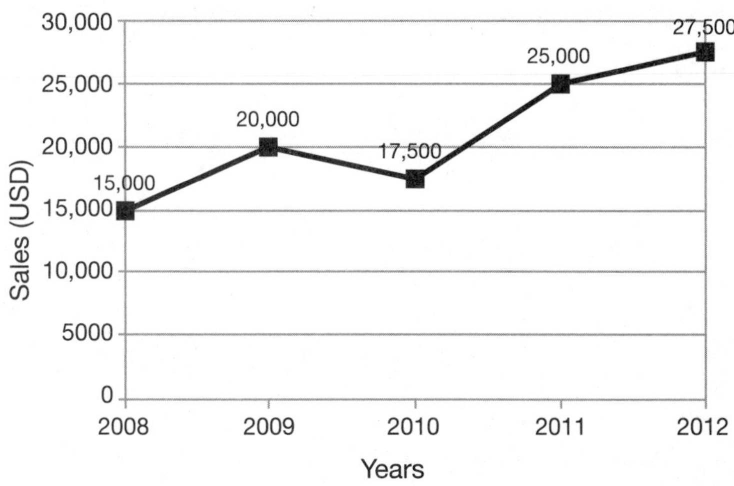

1. **Between what two years was the rate of change the greatest?**
2. **Between what two years did the company's sales have the slowest increase?**
3. **Was there a period where the rate of change was negative?**

When is a function neither increasing nor decreasing? How can that point be identified?

1. The rate of change was greatest from **2010 to 2011**.
2. The slowest increase was from **2011 to 2012**.
3. The rate of change was negative from **2009 to 2010**.

The point where a function changes from increasing to decreasing, or vice versa, is the point where a function is said to be neither increasing nor decreasing.

Looking at the following graph, identify the interval over which this function increases and has a nonnegative slope.

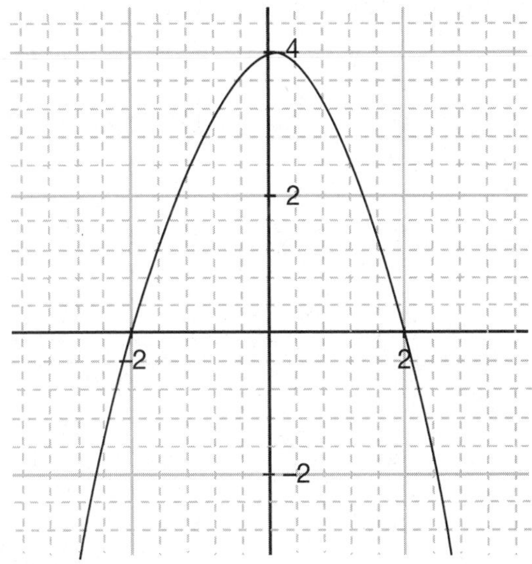

When using interval notation, what is the difference between parentheses and brackets? Discuss the differences between:

A. $(0,\infty)$ and $[0,\infty)$

B. $(-2,5)$ and $[-2,5]$

The interval over which this function increases and has a nonnegative slope is from negative infinity to 0, which is written as **(–∞,0)**.

A **parenthesis** indicates that the interval does not include the number next to it, and a **bracket** indicates that the adjacent number is part of the solution set.

A. (0,∞) is the interval of values greater than 0 up to infinity; [0,∞) is the interval of values beginning at zero and going up to infinity. (Infinity is not a real number, so it is always used with a parenthesis.)

B. (–2,5) consists of all numbers between, but not including, –2 and 5; [–2,5] is the interval beginning at –2 and going up to 5.

Looking at the following graph, is it correct to say that this function is increasing from (0,∞), [0,∞], [0,∞), or (0,∞]?

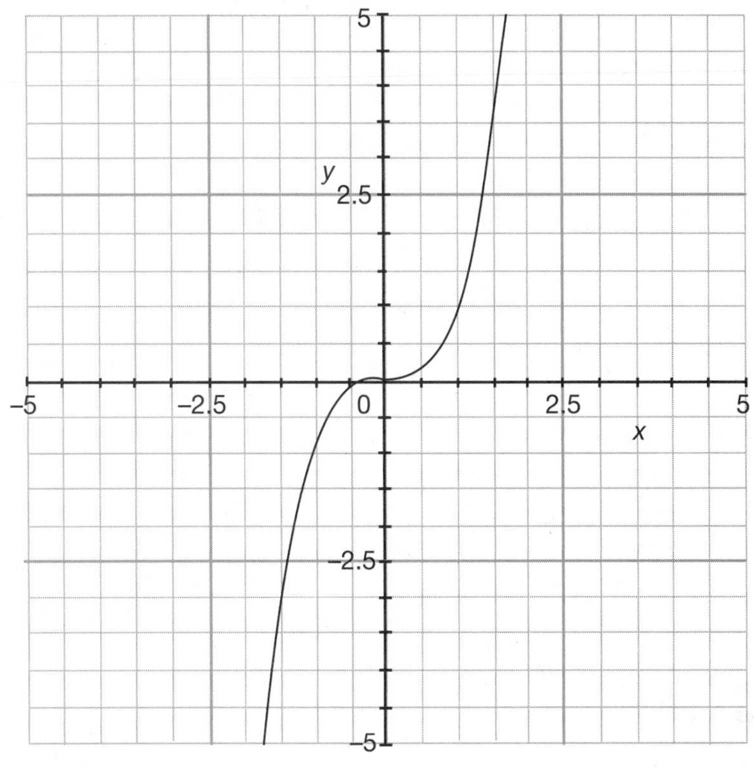

A parenthesis means that the interval does not include the number next to it, while a bracket means that the adjacent number is part of the interval. Infinity is not a real number, so it is always used with a parenthesis and not a bracket. Since this function is neither increasing nor decreasing at $x = 0$, the correct way to express the interval over which this function is increasing is **$(0,\infty)$**.

Estimate the approximate interval(s) over which the following function is increasing. Over which interval(s) is *f*(*x*) decreasing?

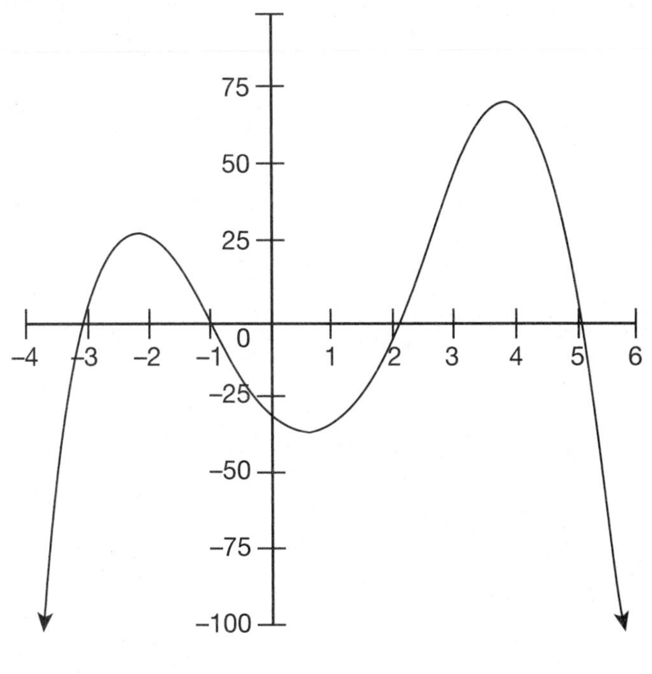

What are the *maximums* and *minimums* of a function?

x-values define the intervals over which y is increasing or decreasing. $f(x)$ is increasing from **$(-\infty,-2.1)$** and **$(0.8,3.9)$**, and $f(x)$ is decreasing from **$(-2.1,0.8)$** and again from **$(3.9,\infty)$**.

The **maximums** and **minimums** of a function are the highest and lowest points of a function.

Look at the two functions below. Determine which function has the greater maximum.

A.

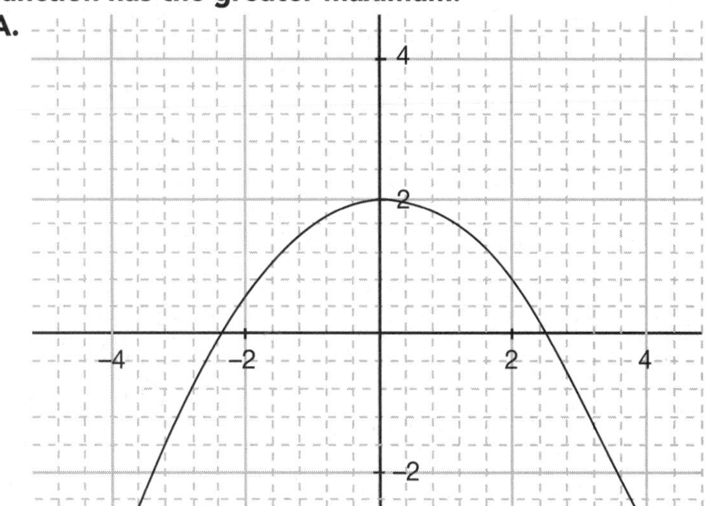

B. $f(x) = -x^2 + 5x$

What is the *relative maximum* and *relative minimum* of a function?

How can the relative maximum and relative minimum of the following functions *l*(*x*) and *h*(*x*) be identified?

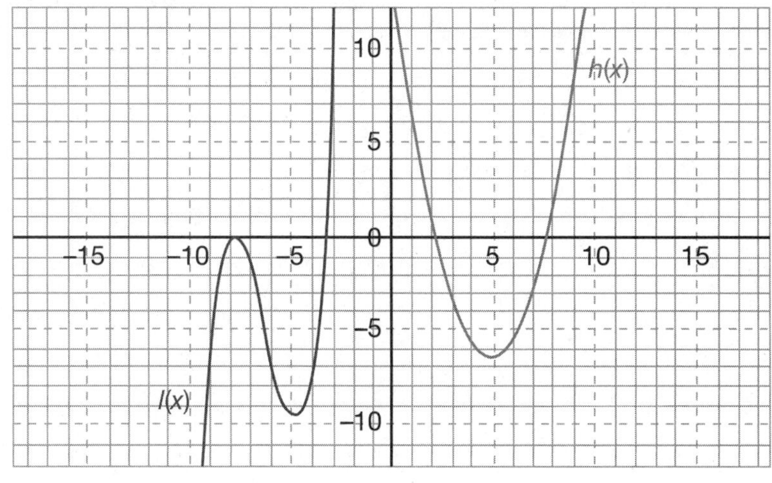

For function *A*, we can see that the maximum value is $f(x) = 2$.

For function *B*, the vertex will be the maximum value since the coefficient to x^2 is negative and it will be a downward facing parabola. For the vertex, begin with:

$x = \frac{-b}{2a} = \frac{-5}{(2)(-1)} = \frac{-5}{-2} = \frac{5}{2}$

Plug $\frac{5}{2}$ back into the function $f(x) = -x^2 + 5$:

$f(\frac{5}{2}) = -(\frac{5}{2})^2 + 5(\frac{5}{2})$

$f(\frac{5}{2}) = -\frac{25}{4} + \frac{25}{2}$

$f(\frac{5}{2}) = -\frac{25}{4} + \frac{50}{4} = \frac{25}{2} = 6\frac{1}{4}$

The vertex of the function given in *B* is at $(\frac{5}{2}, 6\frac{1}{4})$, so ***function B*** has the greater maximum.

The **relative maximums and minimums** are the peaks and valleys of a function. They are not the highest or lowest points in the function, but are relatively higher or lower than the points surrounding them on both sides. In the graph, $h(x)$ has only a minimum of (5,–6) but it does not appear to have a relative minimum. The function $l(x)$ has a relative maximum at (–8,0) and a relative minimum at (–5,–10).

At what point does the function *f*(*x*) have a relative maximum?

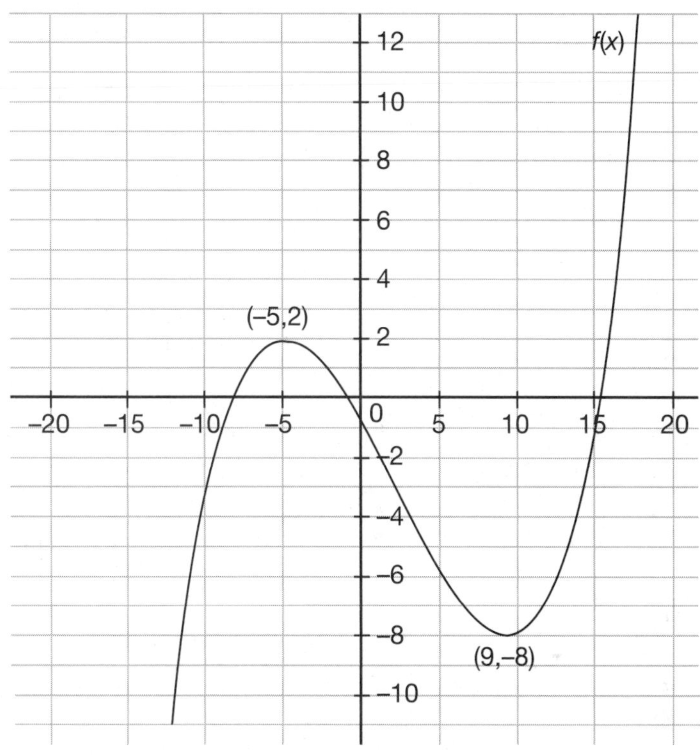

The graph switches from increasing to decreasing at the point **(–5,2)**, making it a relative maximum.

At what point does the function *f*(*x*) have a relative minimum?

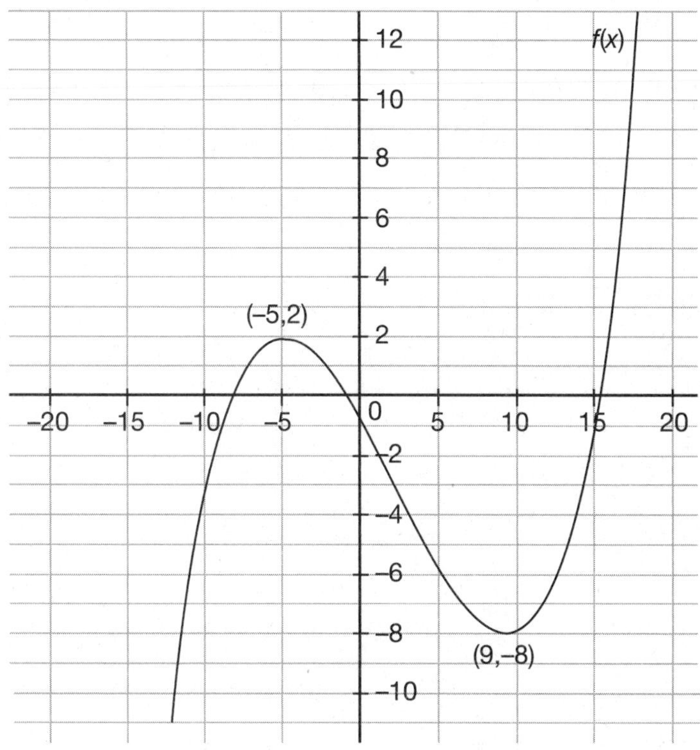

What does it mean for a graph to have symmetry along the *x*-axis?

The graph switches from decreasing to increasing at the point **(9,–8)**, making it a relative minimum value.

A graph has symmetry along the *x*-axis if it is a mirror image over the *x*-axis. This means that *y* and –*y* will both have the same *x*-value. For example, a graph with *x*-axis symmetry could contain the points (3,5) and (3,–5). Graphs that have *x*-axis symmetry are NOT functions because they will fail the vertical line test.

What does it mean for a graph to have symmetry along the *y*-axis?

If this graph is symmetrical along the *x*-axis, sketch the rest of the graph.

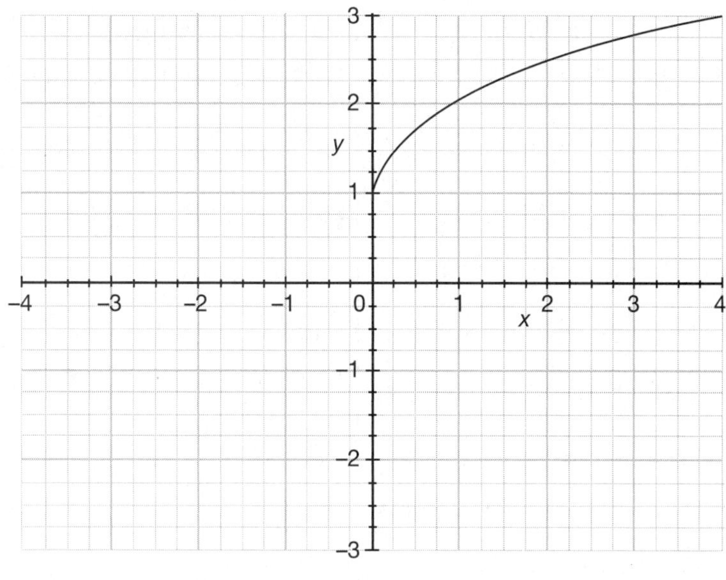

A function has symmetry along the *y*-axis if it is a mirror image over the *y*-axis. This means that *x* and –*x* will both have the same *y*-value, for example, (3,5) and (–3,5). Graphs that have *y*-axis symmetry are functions since they will pass the vertical line test.

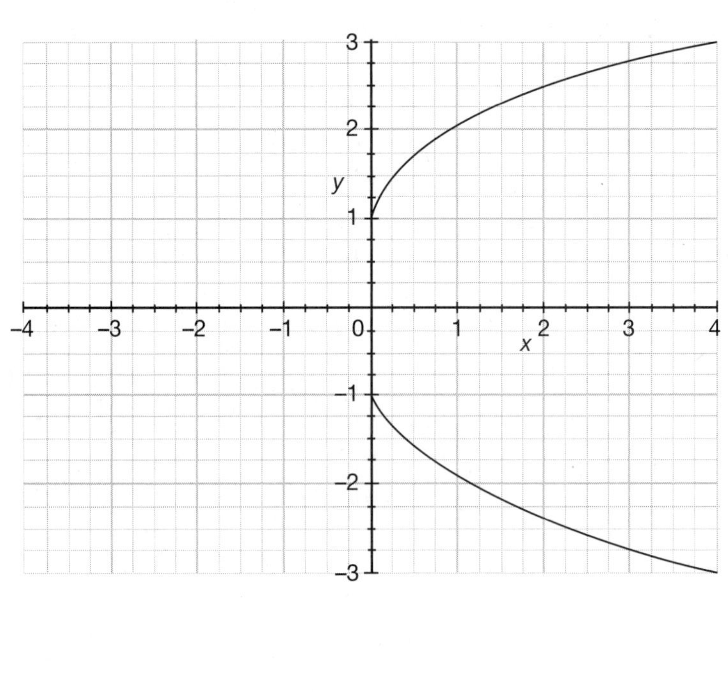

If this function is symmetrical along the *y*-axis, sketch the rest of the graph.

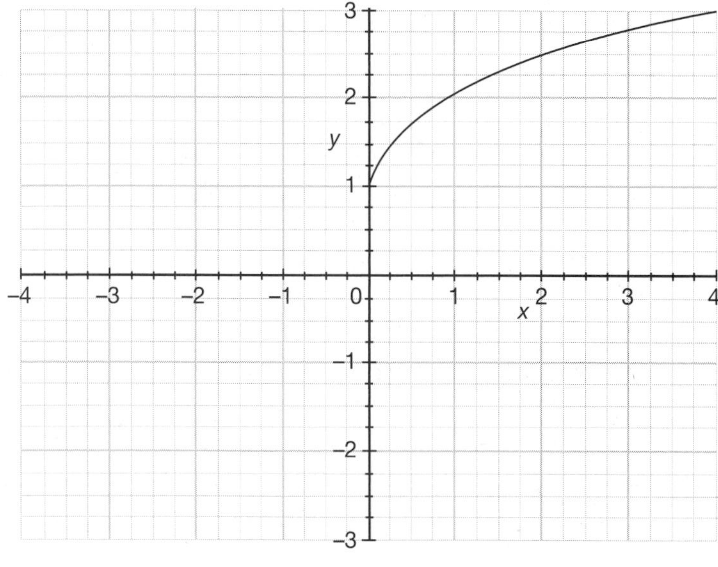

How can you use the equation of a quadratic function to tell when the graph is facing upward and when it is facing downward?

What is the *leading power* of a function and why is it significant?

How is the coefficient of the leading power also significant?

What is the leading power and leading coefficient of the function $y = 5x^2 - 8x + 20$?

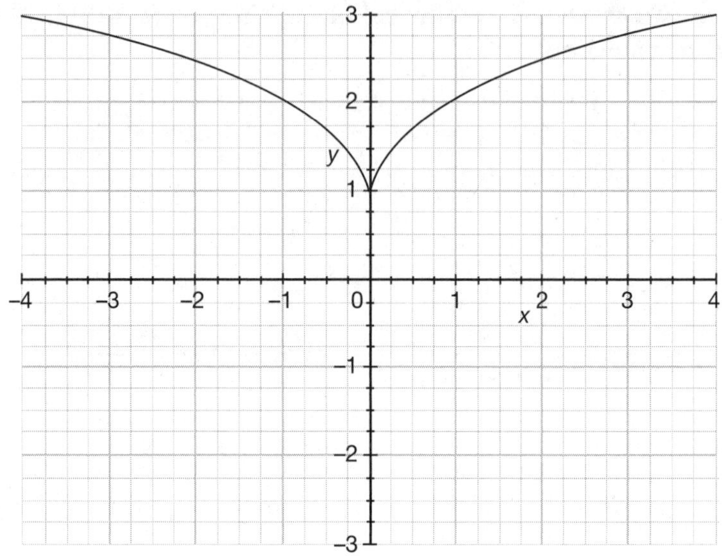

Quadratic equations have the general form $ax^2 + bx + c$. If a quadratic equation has a positive leading coefficient, a, it will be face upward. If a quadratic equation has a negative leading coefficient, a, it will face downward.

The **leading power** of a function is the highest exponent in a given function and determines the general shape of a function's graph.

The sign and size of the coefficient of the leading power impacts the overall direction that a curve opens as well as the steepness of the curve.

The leading power of the function $y = 5x^2 - 8x + 20$ is 2 since 2 is the largest exponent, and 5 is the leading coefficient since it is the coefficient of the term that contains the leading power.

What does it mean to identify the *end behavior* of a function, and which part of a function determines a function's end behavior?

. . . .

How does an *even leading power* affect the appearance of a graph?

How does a negative or positive coefficient of an even leading power affect the end behavior?

. . . .

What is the end behavior of the following functions as x approaches $-\infty$ and ∞?

A. $f(x) = x^2$ as $x \to -\infty$?

B. $f(x) = -x^2$ as $x \to \infty$?

End behavior is investigated in functions that have a leading power larger than 1, such as in quadratic and cubic functions. End behavior refers to what the function is doing as x approaches $+\infty$ or $-\infty$. The leading term of a function determines its end behavior.

If a function has an **even leading power** (x^2, x^4, x^6, etc.), then the function will have a parabolic shape. If the leading coefficient is positive, the parabola will be face up; if the leading coefficient is negative, it will be face down.

When identifying end behavior, only look at the leading term. Both of these functions have an even leading power, so they will be parabolas.

A. $f(x) = x^2$ as $x \to -\infty$: The leading coefficient is positive, so it will face upward, and as $x \to -\infty$, $f(x) \to +\infty$.

B. $f(x) = -x^2$ as $x \to \infty$: The leading coefficient is negative, so it will face downward, and as $x \to \infty$, $f(x) \to -\infty$.

How does an *odd leading power* affect the appearance of a graph?

How does a negative or positive coefficient of an odd leading power affect the end behavior?

KEY FEATURES OF GRAPHS

If a function has an **odd leading power** (x^3, x^5, x^7, etc.), then the function will have a cubic shape. Cubic graphs extend upward in one direction and downward in the opposite direction, so the end behaviors are opposite depending on if x is approaching positive or negative infinity.

Cubics with a positive leading coefficient will exhibit the following end behaviors:

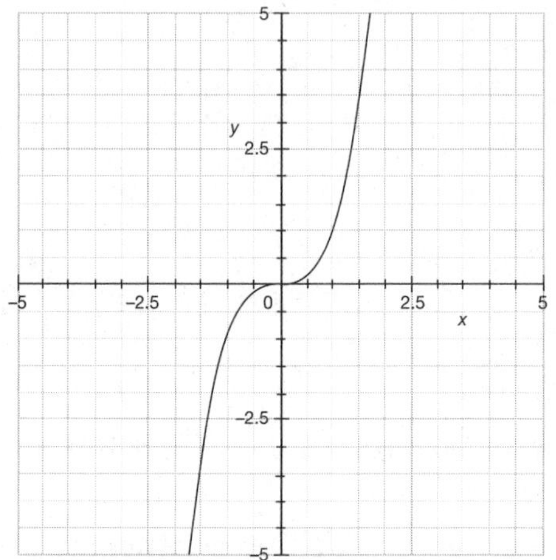

Cubics with a negative leading coefficient will exhibit the following end behaviors:

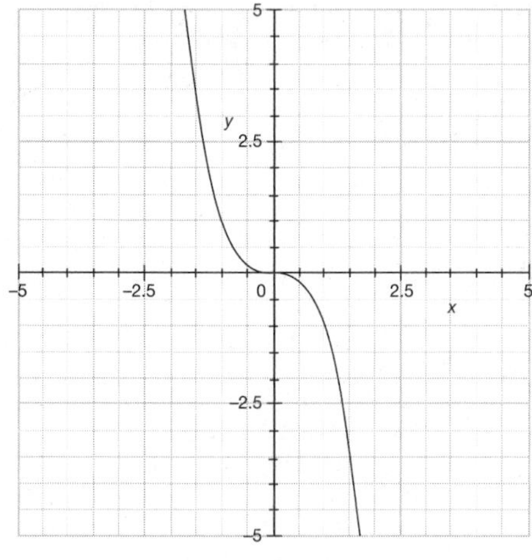

Sketch the following functions on the coordinate grid below:

A. $f(x) = -x^2$
B. $g(x) = x^2$
C. $h(x) = -x^3$
D. $y = x^3$

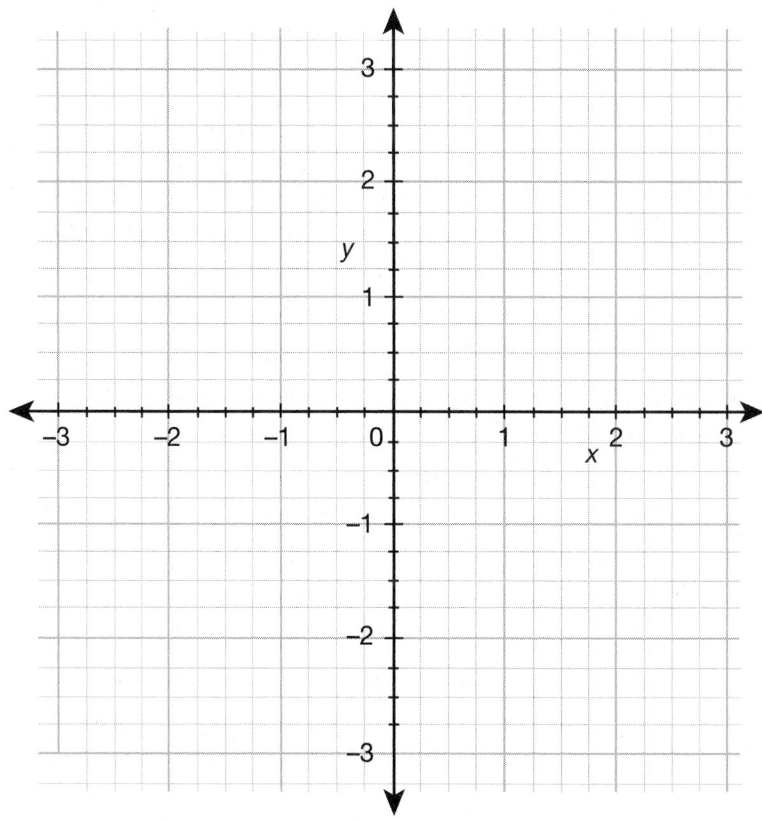

A.

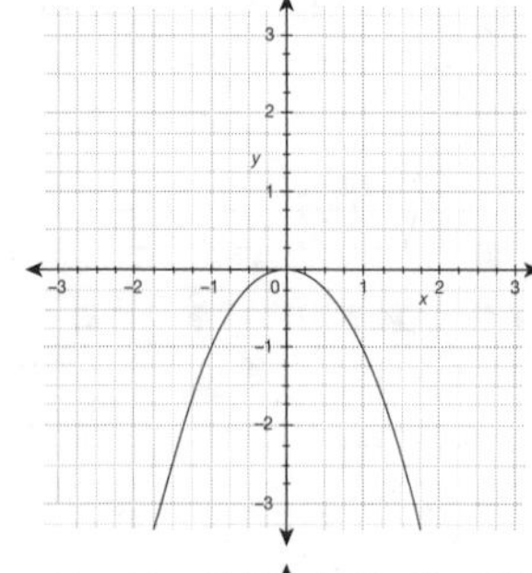

B.

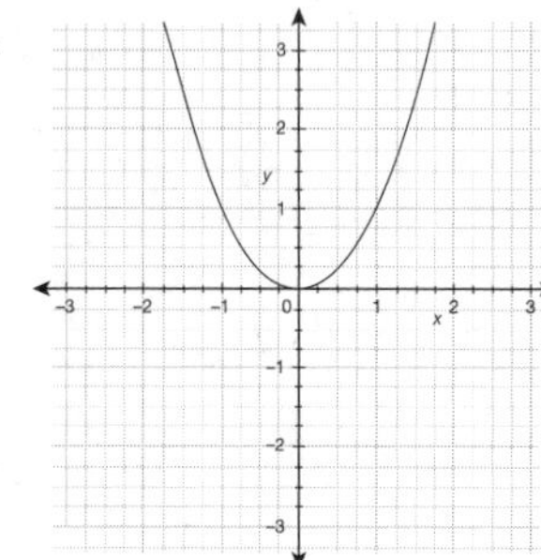

C.

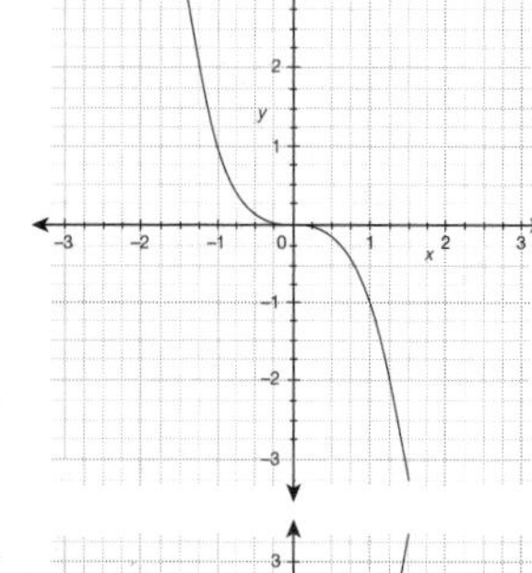

D.

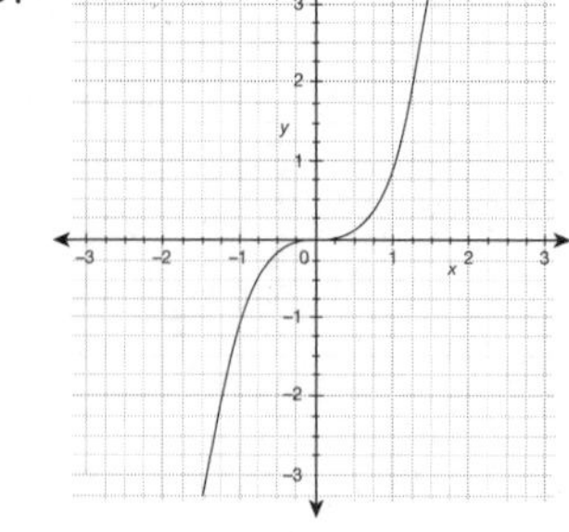

What is the end behavior of the function $g(x) = -3x^3 - 2x + x^4$ as $x \to -\infty$?

. . . .

Suppose that $g(x)$ is a function that has an odd leading power. How will the appearance of $g(x)$ change if the leading coefficient is negative or positive?

. . . .

What is the end behavior of the function $-2x^5 + 3x^3 + x^2$, as $x \to +\infty$?

When identifying end behavior, only look at the leading term of $g(x)$, which is x^4. (Remember, the leading term is not the first term, but the one that has the largest exponent.) x^4 has an even power and a positive coefficient; therefore, it will behave like a parabola with a positive coefficient. The parabolic shape will be upright, so as $x \to -\infty$, $f(x) \to +\infty$.

If $g(x)$ has an odd leading power and a positive leading coefficient, then $g(x)$ will point upward toward the right and downward toward the left. If $g(x)$ has an odd leading power and a negative leading coefficient, then $g(x)$ will point downward toward the right and upward toward the left.

When identifying end behavior, only look at the leading term, $-2x^5$. It has an odd power of 5 and a negative coefficient. Therefore, it will behave like a cubic function with a negative coefficient. The function will generally be decreasing from the left of the graph to the right of the graph, so as $x \to +\infty$, $f(x) \to -\infty$.

Define *perimeter*.

. . . .

What is the perimeter of the following figure?

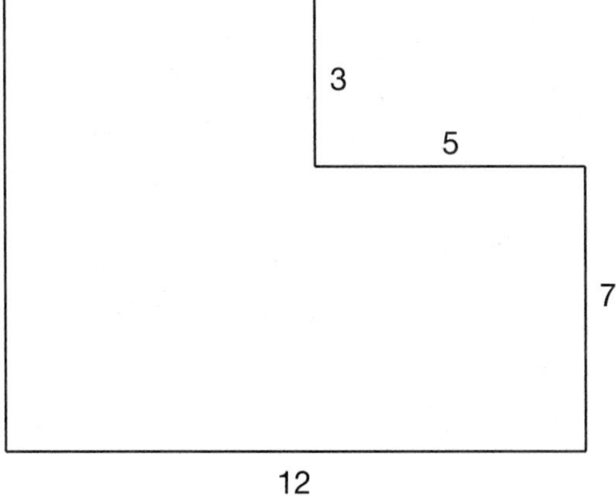

. . . .

What is a *rectangle*? What is a *square*? What makes them different?

Peri means "around" and *meter* means "measure." So, the **perimeter** of any figure is simply the total measure around the figure.

The perimeter is the distance around an entire figure, so add up all of the sides to get 44.

A **rectangle** is a two-dimensional figure that has four straight sides and four right angles. A **square** is a two-dimensional figure that has four equal sides and four right angles. This means that a square is really a rectangle with four equal sides, so all squares are also rectangles! (But all rectangles are not also squares.)

What is the formula for the perimeter of a square?

Find the perimeter of the following square:

6 ft

What is the formula for the perimeter of a rectangle?

$P = 4s$, where s = side length

Perimeter = $4s$

$P = 4(6 \text{ ft.})$

$P = 24$ ft.

There are two possible formulas to use for the perimeter of a rectangle:

$P = 2L + 2W$ or $P = 2(L + W)$

where L = length and W = width

Find the perimeter of the following rectangle:

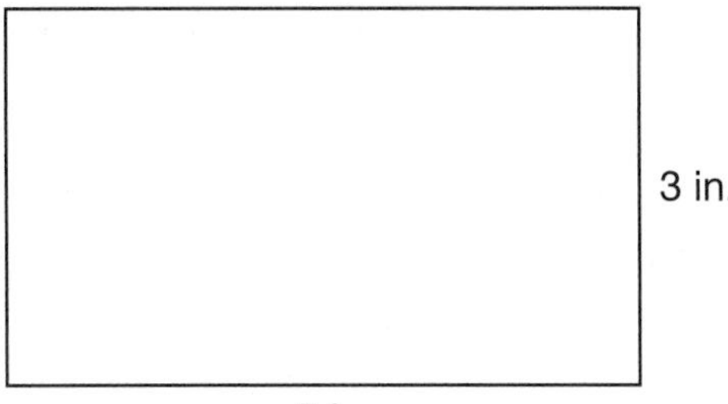

What is the formula for the perimeter of a triangle?

Find the perimeter of the following triangle:

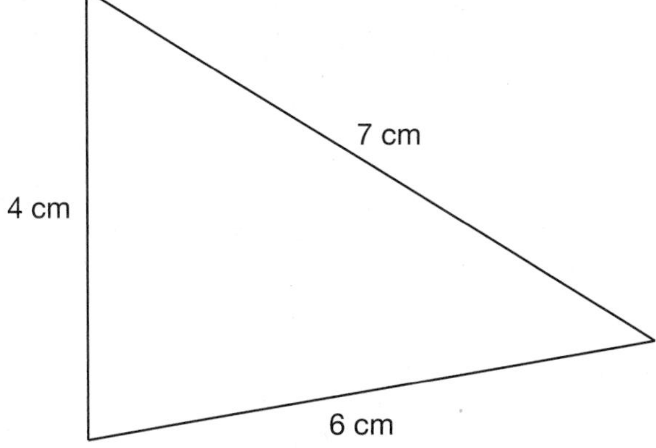

PERIMETER

Perimeter = $2L + 2W$

$P = 2(5\text{ in.}) + 2(3\text{ in.})$

$P = 10\text{ in.} + 6\text{ in.}$

$\boldsymbol{P = 16}$ **in.**

. . . .

There is no specific formula for the perimeter of a triangle, but the perimeter can always be found by adding the lengths of the three sides of a triangle.

. . . .

To find the perimeter of a triangle find the sum of all three sides:

4 cm + 6 cm + 7 cm = **17 cm**

Define *polygon*. What does it mean when a polygon is "regular"?

What are *pentagons, hexagons,* and *octagons*?

What is the formula for the perimeter of a polygon?

PERIMETER

A **polygon** is a straight-sided two-dimensional closed shape with at least three sides. A **regular** polygon is a polygon that has equal side lengths and equal angle measures.

. . . .

Pentagons, hexagons, and octagons are all polygons, which are two-dimensional shapes with at least three sides. A **pentagon** is a five-sided polygon, a **hexagon** is a six-sided polygon, and an **octagon** is an eight-sided polygon.

. . . .

There is not one specific formula for the perimeter of a polygon, since polygons can vary in the number of sides they have. The perimeter of any polygon is found by finding the sum of all of its sides.

Boyd needs to order enough wood to fence in the Wildwood Community Garden grounds, which is in the shape of a regular pentagon with congruent sides. If the fencing costs $12.50 per foot, how much will it cost to fence in the garden?

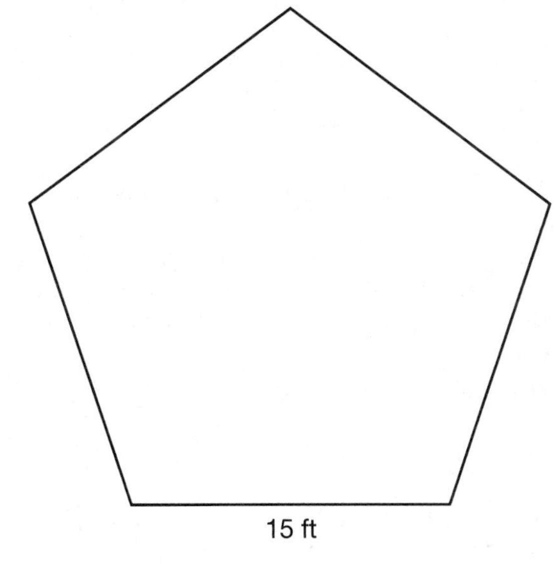

Since the garden is in the shape of a regular pentagon, the side lengths are equivalent. Therefore, the perimeter is $P = 5(15 \text{ ft}) = 75$ ft. The cost of the fencing is $12.50 per foot, so the cost will be (75 ft)($12.50) = **$937.50**.

What is true about the sum of any two sides of a triangle?

What is true about the sum of all three interior angles of a triangle?

What is a *right triangle*?
What symbol is used to indicate that a triangle is a right triangle?

TRIANGLES

The sum of any two sides of a triangle must be greater than the third side.

The sum of all three interior angles of a triangle will always be 180°.

A **right triangle** is a triangle that has exactly one 90° angle. A 90° angle is called a right angle, and it is marked with a small square in the angle.

The following are right triangles:

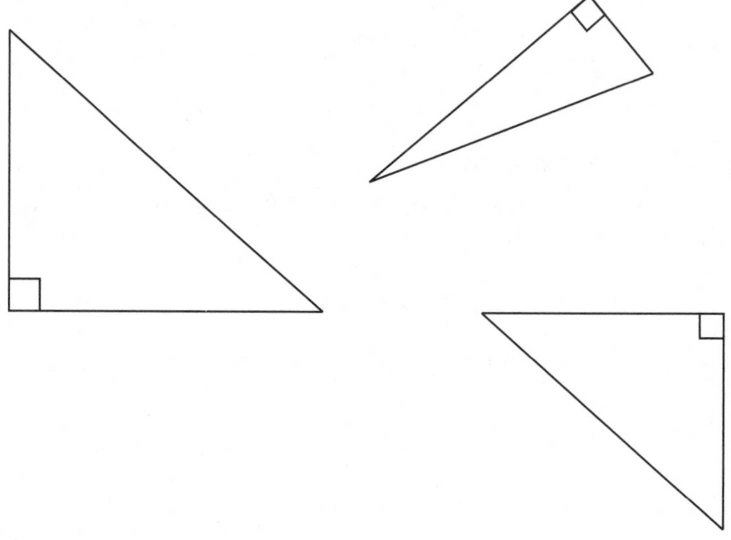

What is the measure of angle *C* in the triangle below?

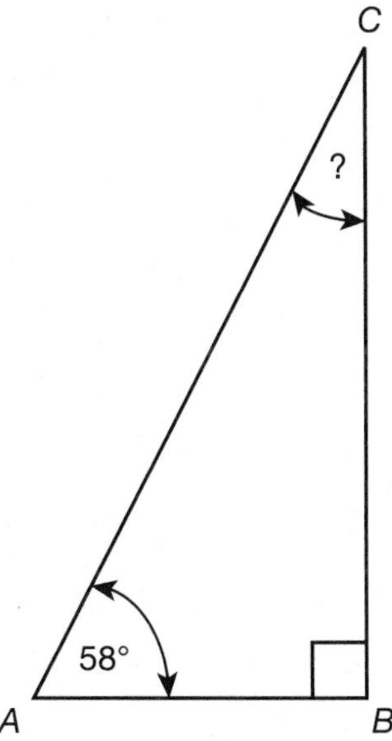

What are each of the sides of a right triangle called?

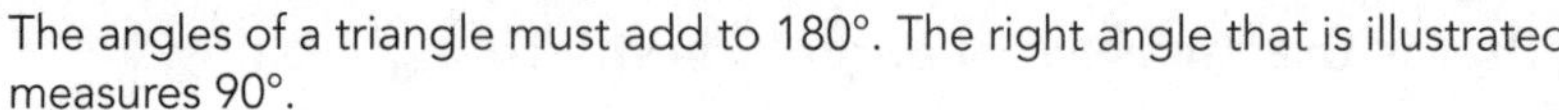

TRIANGLES

The angles of a triangle must add to 180°. The right angle that is illustrated measures 90°.

Therefore, 180° – 58° – 90° = **32°**.

The right angle in a triangle is formed by two sides called the **legs**. The side opposite the right angle will always be the longest side of the triangle, and it is called the **hypotenuse**.

How are the sides and angles of right triangles normally labeled?

. . . .

What is the *Pythagorean theorem* and what is it used for?

. . . .

TRIANGLES

A standard convention in labeling triangles is to use capital letters to label each angle, and to then use the corresponding lowercase letter to label the sides across from each angle.

In right triangles, the legs are customarily named *a* and *b*, and the hypotenuse is normally named *c*. The angles across from these sides have the corresponding uppercase letters, which means that the right angle is normally *C*.

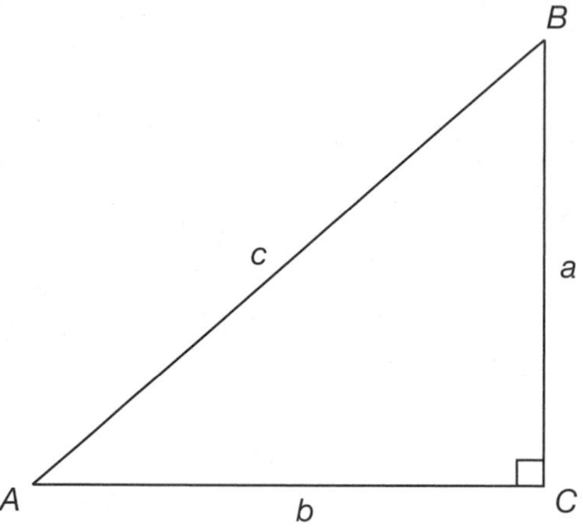

The **Pythagorean theorem** is used to find a missing side in a right triangle. The relationship between the three sides is:

$(\text{1st leg})^2 + (\text{2nd leg})^2 = (\text{hypotenuse})^2$

The standard form of the Pythagorean theorem, where *a* and *b* are the legs and *c* is the hypotenuse, is $\mathbf{a^2 + b^2 = c^2}$.

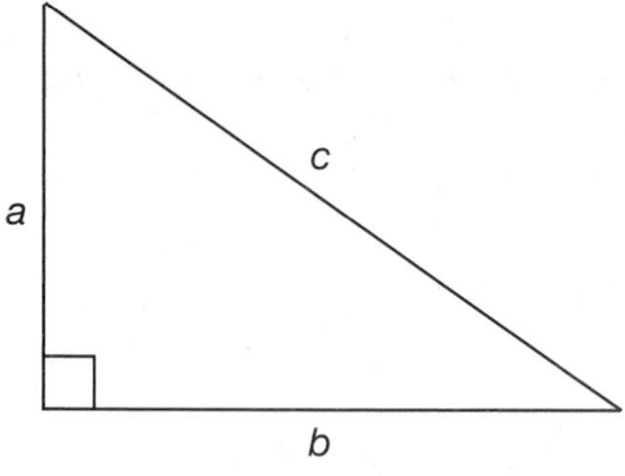

Find the missing side length for the triangle below:

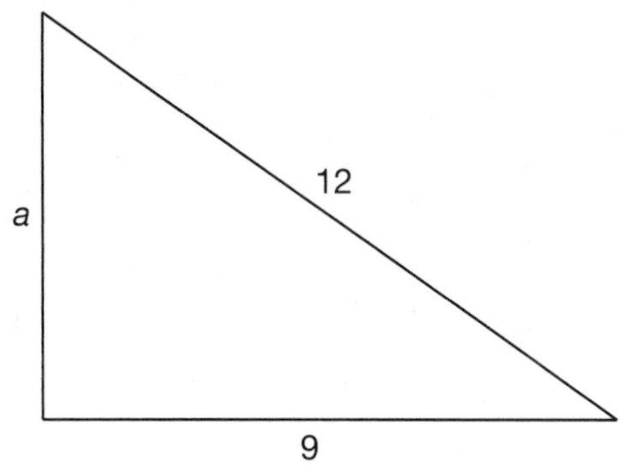

Find the missing side length in the given triangle.

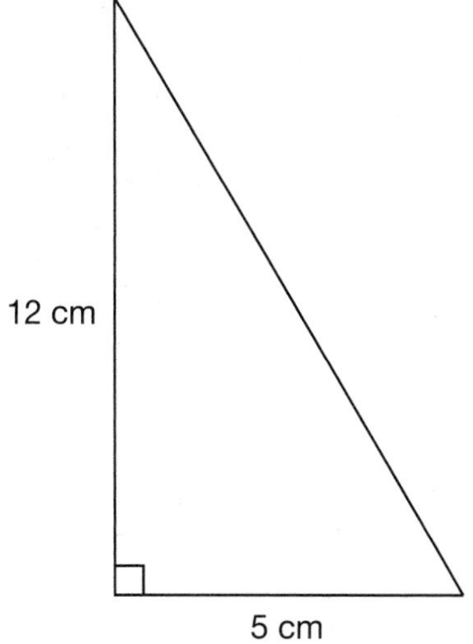

The given triangle has a hypotenuse of 12 and a leg of 9, and the Pythagorean theorem can be used to find the other leg:

$a^2 + b^2 = c^2$

$a^2 + 9^2 = 12^2$

$a^2 + 81 = 144$

$a^2 = 63$

$\sqrt{a^2} = \sqrt{63}$

$a = 7.9$

The given triangle has one leg of 12 cm and another leg of 5 cm, and the Pythagorean theorem can be used to find the hypotenuse:

$a^2 + b^2 = c^2$

$12^2 + 5^2 = c^2$

$144 + 25 = c^2$

$169 = c^2$

$\sqrt{169} = \sqrt{c^2}$

$c = 13$

Ryan bikes to work every day, going 10 miles north from his house on Robert Street and then going 8 miles east on Dodd Road. How much shorter would Ryan's trip be if he used the bike path that cuts through the park instead of his normal route on Robert Street and Dodd Road?

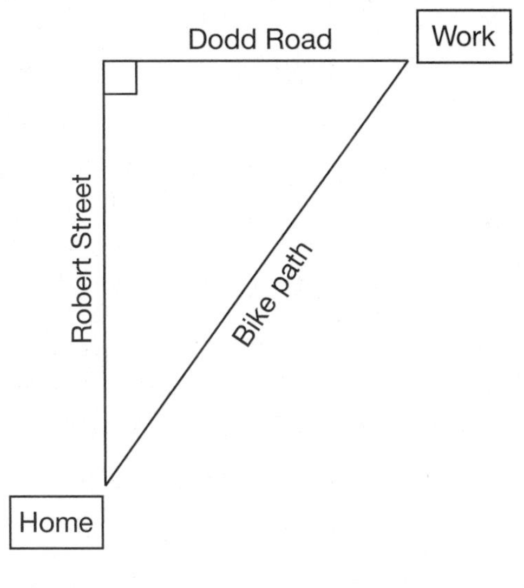

In meters, what is the perimeter of the given triangle?

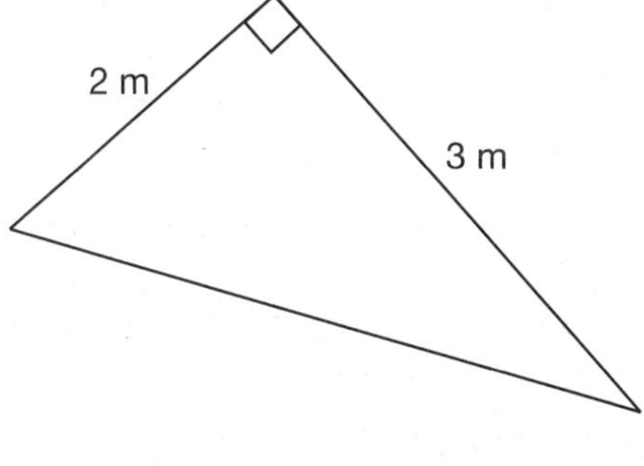

Ryan's regular route is 18 miles. To find out how long the bike path route is, use the Pythagorean theorem.

$a^2 + b^2 = c^2$

$10^2 + 8^2 = c^2$

$100 + 64 = c^2$

$164 = c^2$

$\sqrt{164} = \sqrt{c^2}$

$c = 12.8$

Since $18 - 12.8 = 5.2$, the bike path would be **5.2 miles** shorter for Ryan.

. . . .

First, use the Pythagorean theorem to solve for the hypotenuse: $2^2 + 3^2 = c^2$, so $c^2 = 13$ and $c = \sqrt{13}$. Then, for the perimeter, add all three sides to get $5 + \sqrt{13}$, or **8.6 m**.

. . . .

A 9-foot-long ladder is placed against the side of a building so that the top of the ladder reaches a window that is 6 feet above the ground. To the nearest tenth of a foot, what is the distance from the bottom of the ladder to the building?

A right triangle has legs of length 7 and 4. To the nearest tenth, what is the length of its hypotenuse?

$a^2 + b^2 = c^2$

$a^2 + 6^2 = 9^2$

$a^2 + 36 = 81$

$a^2 = 45$

$\sqrt{a^2} = \sqrt{45}$

$a =$ **6.7 feet**

Using the Pythagorean theorem:

$a^2 + b^2 = c^2$

$7^2 + 4^2 = c^2$

$49 + 16 = c^2$

$65 = c^2$

$\sqrt{65} = \sqrt{c^2}$

$c =$ **8.1**

How is the height of a triangle related to its base?

Looking at the triangle below, James says that $\overline{AC}$ is the base, Patrick says that $\overline{BC}$ is the base, and Erin says that $\overline{AB}$ is the base. What are the corresponding altitudes to each of the three bases that James, Patrick, and Erin are using?

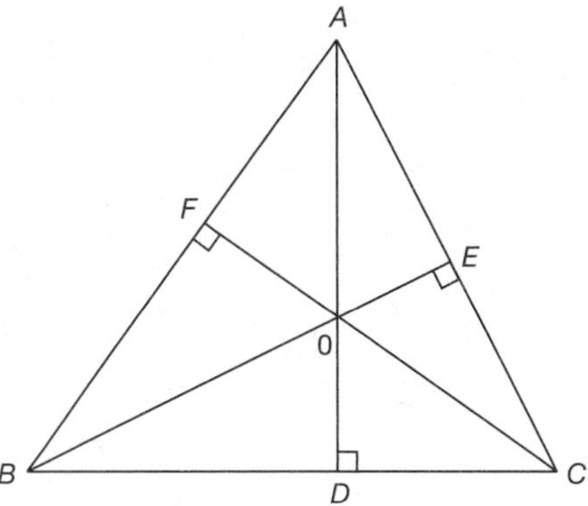

TRIANGLES

The height and base of a triangle are perpendicular to one another. The height is the straight line that perpendicularly rises from one side of a triangle and extends to the opposite vertex. Every side can be considered a base of a triangle as long as the corresponding height to that base is perpendicular to it and terminates at the opposite vertex.

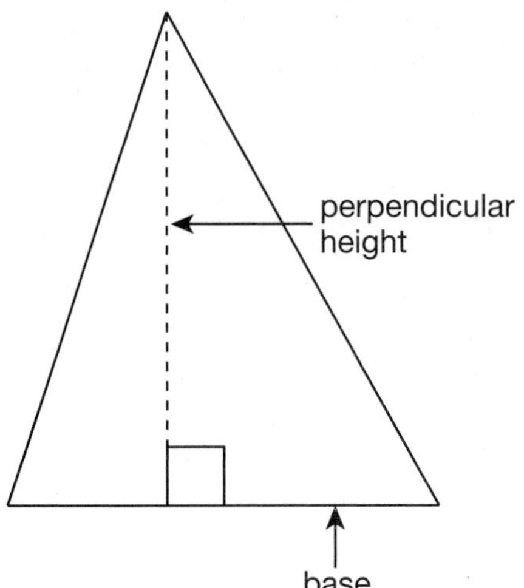

James: $\overline{AC}$ = base, $\overline{BE}$ = altitude

Patrick: $\overline{BC}$ = base, $\overline{AD}$ = altitude

Erin: $\overline{AB}$ = base, $\overline{FC}$ = altitude

Define *radius*.
What is the radius of the following circle?

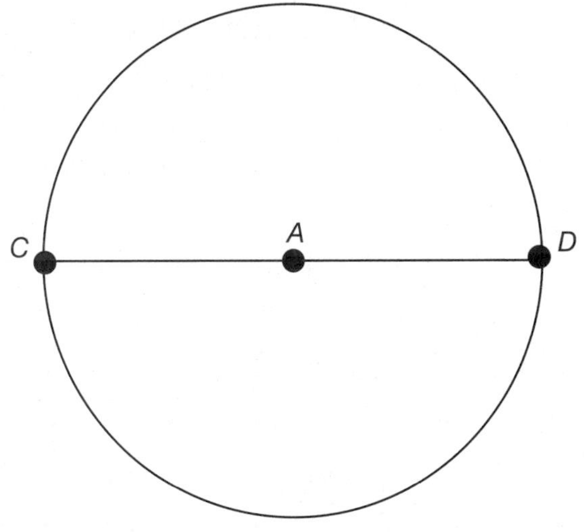

Define *diameter*.
What is the diameter of the following circle?

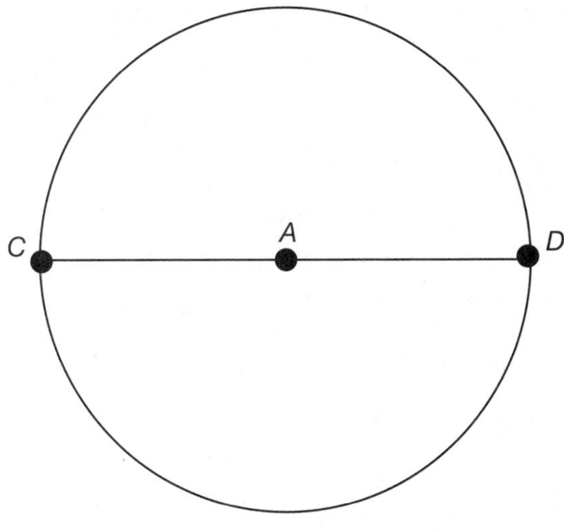

CIRCLES

Any line that is drawn from the center, *A*, to the outside of the circle is called a **radius**. The radius of this circle can be written as $\overline{AD}$ or $\overline{AC}$.

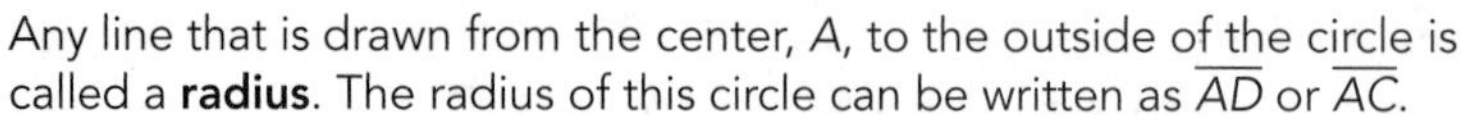

Any line that is drawn from the outside of a circle, through the circle's center, and extending to the other side of the circle is called the **diameter**. The diameter of this circle can be written as $\overline{CD}$ or $\overline{DC}$.

What is the relationship between the radius and the diameter of a circle?

. . . .

What is a reliable estimate to use for π?

. . . .

Define *circumference*.

CIRCLES

The radius of a circle is half the length of the diameter. The diameter is twice the length of the radius.

π is an irrational number, which means that it does not terminate. Acceptable standard values to use for π are **3.14** and $\frac{22}{7}$.

The **circumference** of a circle measures the distance around the circle. This concept is similar to finding the perimeter of a straight-sided figure, but since circles have no straight sides, circumference is calculated differently.

What are the two formulas for the circumference of a circle?

. . . .

What is the circumference of a circle with a diameter of 10 yards?

. . . .

What is the circumference of a circle with a radius of 3 meters?

CIRCLES

$\boldsymbol{C = 2\pi r}$, where r = radius, or

$\boldsymbol{C = \pi d}$, where d = diameter

. . . .

$C = \pi d$

$C = \pi(10)$

$C = 3.14 \times 10 =$ **31.4 yards**

. . . .

$C = 2\pi r$

$C = 2\pi(3)$

$C =$ **6π meters**

If a circle has a circumference of 10 meters, what is its diameter?

What is the radius of a circle with a circumference of 8 yards?

If the circumference of a circle is 62.8 inches, what is the length of the diameter in feet and inches?

$C = \pi d$

$10 = \pi d$

$\frac{10}{\pi} = d$

So the diameter is $\frac{10}{\pi}$, or approximately **3.18 meters**.

. . . .

$C = 2\pi r$

$8 = 2\pi r$

$\frac{8}{2\pi} = \frac{2\pi r}{2\pi}$

$\frac{4}{\pi} = r$

So the radius is $\frac{4}{\pi}$, or about **1.3 yards**.

. . . .

$C = \pi d$

$62.8 = \pi d$

$62.8 = (3.14)d$

$\frac{62.8}{3.14} = d$

So the diameter is **20 inches**, which is 1 foot, 8 inches.

What does *area* measure and how is it measured? Why is area always written with an exponent of 2, like 8 cm^2?

. . . .

How is area different from perimeter? Use a soccer field to give context to your explanation.

. . . .

What is the formula for the area of a square?

AREA

Area measures the space within a two-dimensional object. Area is measured in terms of how many equal sized squares are needed to completely cover a flat space, which is indicated by the exponent of 2 that always follows the unit of measurement.

A closet that is 4 feet long and 2 feet wide will need 8 square tiles, measuring 1 foot by 1 foot, to cover the floor. Therefore, the area is written as 8 ft^2.

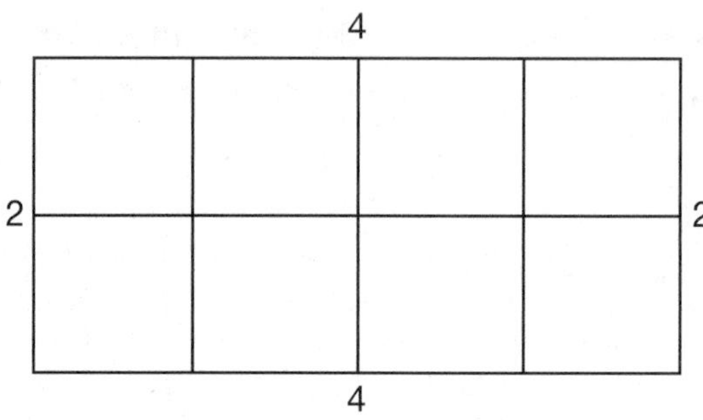

Perimeter refers to the measurement *around* a figure, and area refers to the measurement *inside* a figure. Think of area as being a representation of how much grass is needed to cover a soccer field, and think of perimeter as how much white spray paint is needed to mark the edge of the field.

$\boldsymbol{A = s^2}$, where s = side length

If the area of a square is 81 cm², what is the perimeter of the square?

If the perimeter of a square is 80 cm, what is the area of the square?

What is the formula for the area of a rectangle?

$A = s^2$

$81 = s^2$

$s = 9$ cm

$P = 4s$

$P = 36$ cm

Since $P = 4s$, write $80 = 4s$ and solve for s, which equals 20.

$A = s^2$

$A = 20^2$

$A = 400$ cm^2

Area = $L \times W$, where L = length and W = width

What are the area and the perimeter of the rectangle below?

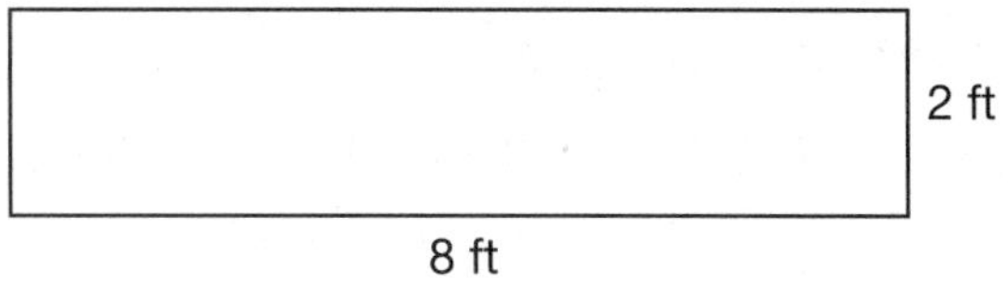

2 ft

8 ft

If the area of a rectangle is 120 cm, and the length measures 48 cm, what is the perimeter?

If the area of a rectangle is 32 in.^{2} and the length is twice as long as the width, find the length and width.

Area = $L \times W = 8 \times 2 =$ **16 ft²**

Perimeter = $2L + 2W = 2(8) + 2(2) =$ **20 ft**

First, use the area formula to figure out the width. Then, plug the width and length into the perimeter formula.

Area = $L \times W$

$120 = 48 \times W$

$W = 2.5$ cm

Perimeter = $2L + 2W$

Perimeter = $2(48) + 2(2.5) =$ **101 cm**

Let width = w

Length = $2w$

Area = $L \times W$

Area = $(2w)(w) = 2w^2$

Since the area is 32 in.^{2}, put that information into the area formula:

$2w^2 = 32$

$w^2 = 16$, so **w = 4 in.** and **length = 8 in.**

What will have a bigger value—the area or perimeter of a rectangle?

What is the formula for the area of a triangle?

What is the area of this triangle?

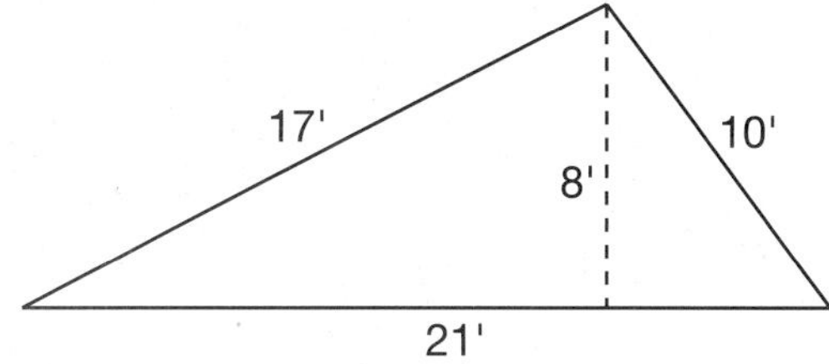

This is a trick question! Although the area is often larger than the perimeter of a rectangle, if a rectangle is long and thin, then it is possible that the perimeter will be greater than the area. This may also be the case if the side lengths are less than 1. There is no specific rule, so it is always best to check!

. . . .

$\boldsymbol{A = \frac{1}{2}bh}$, where b = base and h = height

Remember that the height must always be perpendicular to the base and it must end at the opposite vertex, or angle.

. . . .

$A = \frac{1}{2}bh$

$A = \frac{1}{2}(21)(8)$

$A =$ **84 units²**

What is the area of this triangle?

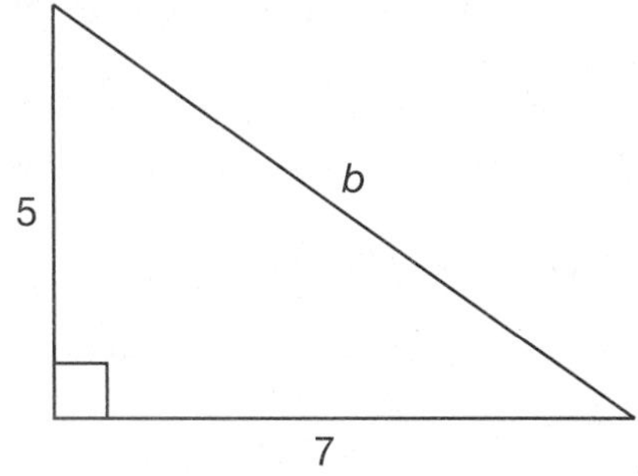

. . . .

What is the area of this triangle?

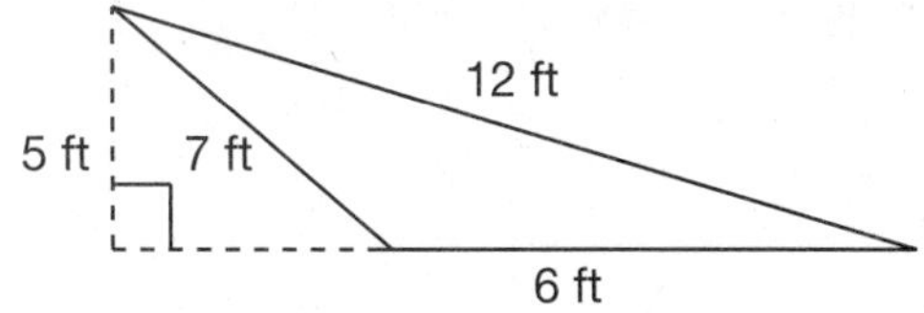

. . . .

The figure below is a rectangle with a half-circle attached. Given the indicated dimensions, what is the area of the entire region in terms of π?

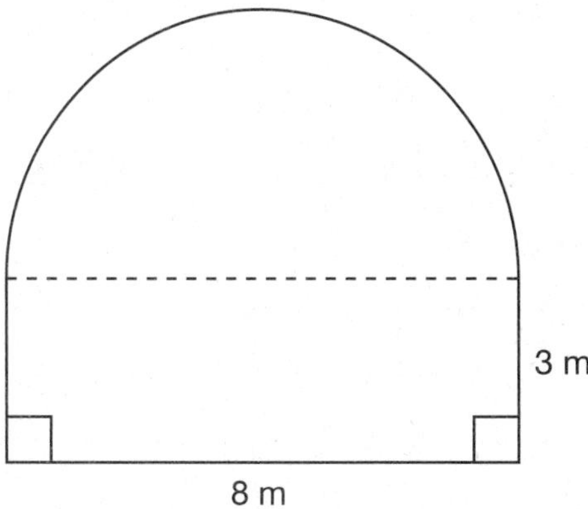

Although one of the sides is missing, the two sides required to find the area are labeled with side lengths.

$A = \frac{1}{2}bh$

$A = \frac{1}{2}(7)(5)$

$A =$ **17.5 units²**

In this case, the height is drawn outside of the triangle, but this is permissible for obtuse triangles.

$A = \frac{1}{2}bh$

$A = \frac{1}{2}(6)(5)$

$A =$ **15 feet²**

The area of the rectangular region is $8 \times 3 = 24$ square meters. The half circle has a radius of 4, so calculate the area of a full circle and divide it by 2:

$A = \pi r^2$

$A = \pi 4^2$

$A = 16\pi$

So the area of the half-circle is 8π, and the entire region has an area of **$24 + 8\pi$ m²**.

If a triangle with a base of 100 meters has an area of 400 m², what is its height?

. . . .

What is the formula for the area of a circle?

. . . .

What is the area of the circle below?

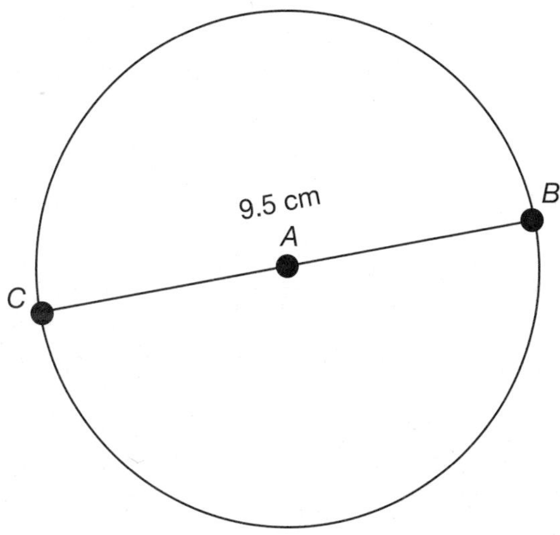

$A = \frac{1}{2}bh$

$400 = \frac{1}{2}(100)(h)$

$400 = 50(h)$

$h =$ **8 m**

• •

$\boldsymbol{A = \pi r^2}$, where r = radius

Note: Be sure to use the radius and not the diameter!

• •

Since the diameter is 9.5 cm, the radius will be half of that, which is 4.75 cm.

$A = \pi r^2$

$A = \pi(4.75)^2$

$A = (3.14)(4.75)^2$

$A \approx 70.85 \text{ cm}^2$

Jocelyn hired a landscaper to turn her dirt-covered backyard into a unique hangout spot. She would like to have a circular deck with a diameter of 10 feet built in the middle of her rectangular backyard. Since the yard is dirt right now, she is going to purchase sod to go around the deck. If the contractor charges $1.20 per square foot of sod installed, how much will Jocelyn be charged for the sod?

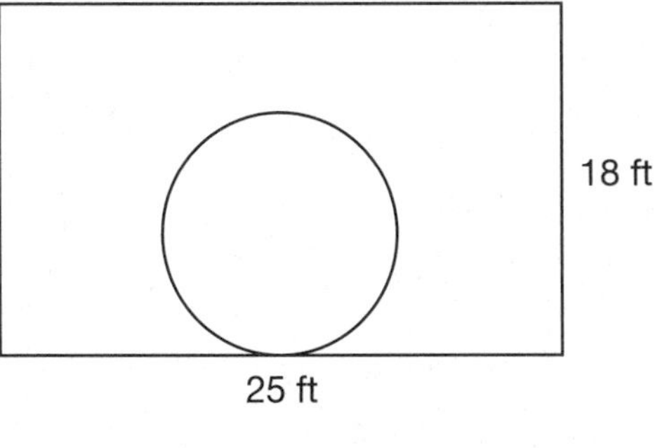

To calculate the amount of sod needed, subtract the area of the circular deck from the area of rectangular yard.

Area of yard = $L \times W = 25 \times 18 = 450$ ft^2

Area of deck = $\pi r^2 = (3.14)(5)^2 \approx 78.5$ ft^2

Area of sod = $A_{Yard} - A_{Deck} = 450 - 78.5 = 371.5$ ft^2

Finally, multiply the number of square feet of sod needed by the cost per square foot to get the total cost of the sod installation:

Cost = 371.5 × $1.20 = **$445.80**

What does *volume* measure?

. . . .

Why is the unit of volume always written with an exponent of 3 after it? (Ex: Volume = 8 cm^3)

. . . .

What is most likely being measured in this image of a rectangular box being broken up into smaller blocks? What would the numerical answer be?

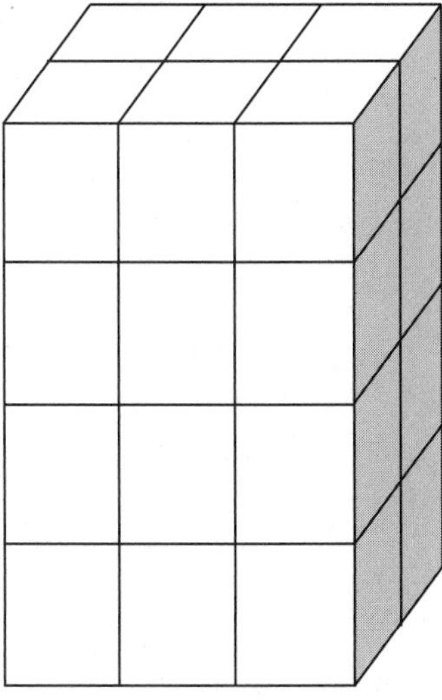

VOLUME

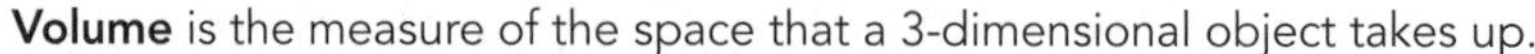

Volume is the measure of the space that a 3-dimensional object takes up.

Volume measures the space *within* a 3-dimensional object. Volume is measured in terms of how many equal-sized cubes are needed to completely fill a space. Imagine how many wooden cubes with a side length of 1 inch it would take to fill a shoebox if they were stacked perfectly against each other without any gaps. That number of cubes would be the volume of that box in cubic inches, which is represented as in.^3 The 3 indicates that there are three dimensions being considered: length, width, and height.

When the amount of 3-dimensional space of an object is being measured, the **volume** is being calculated. Since this box has 3 cubes across the front and is 2 cubes deep, it has 6 cubes on its first level. It is 4 levels high, which means this rectangular prism contains 24 cubes. Its volume is 24 units^3.

How is the volume of a rectangular prism generally calculated? What is the formula for the volume of the rectangular prism below?

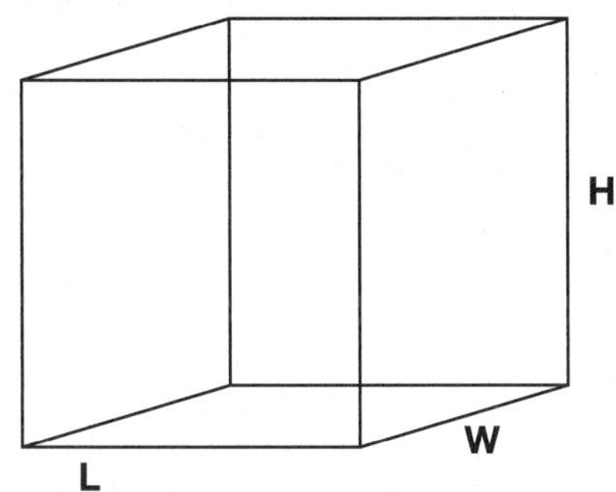

What is the volume of this box? Use the formula Volume = $L \times W \times H$.

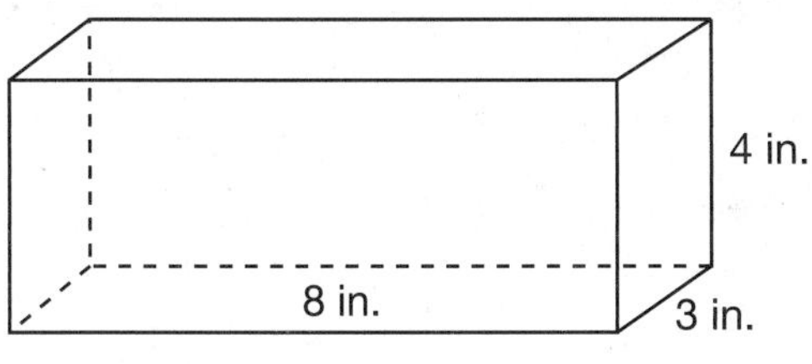

If the height of a rectangular prism is 3 cm and the length of the prism is 8 cm, what is the width of the prism in centimeters if the volume is 96 cm^3? Use the formula Volume = $L \times W \times H$.

VOLUME

The volume of rectangular prisms is generally calculated by multiplying the area of the base by the height. The formula for the area of the given prism is $\boldsymbol{V = L \times W \times H}$, where L is length, W is width, and H is height.

$V = L \times W \times H$

$V = 8 \times 3 \times 4 =$ **96 in.³**

Volume $= L \times W \times H$

$96 = 8 \times w \times 3$

$96 = 24w$

$w =$ **4 cm**

What is the volume of this right triangular prism? Use the formula $V = \frac{1}{2}lwh$.

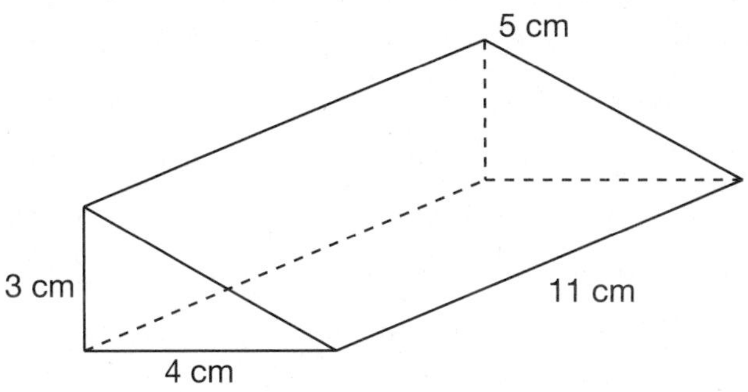

What is the volume of this cylinder? Use the formula $V = \pi r^2 h$.

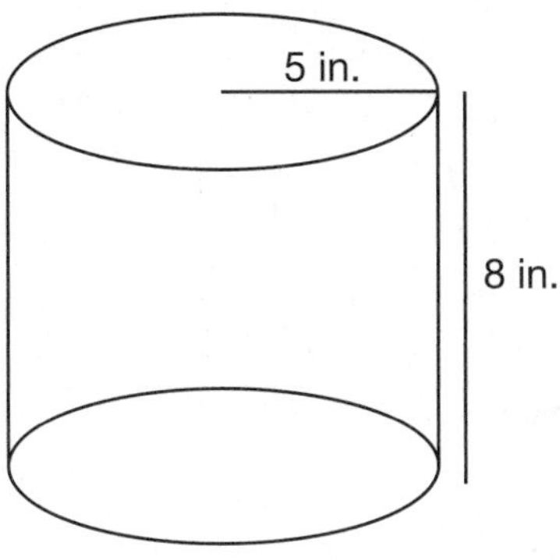

$V = \frac{1}{2}lwh$

$V = \frac{1}{2}(4 \times 3 \times 11)$

$V =$ **66 cm³**

. . . .

$V = \pi r^2 h$

$V = \pi(5)^2(8)$

$V = 200\pi \approx$ **628 in.³**

. . . .

What is the height of the pyramid below if its volume is 54 mm³? Use the formula $V = \frac{1}{3}Bh$, where *B* is the area of the base and *h* is the height of the pyramid.

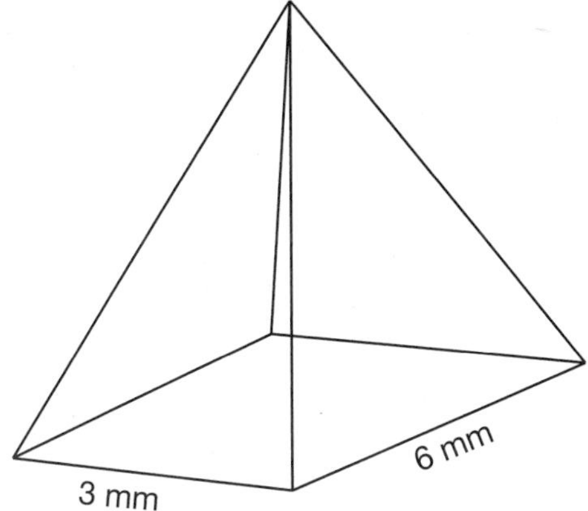

What is the volume of this right circular cone? Use the formula $V = \frac{1}{3}\pi r^2 h$.

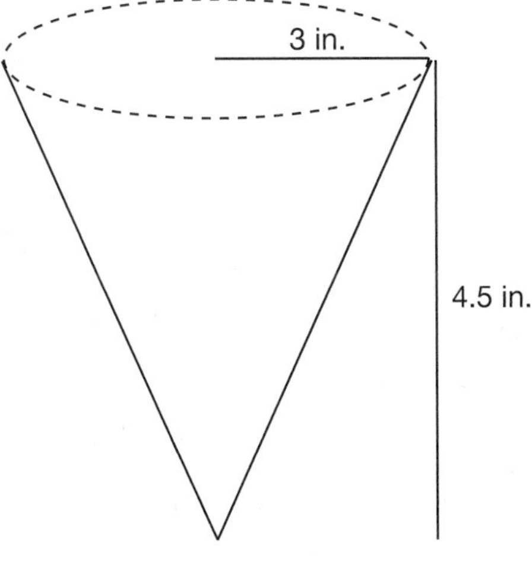

Since B is the area of the base, then $B = 3 \times 6 = 18$ mm^2

$V = \frac{1}{3}Bh$

$54 = \frac{1}{3}(18)h$

$54 = 6h$

$h =$ **9 mm**

• •

$V = \frac{1}{3}\pi r^2 h$

$V = \frac{1}{3}\pi(3)^2(4.5)$

$V = 13.5\pi$

$V \approx$ **42.4 in.^{3}**

• •

Find the radius of a cone if its volume is 148 cm^3 and its height is 7 cm. Use the formula $V = \frac{1}{3}\pi r^2 h$ and round your answer to the nearest tenth of a centimeter.

What is the volume of this sphere if its diameter is 10 mm? Use the formula $V = \frac{4}{3}\pi r^3$.

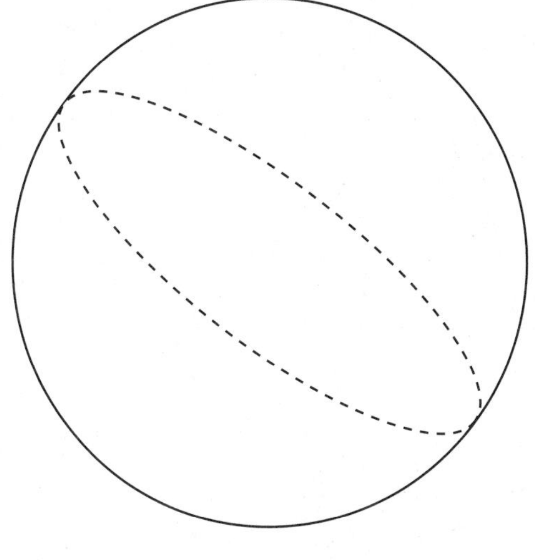

Since $V = 148$ cm^3 and $h = 7$ cm are given, substitute these values into the formula and solve for r:

$V = \frac{1}{3}\pi r^2 h$

$148 = \frac{1}{3}\pi(r^2)(7)$

$148 = \frac{7\pi}{3}(r^2)$

$(\frac{3}{7\pi})148 = (\frac{3}{7\pi})\frac{7\pi}{3}(r^2)$

$20.2 \approx r^2$

$r \approx 4.49$, which rounds to **4.5 cm**

. . . .

$V = \frac{4}{3}\pi r^3$

$V = \frac{4}{3}\pi(5^3)$

$V = \frac{4}{3}\pi(125)$

$V \approx$ **523.3 mm³**

. . . .

Do the following situations require that area, perimeter, or volume be calculated?

1. **The amount of water needed to fill a pool**
2. **The amount of fencing needed to enclose a yard**
3. **The amount of paint needed to paint a wall**

VOLUME

1. The amount of water needed to fill a pool requires **volume**.
2. The amount of fencing needed to enclose a *y*ard requires **perimeter**.
3. The amount of paint needed to paint a wall requires **area**.

Define *surface area*.

. . . .

The formula for calculating the surface area of a rectangular, or right, prism is $SA = ph + 2B$. What do p, h, and B stand for?

. . . .

Calculate the surface area of the rectangular prism below. Use the formula $SA = ph + 2B$.

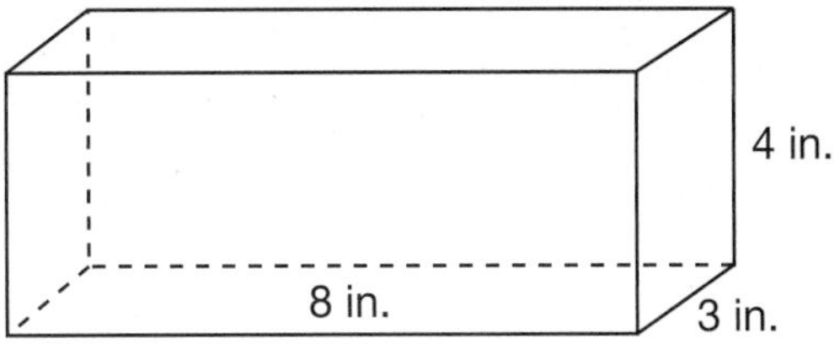

4 in.

8 in.

3 in.

SURFACE AREA

Surface area is a type of measurement that is taken of 3-dimensional figures. The surface area of a 3-dimensional figure is the total combined area of its faces and curved surfaces. Think of surface area as how much wrapping paper is needed to cover a box.

Given $SA = ph + 2B$, $\boldsymbol{B}$ is the area of the base, $\boldsymbol{p}$ is the perimeter of the base, and $\boldsymbol{h}$ is the height.

$p = 2(8) + 2(3) = 22$

$B = (8)(3) = 24$

$h = 4$

$SA = ph + 2B$

$SA = (22)(4) + 2(24) =$ **136 in.^{2}**

The figure below represents a composite part to be manufactured by fusing two solid cubes together. If the cubes used are identical, what is the surface area of the resulting part?

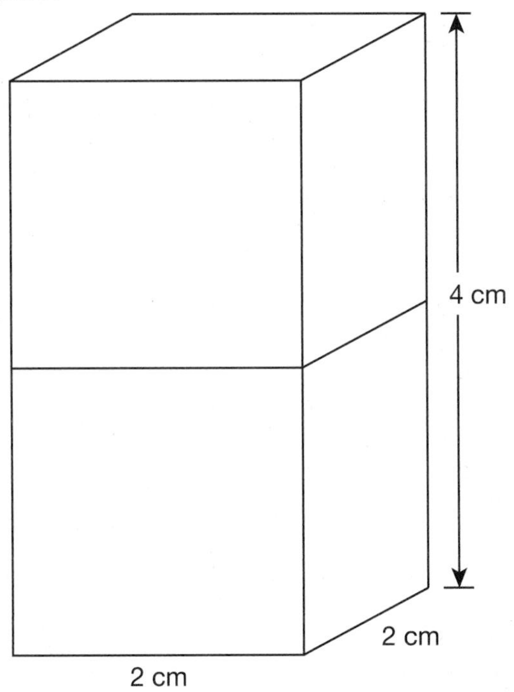

The formula for the surface area of a cylinder is $SA = 2\pi rh + 2\pi r$. What do the variables stand for? Does the surface area of a cylinder include the top and bottom circles?

$p = 2(2) + 2(2) = 8$

$B = (2)(2) = 4$

$h = 4$

$SA = ph + 2B$

$SA = (8)(4) + 2(4) =$ **40 cm²**

Given $SA = 2\pi rh + 2\pi r^2$, ***r*** is the radius, and ***h*** is the height of the cylinder. (Be careful to not confuse the radius with the diameter.) **Yes**, the surface area of a cylinder includes the top and bottom circles.

Calculate the surface area of the cylinder below. Use the formula $SA = 2\pi rh + 2\pi r$.

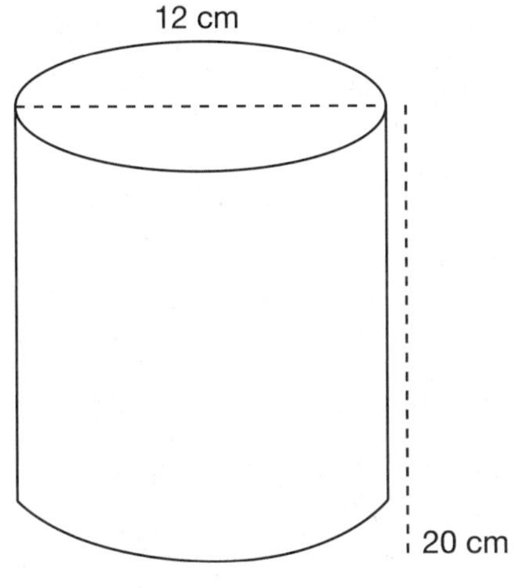

The formula for the surface area of a right pyramid is $SA = \frac{1}{2}ps + B$. What do the variables stand for?

SURFACE AREA

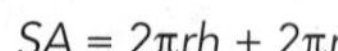

$SA = 2\pi rh + 2\pi r$

$SA = 2\pi(6)(20) + 2\pi(6)^2$

$SA = 240\pi + 72\pi$

$SA = 312\pi \text{ cm}^2 \approx$ **979.7 cm²**

Given $SA = \frac{1}{2}ps + B$, ***B*** is the area of the base, ***p*** is the perimeter of base, and ***s*** is the slant length.

Calculate the surface area of the right pyramid below. Use the formula $SA = \frac{1}{2}ps + B$.

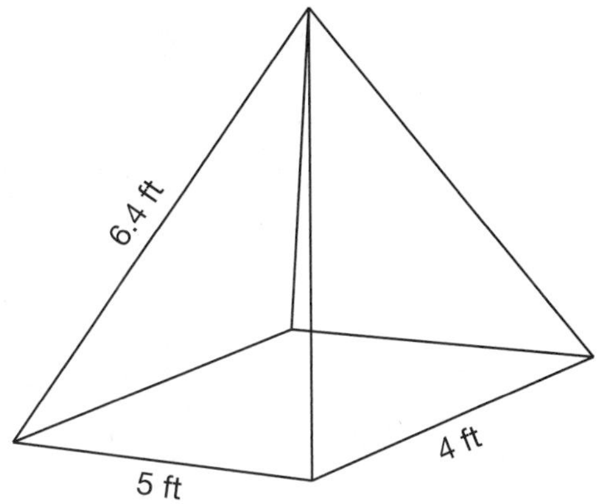

The formula for the surface area of a right circular cone is $SA = \pi rs + \pi r^2$. What do the variables stand for? What might the surface area of a right circular cone be useful for in a real-world situation?

$p = 2(5) + 2(4) = 18$

$B = (5)(4) = 20$

$SA = \frac{1}{2}ps + B$

$SA = \frac{1}{2}(18)(6.4) + 20 =$ **77.6 ft²**

Given $SA = \pi rs + \pi r^2$, ***r*** is the radius and **s** is the slant length. It might be helpful for a business to know how much waffle cookie is needed to make a single right circular ice cream cone, so they know how much of a recipe to make if they plan on making 500 cones for a summer weekend.

Calculate the surface area of the right circular cone below. Use the formula $SA = \pi rs + \pi r^2$.

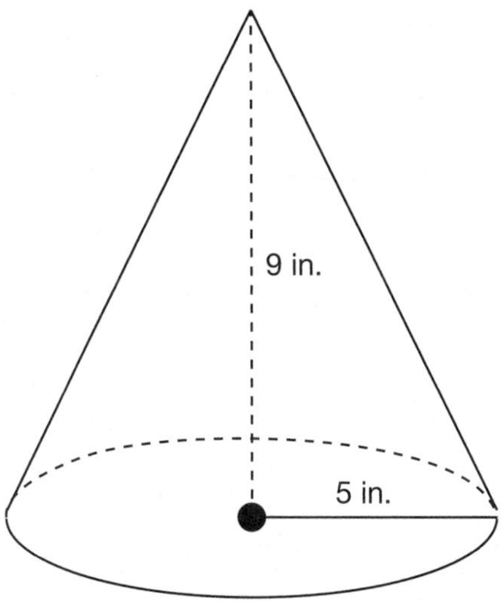

Calculate the surface area of a sphere that has a diameter of 14 cm. Use the formula $SA = 4\pi r^2$.

Calculate the diameter of a sphere if its surface area is 113.04 in.^{2}

Since the slant length is unknown, first use the Pythagorean theorem to calculate the hypotenuse, *c*, which is the slant length:

$5^2 + 9^2 = c^2$

$106 = c^2$

$c = \sqrt{106} \approx 10.3$ in.

$SA = \pi rs + \pi r^2$

$SA = \pi(5)(10.3) + \pi(5)^2$

$SA = 76.5\pi$ in.$^2 \approx$ **240.2 in.^{2}**

. . . .

$SA = 4\pi r^2$

$SA = 4\pi(7)^2$

$SA = 196\pi$ cm$^2 \approx$ **615.4 cm^2**

. . . .

Since surface area is given, the radius can be found and then doubled to get the diameter. Substitute the value of the surface area into the formula and solve for *r*.

$SA = 4\pi r^2$
$113.04 = 4\pi r^2$
$113.04 = 12.56(r^2)$
$\frac{113.04}{12.56} = \frac{12.56r^2}{12.56}$
$9 = r^2$
$r = 3$ in.

So, the radius of the sphere is 3 inches, and the diameter is **6 inches**.

The surface area of a sphere is 36π cubic meters. To the nearest meter, what is the volume of this sphere? Use the formulas $SA = 4\pi r^2$ and $V = \frac{4}{3}\pi r^3$.

Use the surface area formula to find the radius, and then put that into the volume formula.

$SA = 4\pi r^2$

$36\pi = 4\pi r^2$

$9 = r^2$

$r = 3$ m

Put $r = 3$ into the volume formula:

$V = \frac{4}{3}\pi(3^3)$

$V = 36\pi \approx$ **113.04 m³**

What is a *scale factor* and where it is commonly used?

The following two triangles are similar, meaning they have the same general shape and all of their sides vary by the same scale factor. Identify the scale factor and find the length of $\overline{DF}$.

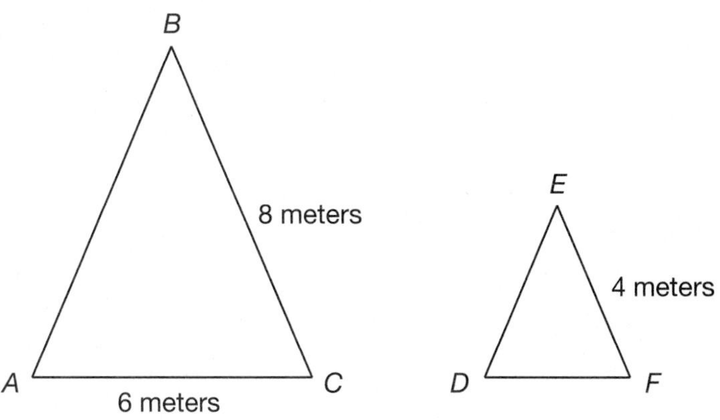

What would be the new area of this triangle if all of its sides were increased by a scale factor of 4?

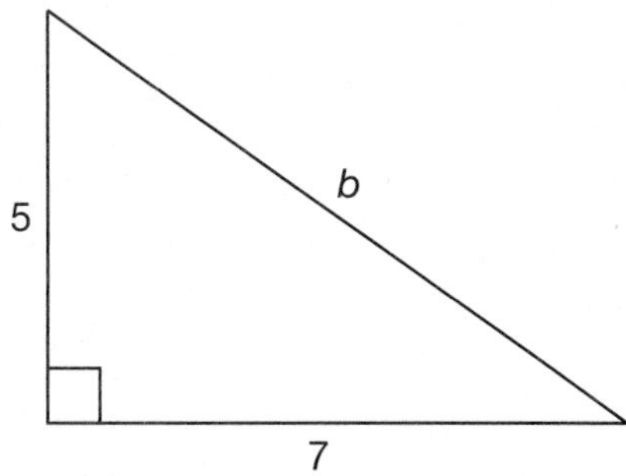

SCALE FACTOR

A **scale factor** is a factor that multiplies a term in order to change the value at a constant rate. Scale factors are commonly used in comparing two similar geometric figures, in drawings for maps or architectural plans, and in transforming the size of items without changing their relative shapes.

• •

The scale factor is $\frac{1}{2}$ going from ΔABC to ΔDEF. That means that all of the sides of ΔDEF are half as long as their corresponding sides in ΔABC. Therefore, $\overline{DF}$ **= 3 meters**.

• •

After applying a scale factor of 4, the base will be 28 and the height will be 20.

$A = \frac{1}{2}bh$

$A = \frac{1}{2}(28 \times 20) =$ **280 units²**

According to the figure below, what are the dimensions of the bedroom in feet? (Note: 1 inch = 3 squares in the drawing.)

Entry Way
Living Room
Porch
Kitchen
Scale: 1 in. = 4 ft
1 in.
Bedroom

According to the figure below, what is the area, in square feet, of this apartment? (Note: 1 inch = 3 squares in the drawing.)

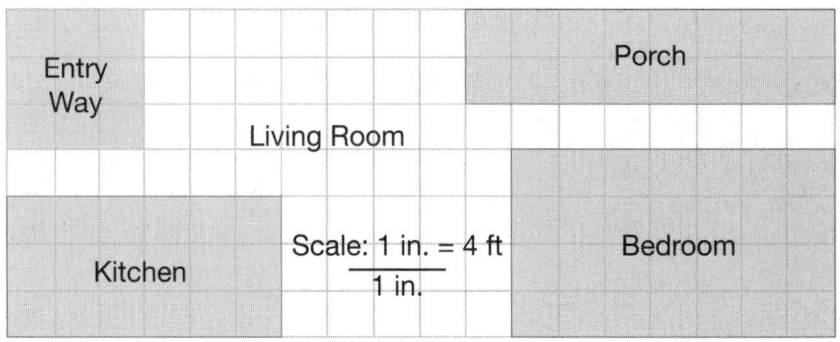

If each centimeter on a map represents 12 miles and Grand Rapids, Michigan, is 27 centimeters from Akron, Ohio, how many miles apart are these two cities?

The scale indicates that 1 inch is equivalent to 4 feet. From the picture, the length of the bedroom is $2\frac{1}{3}$ inches and the width is $1\frac{1}{3}$ inches.

$2\frac{1}{3} = \frac{7}{3}$ and $1\frac{1}{3} = \frac{4}{3}$

To find the actual size of the bedroom, multiply the length and the width by 4.

Length: $\frac{7}{3} \times 4 = \frac{28}{3} =$ **$9\frac{1}{3}$ feet**

Width: $\frac{4}{3} \times 4 = \frac{16}{3} =$ **$5\frac{1}{3}$ feet**

....

The scale indicates that 1 inch is equivalent to 4 feet. From the picture, the apartment is 6 inches long by $2\frac{1}{3}$ inches tall.

6 inches = $6 \times 4 = 24$ feet long

$2\frac{1}{3}$ inches = $\frac{7}{3} \times 4 = \frac{28}{3}$ feet wide

To find the area, multiply the length by the width: $24 \times \frac{28}{3} =$ **224 ft^2**

....

Since each centimeter represents 12 miles, multiply 27 centimeters by 12 to get **324 miles**.

A map is drawn such that 2.5 inches on the map represents a true distance of 10 miles. If two cities are 7.1 inches apart on the map, then to the nearest tenth of a mile, what is the true distance between the two cities?

If m is the number of miles between the two cities, then the following proportion can be set up and solved:

$\frac{2.5 \text{ inches}}{10 \text{ miles}} = \frac{7.1 \text{ inches}}{m \text{ miles}}$

$10(7.1) = 2.5(m)$

$71 = 2.5m$

$m =$ **28.4 miles**

How do you find the average of *x* numbers?

. . . .

What is the *mean* of a group of numbers and how is it calculated?

. . . .

Kai got the following test scores in his Spanish class: 78, 83, 88, 95, 98. Calculate his average test score.

MEASURES OF CENTRAL TENDENCIES

The average of a set of numbers is calculated by dividing the sum of the set of numbers by the quantity of numbers in the set. (Recall that "sum" means addition.)

Average = $\frac{\textbf{Sum of } \boldsymbol{x} \textbf{ numbers}}{\boldsymbol{x}}$

• •

The **mean** is the same thing as the average.

Mean = $\frac{\textbf{Sum of } \boldsymbol{x} \textbf{ numbers}}{\boldsymbol{x}}$

• •

Mean = $\frac{\text{Sum of } x \text{ numbers}}{x}$

Mean = $\frac{72 + 83 + 88 + 95 + 98}{5}$

Mean = $\frac{436}{5}$ = **87.2**

Mr. Carlo's class is learning about frogs. He took his class to the pond to observe them in person. One of the assignments was for each of the 14 students to measure one frog, and then the data was all combined in order to calculate the mean length. The mean length was 2.35 inches. Using the data below, calculate the length of the 14th frog.

Frog	Length (in.)
1	2.3
2	1.9
3	2.0
4	2.4
5	2.5
6	3.0
7	2.7
8	2.6
9	2.5
10	2.4
11	2.3
12	2.1
13	2.4
14	——

Assign a variable to the missing length, x. Write an equation for the average, then solve for x.

Mean = $\frac{\text{Sum of x numbers}}{x}$

$2.35 = \frac{2.3 + 1.9 + 2.0 + 2.4 + 2.5 + 3.0 + 2.7 + 2.6 + 2.5 + 2.4 + 2.3 + 2.1 + 2.4 + x}{14}$

$2.35 = \frac{31.1 + x}{14}$

$2.35(14) = (\frac{31.1 + x}{14})(\frac{14}{1})$

$32.9 = 31.1 + x$

$x =$ **1.8 inches**

Miss Reba keeps track of how many students drop in Monday through Thursday to study for their GED® test. Below is a chart of last week's numbers. Each number on the plot represents how many students came in each group. Miss Reba forgot to write down two numbers for Wednesday. If the average number of students per group was 3.2, and one of the unknown groups had one more student than the other unknown group, how many students in total did Miss Reba see on Wednesday?

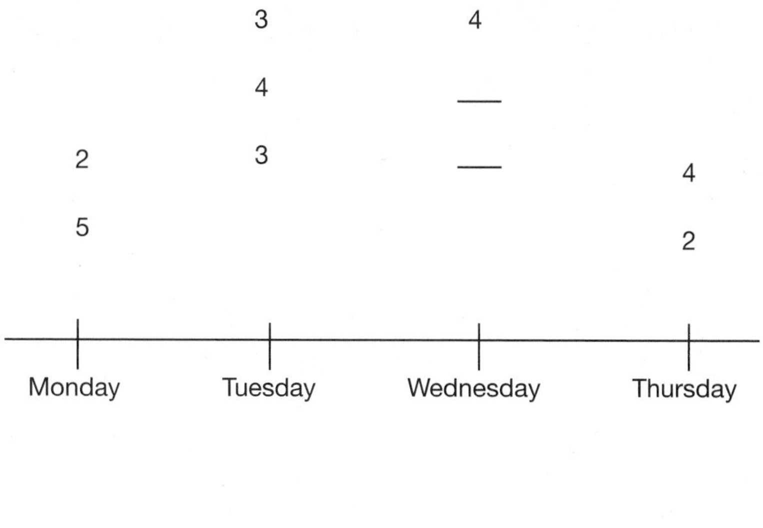

What is the *median* of a group of numbers, and how is it calculated?

Since one of the Wednesday groups has one more student than the other, assign x to one of the groups and $x + 1$ to the other.

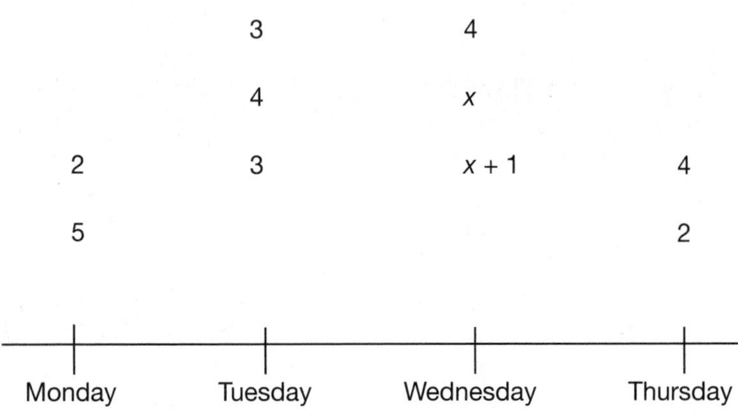

Next, fill in all the known information into the average equation and solve for x:

$\text{Mean} = \frac{\text{Sum of } x \text{ numbers}}{x}$

$3.2 = \frac{2 + 5 + 3 + 4 + 3 + 4 + x + x + 1 + 4 + 2}{10}$

$3.2 = \frac{28 + 2x}{10}$

$3.2(10) = (\frac{28 + 2x}{10})(\frac{10}{1})$

$32 = 28 + 2x$
$4 = 2x$
$x = 2$

One of the Wednesday groups had 2 students, and the other had 3 students ($x + 1$). This means that Miss Reba saw a total of 4 + 2 + 3 = **9 students** on Wednesday.

The **median** of a data set is the middle value of a chronologically arranged set of data. To find the median, first rewrite the numbers in order of least to greatest. Then, find the middle number that has the same quantity of numbers above and below it. If there is an even amount of numbers, the median is the average of the center two numbers.

Find the median of the following set of data: 23, 10, 31, 5, 39, 33

. . . .

What is the *mode* of a group of numbers, and how is it calculated?

. . . .

Can a group of data have no mode?
Can a data set have more than one mode?

First, rewrite the values in chronological order:

5, 10, 23, 31, 33, 39

The two middle numbers are 23 and 31:

5, 10, [23, 31], 33, 39

The median of this data set is the average of 23 and 31.

$\frac{23 + 31}{2} = \mathbf{27}$

The **mode** of a data set is the number that appears the most often.

If a set of data does not have any number that occurs more than once, then the set does not have a mode. For example, {1, 4, 8, 12, 15} has no mode. A data set can also have more than one mode if two or more numbers occur equally more than the other numbers. For example, {1, 1, 4, 4, 4, 8, 8, 12, 12, 12, 15} has two modes, 4 and 12, since they each occur three times in the data set.

What is the mode of the following data set?
45, 56, 23, 36, 79, 45, 12, 12, 56, 38

Identify the mode in the following data set:
100, 96, 94, 101, 106

What is the *range* of a data set, and how is it calculated?

There are three modes in this data set: **12**, **45**, and **56** all appear twice.

Since there are not any numbers that appear more than once in this data set, we can say that there is **no mode** for this set of data.

The **range** of a data set is the distance from the smallest to the largest number in the data set. It is found by subtracting the smallest number in a data set from the largest number.

Find the range of the data set {9, 7, 4, –15, 3, 12, 4, –8, 7}.

The following table shows the compensation of the CEOs of major health insurance providers in 2011. What was the mean CEO compensation for the listed companies?

I	$300,000
II	$275,000
III	$250,000
IV	$325,000
V	$300,000

Two high school biology classes hosted a bird watching day where students kept track of how many different species of birds they observed in a nearby park. The dot plot below represents the number of species observed by many of the students. Find the mode number of birds seen.

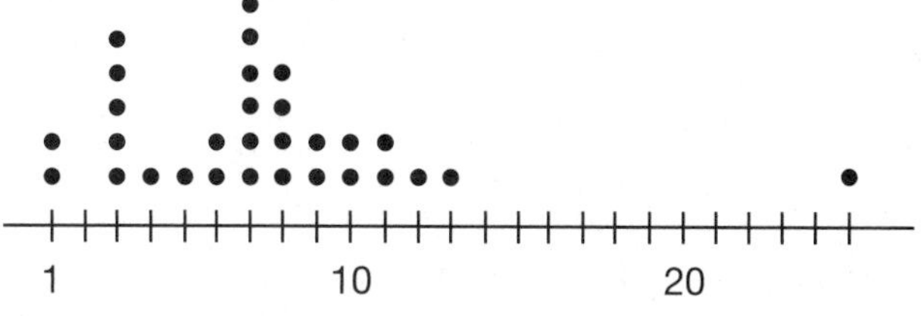

The data set {9, 7, 4, –15, 3, 12, 4, –8, 7} has a minimum of –15 and a maximum of 12, so the range is 12 – (–15) = **27**.

The mean is the average, so add all of the salaries together and divide by 5.

Mean = $\frac{\text{Sum of } x \text{ numbers}}{x}$

Mean = $\frac{\$1{,}450{,}000}{5}$ = **$290,000**

Do not confuse the mean with the mode or median, which are both equivalent to $300,000 in this particular case.

The most frequent number of birds spotted by students was 7 birds, so **7** is the mode.

When is it necessary to calculate a *weighted average*?

. . . .

Stephanie owns a bakery and is purchasing supplies. If she buys 20 cans of peaches for \$6.50 each and 28 cans of cherries for \$9 each, what is the average price per can of fruit?

. . . .

The following table illustrates the number of miles each student travels one way to get to Ms. Bradley's viola class. Find the average number of miles that Ms. Bradley's students travel one way:

Number of Miles Traveled One Way	Number of Students
1	4
2	3
3	5
4	6
5	3

A **weighted average** accounts for finding the average for several different sized groups of terms that have different values. If 15 households have 0 cars, 20 households have 1 car, and 75 households have 2 cars, and you were looking for the average number of cars per household, a weighted average would be required, since it would be incorrect to simply find the average of 0, 1, and 2.

• •

Since the different fruits have different prices, each type must get multiplied by the quantity that was purchased before the average can be found:

Mean Price per Can = $\frac{\text{Total cost of all cans of fruit}}{\text{\# of cans of fruit}}$

Mean Price per Can = $\frac{\$6.50(20) + \$9.00(28)}{20 + 28}$

Mean Price per Can = $\frac{\$382}{48}$ = **$7.96**

• •

Since there is a different number of students in each category, it is necessary to find the total number of miles traveled one way by *all* of Ms. Bradley's students and divide that by the number of total students in her viola class.

Total number of one-way miles: 1(4) + 2(3) + 3(5) + 4(6) + 5(3) = 64

There are 21 students in total, so $\frac{64}{21} \approx 3.05$

On average, Ms. Bradley's students travel about **3 miles** each way to get to her viola class.

Five-year old Larry made up a card game using four 10s, three Jacks, two Queens, and one King. He assigned a point value to each of the cards, which is found in the table below. What is the average point value of each card?

Card	Frequency	Point Value
10	4	5
Jack	3	10
Queen	2	15
King	1	20

The following table shows all of the assessed work in Chad's math class and how these assignments are weighted to create a final score for a student's performance in the course. Each assignment is worth 100 points. Use Chad's scores in the second table to find his final grade for the course.

Assignment	Number	Percentage
Tests	4	70%
Homework	6	10%
Final Exam	1	20%

Assignment	Chad's Scores
Tests	78, 85, 88, 90
Homework	87, 90, 83, 93, 91, 90
Final Exam	82

Since each card is assigned a different value, a weighted average must be calculated.

To do so, first multiply the number of each card by its point value, then add up the total value.

4(5) = 20

3(10) = 30

2(15) = 30

1(20) = 20

20 + 30 + 30 + 20 = 100

Next, divide the total value of all the cards by the number of cards used in the game. There are 10 cards used in the game (4 + 3 + 2 + 1).

So, the (weighted) average value of each card is:

$\frac{100}{10}$ = **10 points**

. . . .

To find Chad's final grade, each assignment needs to be weighted differently. First, find the average of each type of assignment, then multiply each category's average by the percentage assigned to it. Then, add the percentages together to find Chad's final grade.

Final Grade = $(\frac{78 + 85 + 88 + 90}{4}) + 0.10(\frac{87 + 90 + 83 + 93 + 91 + 90}{6}) + 0.20(82)$

Final Grade = 0.70(85.25) + 0.10(89) + 0.20(82)

Final Grade = 84.975% ≈ **85%**

. . . .

1. **What is *probability* and how is it notated?**
2. **How is the *simple probability* of an event happening calculated?**
3. **What is the probability of rolling an even number with a six-sided die?**

. . . .

What is the probability of grabbing a blue M&M out of the bag with the following contents?

Green	6
Yellow	5
Brown	10
Red	8
Blue	7
Orange	6

. . . .

What is *compound probability* and how is it calculated? What is the compound probability of rolling a 5 with a die and flipping a tail with a coin?

PROBABILITY

1. **Probability** is the likelihood of an event happening; *P*(A) means the "probability of event A."
2. **Simple probability** is calculated by expressing the number of outcomes that fit a specific criterion and the number of total outcomes as a ratio. It is often expressed as a decimal and sometimes as a percentage.
3. When considering the probability of rolling an even number with a die, there are three even numbers and six total possible outcomes:

$\text{Probability} = \frac{\text{\# of outcomes that fit the specified criterion}}{\text{total \# of total possible outcomes}}$

$P(\text{Even \#}) = \frac{3}{6} = \frac{1}{2}$

There are seven blue M&Ms in the bag. To find the probability that a blue one is selected, add up the total number of M&Ms in the bag and divide 7 by the total number.

$P(\text{Blue}) = \frac{7}{6 + 5 + 10 + 8 + 7 + 6} = \frac{7}{42} = \frac{1}{6}$

The probability of choosing a blue M&M from the bag is $\frac{1}{6}$.

Compound probability is used with events where more than one condition must be satisfied. To find compound probability, multiply the individual probabilities of each event together, and the product is the compound probability. For example, the compound probability of rolling a 5 with a die and flipping a tail with a coin is $\frac{1}{6} \times \frac{1}{2} = \frac{1}{12}$.

A six-sided die is rolled three times. What is the probability of rolling a 3, followed by any even number, followed by rolling a number greater than 4?

. . . .

What does it mean if a second trial is done "with replacement"? How does "with replacement" affect the probability of a follow-up event happening? How is the compound probability of both events happening affected by "with replacement"?

. . . .

The probability of pulling a fork out of a drawer is $\frac{4}{13}$. If the second fork is pulled out of the drawer with replacement, what is the probability that the second utensil removed will be a fork? What is the compound probability of both utensils being forks?

The probability of rolling a three is $\frac{1}{6}$. The probability of rolling an even number is $\frac{3}{6}$. The probability of rolling a number greater than 4 (which means a 5 or a 6) is $\frac{2}{6}$. The compound probability of all three of these events happening is the product of these individual probabilities:

$\frac{1}{6} \times \frac{3}{6} \times \frac{2}{6} = \frac{6}{216} = \mathbf{\frac{1}{36}}$

When a trial is done "with replacement," it means that any sample that was removed from the pool will be replaced before a second trial is run. When a follow-up event is happening "with replacement," the second event will have the same probability as the initial event. The compound probability of an event happening twice in a row, "with replacement," would be the square of the event happening one time.

If a follow-up event is happening with replacement, the second event will have the same probability as the initial event. Since the probability of pulling a fork out of the drawer is $\frac{4}{13}$, the probability of the second utensil being a fork is also $\mathbf{\frac{4}{13}}$. The compound probability of both utensils being forks is $\frac{4}{13} \times \frac{4}{13} = \mathbf{\frac{16}{169}}$.

Robert would like to pick two students from his class of 30 to be class leaders. His class has 16 girls and 14 boys. If Robert picks these students one at a time, without replacement, what is the probability that both class leaders are boys? Round your answer to the nearest whole percent.

. . . .

Given six different possible outcomes that have equal likelihood, *A*, *B*, *C*, *D*, *E*, and *F*, how would the probability of outcome *A* or *E* happening be calculated? Is this simple probability or compound probability?

. . . .

Kaoru's purse contains 12 pink marbles, 8 purple marbles, and 2 blue marbles that are all the same size. If Kaoru removes two marbles in a row out of her purse, without looking, what is the probability that both of them will not be pink?

P(first student being a boy) = $\frac{14}{30}$

P(second student being a boy) = $\frac{13}{29}$

For compound probability, multiply both of these probabilities:

$\frac{14}{30} \times \frac{13}{29} = \frac{182}{870} = 0.21 =$ **21%**

• •

Compound probability refers to events where one condition AND a second condition must happen together. When either one event OR another event is considered desirable, that is not compound probability. This is **simple probability**, where the total number of desirable events is divided by the total number of possible events. In this case, the probability of A or E happening is $\mathbf{\frac{2}{6}}$.

• •

There are 22 marbles in total. Since 10 of the marbles are not pink, there is a $\frac{10}{22}$ chance that the first marble will not be pink. Then, there is $\frac{9}{21}$ chance that the second marble is also not pink. The compound probability that neither of the 2 marbles will be pink is $\frac{10}{22} \times \frac{9}{21} = \frac{90}{462} = \frac{15}{77} \approx$ **0.19**.

There are 48 total applicants for a job. Of these applicants, 20 have only a college degree, 15 have only five years of work experience, five have neither a college degree nor five years of work experience, and eight have both a college degree and five years of work experience. If an applicant to the job is randomly selected, what is the probability, to the nearest tenth of a percent, that the applicant has at least a college degree?

. . . .

How is *n*! read and what does *n*! mean? Calculate 5!

. . . .

***Combination* and *permutation* are terms used to define two different types of counting techniques. Define the circumstances under which the combination method is used for a counting problem.**

What is an example of a type of problem that would use combination?

Divide the total number of desirable events by the total number of possible events to calculate this type of probability. In this case, 20 have a college degree and eight have a college degree in addition to work experience, so $\frac{28}{40}$ will meet the requirement of having at least a college degree, which is **0.7**.

. . . .

n! is read as "*n* factorial." *n*! is the product of all positive integers less than or equal to *n*.

$5! = 5\times4\times3\times2\times1 =$ **120**

. . . .

The counting technique of **combination** is used for problems where the order of events is not significant. Under combination, the grouping *a-b-c* does not get counted differently from *b-c-a* or *c-b-a*, so all of those groupings count as just a single option. If three out of 100 students were getting chosen to all receive a $500 award, it would not matter if the awards went to Ryan, Holly, and Steven, or if they went to Holly, Steven, and Ryan, since in either case, all of them would be getting an equivalent award. This is an example of where the combination technique would be used.

Combination **and** ***permutation*** **are terms used to define two different types of counting techniques. Define the circumstances under which the** ***permutation*** **method is used.**

What is an example of a type of problem that would use permutation?

. . . .

Maya is trying to decide which 3 toppings she wants on her pizza; there are 12 options on the menu. Is this an example of combination or permutation?

. . . .

Chris is trying to create a four-digit pin to use with his bankcard. Is this an example of combination or permutation?

Permutations are combinations where the order is significant. With **permutation**, the groupings *a-b-c* and *b-c-a* would count as two separate options. If three out of 100 students were getting chosen to receive awards that were $500 for first place, $250 for second place, and $100 for third place, then the order in which the awards are given to the three students certainly makes a difference, and *a-b-*c and *b-c-a* would be counted as two different options.

Whether Maya orders olives, onions, and mushrooms or mushrooms, olives, and onions, her pizza will be the same. Since order does not matter in this case, this is an example of **combination**.

If Chris selects 1-2-3-4 for his bankcard, he will not be able to access his account if he enters the pin 4-3-2-1. Since order of the numbers matters in this case, this is an example of **permutation**.

What is the method for calculating permutations? Write the formula for the number of permutations there are for selecting *k* items out of *n* options.

. . . .

What is the method for calculating combinations? Write the formula for the number of combinations there are for selecting *k* items out of *n* options.

. . . .

If Miss Murphy was trying to calculate the number of ways that first, second, third, and fourth place trophies could be awarded to 15 different teams in a talent show, is she looking to calculate a permutation or a combination? Find out how many different ways these trophies could be awarded.

$P(n,k) = \frac{n!}{(n-k)!}$, where n is the total number of options to choose from and k is the number of items selected.

$\mathbf{C(n,k)} = \frac{n!}{k!(n-k)!}$, where n is the number of options to choose from and k is the number of choices made.

Since getting the first place trophy is very different from getting the fourth place trophy, order matters and this is an example of a **permutation**.

$P(n,k) = \frac{n!}{(n-k)!}$

$P(15,4) = \frac{15!}{(15-4)!} = \frac{15!}{11!}$

$P(15,4) = \frac{15!}{11!} = \frac{15 \times 14 \times 13 \times 12 \times 11!}{11!}$

$P(15,4) = 32{,}760$

There are **32,760** ways that these four trophies can be awarded.

A student council committee is ordering 3 different colors of balloons to decorate the school on spirit day. There are 12 colors to choose from. Is this an example of a permutation or a combination? Find out how many different ways the balloon colors can be ordered.

President Obama is giving a commencement speech at UCLA. Three students in the Community Service Club are being invited to sit alongside him on stage, in recognition for the good works they have done in the community. One student will get to sit next to Obama, another student will be two seats away from him, and a third student will be the farthest from him. There are 14 students in the Community Service Club, and the three seats will be awarded in the order that their names are randomly pulled from a hat. How many different ways can the three chairs next to President Obama be occupied?

There are ten different colored note cards that orientation participants can choose from. A participant is asked to select four different colored note cards. How many different color combinations could result?

The order in which the colors are chosen does not matter, so this is an example of a **combination**:

$C(n,k) = \frac{n!}{k!(n-k)!}$

$C(12,3) = \frac{12!}{3!(12-3)!}$

$C(12,3) = \frac{12!}{3! \times 9!} = \frac{12 \times 11 \times 10 \times 9!}{3 \times 2 \times 1 \times 9!}$

$C(12,3) =$ **220**

Since the order that the names get pulled will determine the order that the students are sat on stage, this is a permutation of $P(14,3)$:

$P(n,k) = \frac{n!}{(n-k)!}$

$P(14,3) = \frac{14!}{(14-3)!}$

$P(14,3) = \frac{14!}{11!} = \frac{14 \times 13 \times 12 \times 11!}{11!}$

$P(14,3) =$ **2,184**

This is an example of combination since the order does not matter:

$C(n,k) = \frac{n!}{k!(n-k)!}$

$C(10,4) = \frac{10!}{4!(10-4)!}$

$C(10,4) = \frac{10!}{4! \times 6!} = \frac{10 \times 9 \times 8 \times 7 \times 6!}{4 \times 3 \times 2 \times 1 \times 6!}$

$C(10,4) =$ **210**

A basketball coach has nine players on her team. How many different five-player lineups can she create for the starting team?

. . . .

The *Fundamental Counting Principle* states that if there are *m* ways that one activity can happen and *n* ways that another activity can happen, then the number of ways for both activities to happen is __________.

. . . .

If Ella flips a coin and rolls a die, how many different outcomes are there?

The order in which the starting players are selected is not significant, so use combination:

$C(n,k) = \frac{n!}{k!(n-k)!}$

$C(9,5) = \frac{9!}{5!(9-5)!}$

$C(9,5) = \frac{9!}{5! \times 4!} = \frac{9 \times 8 \times 7 \times 6 \times 5!}{5! \times (4 \times 3 \times 2 \times 1)}$

$C(9,5) = \mathbf{126}$

. . . .

If there are *m* ways that one activity can happen and *n* ways that another activity can happen, then the number of ways for both activities to happen is $\boldsymbol{m \times n}$.

. . . .

Use the Fundamental Counting Principle: there are 2 possible results for a coin toss and 6 possible results for rolling a die, so there are 2×6 = **12** unique outcomes for flipping a coin and rolling a die.

If Margo flips a coin and rolls a die, what is the probability that she will roll a 5 and get tails?

Ferd's Falling Station offers a special menu that has an appetizer, main course, and dessert for $22.99. There are three appetizers, five main courses, and four desserts to choose from. How many different variations of the three-course menu special are there?

Use the Fundamental Counting Principle to first determine how many possible events there are: there are 2 possible results for a coin toss and 6 possible results for rolling a die, so there are $2 \times 6 = 12$ unique outcomes for flipping a coin and rolling a die. Only 1 of those options is a 5 and a tail, so the probability is $\frac{1}{12}$.

. . . .

Each course is unrelated to the previous course, so multiply the number of choices for each course together to see how many unique combinations there are: $3 \times 5 \times 4 =$ **60**.

. . . .

NOTES

NOTES